DYING TO BE YOUNG

A COSMETIC NIGHTMARE,
A SPIRITUAL AWAKENING

DR. ERIC KAPLAN

DYING TO BE YOUNG

Pegasus Books LLC
45 Wall Street, Suite 1021
New York, NY 10005

First Pegasus Books edition 2008

Library of Congress Cataloging-in-Publication Data is available.

ISBN: 978-1-60598-032-4

10 9 8 7 6 5 4 3 2 1

Printed in the United States of America
Distributed by W. W. Norton & Company, Inc.

MORE ENDORSEMENTS FOR
DYING TO BE YOUNG

"An inspiring story of how people can find faith and strength in even the worst circumstances. A book to strengthen the soul of anyone who reads it."

—Rabbi **HAROLD S. KUSHNER,**
Author of #1 International Best-seller,
WHEN BAD THINGS HAPPEN TO GOOD PEOPLE

The Kaplans' story will provide chicken soup for anyone's spirit or soul. Their book "Dying to be Young" shows Miracles can take place with hard work and the right attitude. Their story demonstrates that you can transform your life into exactly what you want it to be, regardless of your situation, by simply shifting your mindset and creating a renewed reality.

—Jack Canfield, Co-Author,
Chicken Soup for the Unsinkable Soul®

"Dr. Kaplan's gripping story about coming back from the brink of death after a botched [cosmetic] treatment proves once and for all that beauty is an inside job. As Kaplan shows, there isn't a scalpel, pill, lotion or injection that can make us as radiant as an open, loving heart."

—Ken Blanchard, co-author of Best Sellers, **The One Minute Manager®** and **Leading at a Higher Level**

This book inspires you to confront your problems and draw on your inner resources to overcome even the greatest of life's obstacles.
—Brian Tracy, Best-selling author of
more than 40 books, including **Crunch Point**

This book is destined to save lives, changes lives, and inspire anyone because of its impact, inspiration and insight.

—**Les Brown, best selling author of**
Live Life to the Fullest

Your story will motivate and inspire others. I wish you and your wife every success.

—**Wally FAMOUS Amos**

I have known Dr. Kaplan as a friend, the family chiropractor, and an incredible motivator and now as an author who has lived to share his purposeful message. Imagine making one choice that could send you to a place of unimaginable suffering. That's what happened to my friend Eric and his dear wife Bonnie. They could have given up, but chose to turn inward and found a power and insight so far beyond the physical self. Their courageous story teaches us to be grateful in all that God has given and to draw wisdom from all of our challenges. Anyone who reads this book will be blessed and know that yes, we are responsible for our choices but there is so much love and guidance available to us if we just ask, and listen. Living, Loving, "be"ing, accepting the moment and ourselves is the greatest gift!! Thank you Eric, for stepping so deeply into the divine space and bringing back such wisdom to share. If anyone would live to uplift others I knew it would be you!

—**Marla Maples**

The Kaplans' story is an inspiring read and a clarion call to America about the dangers of [botulism] and the horrible consequences if ever used as a weapon of terrorism.

—**Thomas McMillen, Rhodes Scholar, Former Congressman,**
Former Chairman President's Council
on Physical Fitness and Sports, 11 year NBA veteran

Dr. Kaplan's book clearly represents the strength it takes to survive and succeed. He is living proof that it starts with a Dream. His story and message show that if you visualize your Dream and make a commitment anything is possible. Their comeback story is what makes life exciting. This book will teach anyone to never underestimate the power of a Dream. It will change your life as the Kaplans changed theirs.

—Rudy Ruettiger, whose life story was the basis of the 1993 TRISTAR blockbuster film, "RUDY"

Two is better than one if two can act as one. Obviously, the Kaplans acted as one in their courageous fight to overcome obstacles which seemed impossible. I am so excited that they are sharing this story with us. It is inspiring.

—Mike Krzyzewski, Head Coach, Basketball, Duke University

As a cosmetic dentist and Mrs. America 2005, I have seen first hand the measures some take in trying to achieve what they consider beauty. In this amazing true life story, the Kaplans' message helps exemplify true beauty, inner beauty. Their courage should never be forgotten.

—Dr. Chiann Fan Gibson DMD

...I have always been against cosmetic procedures and have considered them malpractice since I became an M.D. Good luck on your crusade to change the way the world thinks about cosmetic procedures... Please give your life to peace, justice and care.

—Patch Adams, M.D., Author

I know first hand Dr. Eric Kaplan as a Public Speaker and an Author. Eric walks the walk and talks the talk. His story told in his book "Dying To Be Young" is a spellbinding story that will make you laugh, make you cry, and teach you the empirical laws for health, success and inner healing. If you are looking for an inspirational story, this is the book.

—Dottie Walters
Walters Speakers Bureau, Founding member of the
National Association of Speakers,
Editor and Publisher of "Sharing Ideas Magazine"
Bestselling Author of <u>Speak and Grow Rich</u>.

Being in the NFL as a defensive end for 10 years, I understand a good fight. The Kaplans' story is an amazing story of amazing people. Their ability to overcome adversity makes them champions in my book. I recommend this book to anyone who wants to be the best they can be."

—Duane Clemens, Cincinnati Bengals Defensive End

Dr. Kaplan's story depicts how the power of love, faith and family can triumph in the face of adversity. Faced with what many considered certain expiration of life as we know it, Dr. Kaplan and his family banded together and used the power of love and faith to turn an almost certain tragedy into success. I am inspired by their story.

—Barry Larkin, Cincinnati Reds,
President/CEO Champions Sports Complex

...[It's] an honor to endorse your book. Thanks for all you do while making the world a healthier place.

—Lee Haney, Eight time Mr. Olympia, Author
Former Chairman President's
Council on Physical Fitness and Sports

Your book is a Homerun!

—Johnny Damon,
Two-time, All Star Centerfielder, New York Yankees

Dr. Kaplan's new book reminds us that experiencing pain and adversity can arm us with incredible resiliency. Dr. Eric and Bonnie Kaplan's extraordinary journey teaches us lasting lessons which will help us overcome the daunting obstacles of the challenging gift we call life.

—Rabbi Joel Levine, Temple Judea,
Palm Beach Gardens, Florida

Dying to be Young is a moving and spiritual book. Eric's and Bonnie's journey to renewed faith and healing is made possible by using, in Eric's words, "the power of the I AM" When Moses asked God who He was, God answered, "I AM WHO I AM" (Exodus 3:14). And just as that name and power led Moses through the Wilderness, "the power of the I AM" led Eric and Bonnie Kaplan through their Wilderness to a place of healing. Their book will guide anyone to the reality of God and to the joy of Oneness with the Creator.

—Lamar Helms, Associate Chaplain,
Big Canoe Chapel, Big Canoe, Georgia

Bonnie and Eric Kaplan's story is a true story of hope...and faith... and true unconditional love. Dr. Kaplan is an inspiration to everyone. He is my inspiration.

—Jaki Baskow, CEO Baskow & Associates

Dying to be Young is a book you will not be able to put down. Bonnie and Eric Kaplan have always been leaders in our community. For months our community both struggled with the tragedy of their experience and prayed that again they would be back with us assuming their important roles. Dr. Kaplan's book will make you cry and understand that life is far more precious and important than many of us understand.

—Mayor Joe Russo, Palm Beach Gardens, Florida

Dr. Kaplan's book makes you stop and think about life and the pressures that society places upon us to look beautiful, no matter the price. We need to focus inward and teach our children that beauty comes from "who" we are, and not "what" we look like. The tragedy certainly became a triumph for the Kaplans. The greatest gift a person can obtain is the gift to understand what your purpose in life is. This gift was bestowed upon the Kaplans as they fought for their lives. They are blessed to know their mission and this book is an excellent tool for their teachings. Dr. Kaplan's book opens your eyes and helps you see what really matters in life. Compelling book, excellent dialogue, very inspirational.

—Jodi A. Pliszka, M.S.
ABC'S AMERICAN INVENTOR TOP 12 FINALIST, Award Winning Author, Clinical Therapist, Motivational Speaker, Entrepreneur, Mommy

If you've ever thought about having [cosmetic procedures to remove wrinkles], you will change your mind after reading this book. It's not only a compelling love story, it is a moving narrative about survival and the miraculous proof that angels are all around us.

—Yvonne Perry, Author of <u>More than Meets the Eye: True Stories about Death, Dying, and Afterlife</u> and <u>Right to Recover: Winning the Political and Religious Wars over Stem Cell Research in America</u>

Dr. Eric Kaplan's Dying to be Young is so much more than a chronicle of his journey [surviving] botulism; it is a remarkable guide to aging with grace and dignity.

—Reader Views

Lifestyle of the Fit & Famous

"The Taj Mahal of health books." —**Donald Trump**

"It is my sincere prayer your book will be a help and blessing to many people." —**Norman Vincent Peale**

"A must read book for anyone thinking of losing weight and keeping it off." —**Dr. Earl L. Mindell**

"If you want to get thin and win, Dr. Kaplan's Lifestyle of the Fit & Famous is the one to ingest and digest for immediate progress."
                                                          —**Mark Victor Hansen**

Very Motivational and inspirational.
                              —**Gary Carter, Hall of Fame Catcher**

I would consider it mandatory reading for anyone who is serious about maintaining a healthy body and happy disposition.
       —**Nathaniel Crosby, 1981 U. S Amateur Champion**

Dr Kaplan's book is more than highly motivational. It is a must -read for anyone who wants to live a healthier, happier lifestyle.
                         —**Billy Cunningham, Hall of Fame**
                              Basketball Player and Coach
Enjoyed the book, I highly recommend it.
                    —**Kevin Loughery, NBA Veteran,**
                         Former Coach Miami Heat

TABLE OF CONTENTS

Dedication

I dedicate this book to Bonnie Kaplan, my wife, my life partner, and my best friend for 26 years. Bonnie survived as a youth abandoned by her parents and raised by the state. She went on to educate herself as she worked her way through school. In 1997, Bonnie was diagnosed with colon cancer and was originally given six months to live. She is now eight years cancer-free. She went on to conquer botulism and its crippling effects. She has done all this while enduring me! Our story is more than a story of botulism; it is a love story of two people fighting for the love they held dear. Bonnie has always led by example and provided strength, wisdom and insight. She is the person I respect and love the most. It was from her strength that I found the power to write this book.

Acknowledgements

I would like to give special thanks to my brother, Steven, and his wife, Gloria, who put their lives on hold to tend to our needs. They truly held our family and our lives together. Thank you for being at the hospital with us every day. You helped us physically, emotionally, and spiritually more than I could say with words.

To my neice's and nephew Richard, Tracey and Beth Kaplan for their ongoing visits, presents, calls, e-mails and gifts. I am proud to call you family.

I would also like to thank everyone who visited us, wrote us, e-mailed us, called our family, rooted for us or prayed for us. We are thankful to all of our friends for being true friends, and to all our family for standing behind us.

To the law firm of Grossman & Roth—especially Stuart Grossman and his assistants, Rodney Bryson, Esq. and Donna Burroughs—not only for representing us, but also for caring about us as human beings and for making a stand with the government about their policies in regard to these horrific toxins. Mr. Grossman is a man among men, a true gladiator, he has remained focused on eliminating this terrible toxin from the public. Only a "man of steel" would stand up and challenge the Federal Government for its ineptness. We are grateful to him and his team for assisting us in preventing this from happening to anyone else.

I would like to offer special thanks to Bear Lakes Country Club, to the Board of Directors and membership for there humane understanding. I would like to pay tribute to my Saturday-morning golf group for keeping me in the loop and for their patience for playing golf with me as I re-learned the game. I thank Andy Brock, Harvey Golden, Keith Hammond, Rich Kaufman, Rich Palladino, Sandy Meyers, Rich Lubin, Bob Shalhoub, Warren Zwecker and Bill Meyer. Special thanks go to Bear Lakes staff, especially David McClymont and Steve Pembrook, and Professionals Kevin Murphy, Matt Messer, Toby Hill and Ted Strelec for their patience and ongoing support.

Thanks to all my friends and neighbors at Big Canoe for their kind hearts and endless meals. Our appreciation to the developer Bill Byrne and his marketing guru Ann Young, for their ongong support. The womens guild at Big Canoe for there constant letters and prayer. We would especially like to thank Minister Lamar Helms of the Big Canoe Chapel for visiting us at the Shepherd Center weekly for prayer and helping us feel welcome in our new community. To Carolyn & Sonny Miracle and Tom, TJ and BobbieMeany for making our Georgia house a home and a comfortable place to recover. To the Beechlers, Fox's and Alfonso's for their visits and ice cream. To David O'Connor, Linda, Trish and all the golf staff. Finally, to all the staff at the Fitness center for aiding us in our rehabilitation, thanks to Tina, Steve and staff for their support and Alannah for nursing us back to health.

I thank my good friend and partner, Dr. Gerry Mattia and his wife, Paulette, who assisted in managing my business affairs. I am blessed to have such loyal friends and business partners. I would also thank Pam Billinski, my billing expert, who covered for me while I was sick by answering questions for my clients. Pam along with my good friends Dr. Neil Brown and Dr. Gerry Mattia were life savers. These three people along with my brother Steve and Stephanie Juergon single-handedly kept my business afloat.

To my great friend and attorney Thomas Dougherty whose friendship, insight and legal help was germane during our recovery. To my sports friend and attorney Howard Newman for his ongoing legal help and support.

To the congregation of Temple Judea: Your love, cards, e-mails, prayers and support helped us in our healing, especailly the Savel, Levy, Hoffinger , Rosen and Schneiderman families. Special thanks to Rabbi Joel Levine my spiritual friend who assisted me through the detours of life, his wife, Susan, daughter Rachel, and to Cantor Rita and Ira Shore for singing at our bedside to lift our spirits.

We want to thank all the staff, parents and students of the Batt Private School. Your ongoing cards, e-mails, dinners, notes and love for us were cherished daily. Special appreciation to the school's owner, Judy Batt, and in memory of her husband Roy, who passed on during the writing of this book.

A special thanks to the following people for being there 24/7: the Axelrods, Balas's, Bards, Bernsteins, Beers, Beiges, Birnbaums, Brailes, Brocks, Burkes, Buschs, Chapnicks, Daniels, Dickens, Doughertys, DiMayos, Egittos, Fischers, Garfunkels, Gotkins, Greggs, Griswalds, Gutsteins, Harmons, Harveys, Hicks, Hoxies, Juergans, Kaufmans, Kerners, Kings, Larussos, Levines, Littenbergs, Marcus's, Mandels, McMillens, Meyers, Newmans,

Osbornes, Prestons, Prices, Punyons, Rosens, Russos, Scherbaks, Siegelmans, Smiths, Yeckes, Zucks, and Zweckers. Also, special thanks to Uncle Jack Segall, Uncle Buddy Adler, my cousin Steven Daniels and my Aunt Gloria Punyon for coming to the hospital every day, rain or shine.

Thanks to the LPG Company for their love and support and for not giving up on my partner or me. Also, a special thanks to Thierry & Natalie Phillipe and family.

To Dr. Dennis Egitto and his wife, Barbara. Dennis has been a best friend for over 20 years. It was his foresight and keen medical awareness that saved our lives. To this family ,whom we love so much, we will forever be grateful and indebted.

Thanks also to all the doctors and nurses at Palm Beach Gardens Hospital, with special thanks to Drs. Koerner, Taub, Sanchez, Price, Tuckman, Ooh, and Vasquez, and to all the nurses, therapists and staff who cared for us—especially my Angel, Shelly.

To the Shepherd family and the Shepherd Center, this is truly a place of miracles. To all the doctors, nurses, therapists and staff for caring so much about us. With special thanks to Drs. Bowman, Gutay, Leslie and Karen Kline. Their help restored our lives when we faced an insurmountable health trauma.

To the American Chiropractic Magazine for standing behind me during my recovery with special thanks to the Busch Family and blessings to their editor and my friend, Jacklyn Busch Touzard.

My special thanks to the Chiropractic Profession and specifically, New York Chiropractic College for providing me the training, philosophy, insight and peers, which allowed me to heal myself and my wife to a higher level of health than anyone ever expected to be possible after botulism poisoning.

I would like to honor my cousin and adopted aunt Ruth Zuck, who has battled lung cancer for over four years. Her desire to live and beat all odds inspired us on our journey. She is our hero.

And lastly, but most importantly, thanks to my two sons, Michael and Jason, who became men overnight, for putting their lives on hold and showing us that our own lives were worthy of two great young men. No children should ever see what our sons have seen. Their love for us was our best medicine.

A percentage of the proceeds from the sale of this book will be donated to Shepherd Center in Atlanta, Georgia.

Prologue

My goal is to pour out my heart and try to develop a book that deals with a real situation. Botulism poisoning is fatal in most cases, yet my wife and I beat the odds and are living today to tell our story. What we went through emotionally, physically and mentally during our recovery could qualify for no less than hell on earth. What we learned spiritually could be no less than heaven.

This book is not a tragedy, a comedy, a saga, or a soap opera. If it were a soap opera, it would be entitled "One Life to Give." This is a book about survival and conquering all odds. It is a book about the love and support offered to us by family, friends, doctors, nurses and even strangers. It's about the lessons I learned while fighting for my life.

There is one thing we all know about life on earth, that we do not get out of here alive! However, some of us die and come back, as I did. It was through my encounter with death that life itself developed a greater meaning. The experience opened my inner eye, to see what so few can see: that life is for living, loving, laughing and learning, not for whining, worrying, and working. I want this book to be a guide to your inner eye—to open your mind to the gift of life and to understand that your spirit is eternal. I want you to realize that no matter what you are going through, you are not alone in this universe. Although God is abundant in my thoughts and actions, this is not a religious book. Through it, you will learn to believe in life, love and the power of the human spirit. Belief is a sign of faith, and faith has nothing to do with religion.

There are only two types of people on earth. There are those who believe there is no order in the universe, and that whatever happens occurs randomly and for no apparent reason. These people are usually angry or lonely. Then, there are those who believe that everything happens for a purpose and that nature makes no mistakes. They understand the perfection of life and see every circumstance as part of a larger picture. They see balance in the universe. I am of the latter category. I understand that darkness follows light, summer follows winter, and I believe that as surely as the sun rises and sets each day, there is order to the universe.

Prior to November 23, 2004, no one in the world had ever been poisoned by fake Botox or injections of raw botulinum toxin. The dosage we received should have been fatal. Thankfully, it was *not* fatal and good has triumphed over a bad situation. My body has been altered physically and may never be the same, but mentally and spiritually, I am stronger than ever. I have learned that our mental attitude dominates our physical condition. Yes, brains are superior to brawn! The power of our mind, spirit and soul is stronger than any muscle in our body; and the stronger our spirit becomes, the more we empower our body to heal.

It is my heartfelt desire that this book inspires you to see beyond the mundane and become thankful for the little things in life—the ability to blink, to breathe, to move, to laugh, to cry, and to love and be loved.

Dr. Eric Scott Kaplan

Introduction

Thinking about wrinkle reducing injections? Think twice!

If someone came to you with a syringe filled with anthrax and told you it would make you look younger, would you let them inject you? Of course not. Now suppose someone comes to you with a syringe of botulism toxin and told you it would make you look younger and remove wrinkles, would you let them inject your face? Last year over seven million Americans said yes.

How have so many people been persuaded to receive injections of this deadly toxin? Because we naïvely trust pharmaceutical marketing, our government and the health care delivery system to protect us. We don't ask questions about the materials doctors use to make us look younger.

Since the FDA approved it for cosmetic use in 2002, Botox has become a household word and many people have been injected with the drug at the site of a facial line to paralyze the nerve and make the skin appear wrinkle free. This FDA-approved and licensed Botulinum Toxin Type A is derived from the waste of the bacterium *Clostridium botulinum*—the same toxic byproduct that causes botulism food poisoning. Botulinum toxin is the most poisonous substance known to man. Because of its extreme potency and lethality, the ease of production, transport, and misuse, Botulinum toxin is considered a bioweapon. A single gram of crystalline toxin, evenly dispersed as an aerosol and inhaled, would kill more than one million people. The name Botox is cute, but remember it is short for botulism toxin.

The media, pharmaceutical companies and doctors have made it seem so safe that many people receive this plastic surgery procedure at a social event known as a Botox party. What happened to my wife and me was no party. We voluntarily took what we were told and thought were legal Botox treatments—actually paid for them—and ended up with botulism because the doctor had used an illegally obtained raw botulinum toxin A substance instead of the FDA approved Botox serum. Within seventy-two hours we were hospitalized, on life support, and unable to move a single muscle in our bodies. We almost died! On a misguided journey looking for youth, seeking heaven on earth, we found ourselves in hell.

Cosmetic procedures gone wrong are the quiet epidemic sweeping America that no one in the drug industry wants you to know about. Few of us realize we could be risking death when we ask doctors to help us preserve our youth. Bonnie and I learned from our mistake and we want to share our insight with you. For those who are thinking of cosmetically altering your appearance, do your research and ask questions about what is going into your body. If you have already been damaged by drugs and medical procedures gone awry, perhaps this book will help you find encouragement in the midst of your suffering and injustice.

While I was facing death, unable to communicate and in a paralyzed state, I wanted to die. Bonnie and I were in terrible pain as we faced a long uphill battle—a battle that offered no assurance that we would recover and live normal lives. I was deeply depressed and even prayed for God to take me out of my suffering. Ironically, I also bargained with God and prayed to live—but only if Bonnie and I could both recover and be healthy again. My prayers were answered in an unusual way and that is part of my story. I had three angelic visitations—each one giving me a message and encouraging me to use my will power and mental authority to live and recover. For those reading this book who feel you are alone in life and want to die, I want you to know that angels are everywhere, even in your personal hell. I pray this book will help you find your inner power and give you confidence to recover from illness.

Although our experience was a nightmare, I know that something good will come of it. I believe that I am divinely inspired to write this book to encourage others. Perhaps you are facing the death of your physical body and have doubts or worries about what comes next. In reading my story, you will be presented with compelling evidence that there is life after death and that the afterlife is a wonderful place to learn, love, plan and continue spiritual growth. I now believe that our soul or spirit is our true identity with an eternal consciousness that will continue in other realms and dimensions. Death is merely a portal or tunnel to another realm of consciousness, spiritually akin to the physical one we pass through as an infant when coming into this life through our mother's womb. After my experience, I feel there is truly nothing to be afraid of regarding this transition.

By sharing our knowledge and our story with you, it is our hope and prayer that you are helped and encouraged to be the best *you* can be.

DYING TO BE YOUNG

Chapter One

The Genesis of Our Degeneration

The room was cold and I was drifting in and out of consciousness as I lay in an uncomfortable bed wondering what could have happened to me. I was surrounded by the clamour of chaos and unfamiliar sounds that offered only to confuse my senses. There were machines making noise around me, but I did not know where I was, how I had gotten there or how long I had been in this condition. Voices of strangers scurried around me as I kept trying to figure out what was going on. I recognized the voices of my loved ones; some were crying as if someone had died. *Are they crying for me? Am I dead? Is this my funeral? No, I am alive. God, what is happening to me?*

I heard my brother's voice, "Eric, it's Steve. Can you hear me?"

I tried to speak, but my lips would not move and I could not utter a sound. *This can't be real. I must be dreaming. If this is a dream, I can just open my eyes and wake up. Open your eyes…I can't! I can't open my eyes! Why can't I wake up? Am I alive? Oh God, I am helpless! I can't move! I must be dead! Wait…how can I think, if I'm dead? I can hear, so I can't be dead, right? Someone is touching me. I can feel, so I MUST be alive. Come on, Kaplan. Open your eyes!* I screamed within my own head, but no one heard me. *I cannot open my eyes. OH GOD, I CAN'T MOVE. Why can't I move? I'M ALIVE! I'M TRAPPED IN MY BODY! Help me! Somebody help me! I can think, but I cannot talk. I must have died. Oh my God, I am not in heaven. I am in hell!*

My bewilderment changed to panic when I heard a stranger's voice say, "Your parents are in bad shape. They may be like this for a year to eighteen months. It could be six months before they are even able to open their eyes."

Who is this man and who is he talking to? He's talking about my wife and me! Eighteen months like this? No way! Where is Bonnie? Is she okay? How did this happen? I want answers! Oh, God, please let this be a dream. Help me wake up.

"Dad?" It was my oldest son, Michael.

Michael? I'm here. I'm trapped. Help me wake up! He couldn't hear me. *My thoughts were racing and I was panicking. Why can't I speak to him?*

"I love you, Dad. You can make it!" Jason, my 19-year old son, was there too. He was holding my hand and cheering me on. I could feel my sons' love and I knew I must be alive.

Alarms were beeping and some kind of machine was pumping air in and out of something—someone—ME! *I must be in the hospital. I must be in bad shape.* Snippets of recent events started coming to me in my brief moments of consciousness. I remembered riding to the hospital with Jason and I vaguely remembered seeing my friend, Dr. Dennis Egitto, after Bonnie and I arrived in the emergency room. *Bonnie! Where is she? Is she alive? Is she paralyzed too?* People were coming in and out of my space testing and probing me, but I still could not imagine what had caused Bonnie and me to become so sick and weak.

"Eric, this is Dennis. I don't know if you can hear me." Dr. Egitto tried desperately to communicate with me, but I could not answer him. "You need to fight this. You have a rough road ahead of you."

28

"How rough?" I wanted to ask.

"I am going to give you something for pain. It will also help you relax."

I was thankful to have something to relieve the terrible aches. My joints and muscles were hurting all over my body. Soon a wild feeling came over me and I couldn't tell what was real from what was imagined. I did not know what was happening to me, but I knew I was loved as I drifted off to sleep.

I awoke again later. How much later? I don't know. Time was immeasurable. It could have been hours; it could have been days. Wanting to believe this was nothing more than a nightmare, I again tried to get out of bed. I was terrified when I realized I could not move my body, speak a word, swallow, or open my eyes. I could feel pain in my throat and I could hear machines around me. Suddenly the stark reality set in. I was in a hospital bed and I was paralyzed. *Am I in a coma? Why am I here? What happened?*

Imagine a world of total darkness where you cannot see, touch, or move. You can hear, feel and think but you cannot communicate with the outside world in any way. Imagine being a prisoner, trapped in a cold, lifeless container that showed no signs of life. That was my plight for weeks as I struggled in a mental stupor with very little physical improvement. To some this may read like another Steven King novel. To me, it was worse. It was my life, it was real, and it was hell. Once I realized I was in Hell, my question was, "How do I get the hell out of here?"

Chapter Two

Instant Replay

"Dad?" Michael called to me from my psychosomatic mist. "You are in the hospital. Can you hear me?"

I could hear my son, but I could not physically answer him. Due to the drugs I was being given, I was in a pseudo-cognizant state. Many times it felt as if I was dreaming while awake. However, being asleep and in my dream world was much better than being awake and having to face my bleak reality. During my sleep, my imagination allowed me to disassociate from what was actually happening around me by creating pleasant scenes to my own liking. Being awakened by a doctor or sudden noise was like having to take a commercial break from my favorite program only to find myself still in hell, still paralyzed and unable to open my eyes or communicate with those around me.

Lying there lifeless, in and out of sleep, I had to know what had happened to cause this horrible condition. When I was awake, my mind was going nonstop at ninety miles an hour. Like a VCR, I kept rewinding scenes of the past few days. It was like watching an instant replay of a sporting event.

The week before being hospitalized, I had given a seminar at the beautiful JW Marriott in Orlando, Florida, which doctors from throughout the country attended. My partner, Dr. Gerry Mattia, and I were pleased to have numerous professional athletes present. Dr. Toia and his partner, Dr. McComb, were there. Their clinic provided a wide array of services and procedures, many designed to bolster patients' image and make them look and feel younger. I was familiar with their success and was flattered by their attendance. At the time of the seminar, I was fighting a mild bronchial infection for which Dr. Toia recommended a round of intravenous vitamins—cutting edge stuff. He called right after the seminar to tell me he had set up an appointment for November 23 for me to have the vitamin cocktail and for Bonnie to have another round of Botox injections. Anti-aging was the hot topic in health care and, like most Americans, we wanted to look and feel younger. Bonnie and I had both been injected with Botox about one year earlier and we had excellent results. Before our first round of treatments, I did my research. There was no mention anywhere of side effects and I believed the media, as millions of Americans did. Imagine removing all lines and wrinkles in minutes; taking years off your life—quick and easy with little pain and no side effects. Since wrinkle reducing cosmetic injections are considered safe, many people elect to have them. Although we never attended one, we had numerous friends who had been injected at a "Botox" party, a common practice in Palm Beach. All data indicated that having these injections was harmless.

Harmless? I thought as I lay there trapped in my body, *You call this harmless? How could I have been so stupid? Kaplan, you, of all people, know that every drug has the potential to be harmful. Yesterday I was healthy, happy, alive and enjoying my life in South Florida. Now I am trapped in hell.*

There was chaos in my room. Someone was pricking me with a sharp object, trying to get me to respond. "Eric? ERIC?"

OUCH! That hurts!

"Eric, can you move your hand?"

I tried with all my might, but I could not make my hand move. In fact, I could not move any part of my body—not even my eyes. I was alive and I was aware. I knew what was going on, but I was unable to respond. The words were in my head but, I could not verbally speak them. I wondered if this is how Lou Gehrig felt before he died.

Unable to communicate with the outside world, I was trapped inside my own body, captive to my own thoughts. The brain is an amazing machine; it has the ability to recall any event in our lives. Nothing is ever lost, only forgotten. Oliver Wendell Holmes once said, "The brain is an amazing instrument. It can turn a heaven into hell, or a hell into heaven." I chose the latter. I had to keep my sanity. I had to bask in the memories of my past to avoid focusing on what was happening in the present or worrying about the future. This form of escape allowed me to travel in time. The VCR in my mind rewound again and the tape began to play...

The day before Thanksgiving started simply enough. It was a beautiful, sunny day in south Florida with the temperatures in the mid-eighties. Michael was home from college for the Thanksgiving holiday. I enjoy being with my family, and Michael is a son any parent would be proud of. He is handsome, intelligent and respectful, and I have always enjoyed his company. Our relationship is more than just father and son; Michael is my friend. Bonnie and I were going to Dr. Toia's office that day, so Michael went with us. While riding in the car for an hour, we were able to talk and catch up with one another. The trip reminded me of myself as a boy riding with my own father to Brooklyn to see his parents, my grandparents. My dad was a stern and quiet man, and I was the child who could not remain quiet for ten seconds. It was during those trips that I got to speak to my dad one-on-one. At home, he would just walk into another room when he tired of hearing me, but in the car, he was my captive audience. Well, on this day so were Bonnie and Michael.

In my efforts to encourage Michael to pursue a career in medicine, I began my discourse about the distinctiveness of the Advanced Integrated Medical Center. "The clinic you are going to see today is unique," I told Michael. Based on my experience and current profession as a chiropractor, I considered myself on top of all the changes in health care.

"In what way?" Michael asked.

"This clinic combines traditional medicine with alternative healthcare options. There are six doctors in this office: one medical doctor, two osteopaths and three doctors of chiropractic."

"Six doctors in one clinic," my son responded.

"Yes, plus many technicians and therapists."

I continued my infomercial until we pulled into the parking lot of the impressive two-story medical complex. As we walked into the first floor waiting room, I could not help but notice how full and busy the facility was. A clean, medicinal smell of success permeated the air. As a chiropractor, author, motivational speaker, and healthcare consultant, I was well-known in the world of chiropractic and I had many friends and acquaintances in the medical field. The staff members at this practice knew me well.

"Dr. Kaplan, good to see you," the receptionist promptly greeted us as we arrived.

"Likewise," I returned her greeting and nodded to Michael. "My son is interested in a career in medicine. Will it be okay if I show him around the facility?"

"Most certainly." We were treated like royalty and were given a tour of every inch of the clinic.

As we walked, I picked up where I left off on my infomercial telling my son that, in my opinion, Advanced Integrated Medical Center was ahead of the curve. Not only did it provide a safe approach to traditional and alternative medicine, it did so in an environment that was modern and comfortable. However, the outward appearances of the facility were deceiving. There was a lot going on behind the scenes that no one knew about. I believed my own sales pitch. For the first time in my life, my instincts were wrong, or perhaps they were correct and God had a bigger plan for me.

Like so many people, I felt invincible and believed nothing bad could happen to me. I trusted my doctors; we all trust doctors. I had been in the medical field for twenty-five years and I had known Dr. Toia for about twenty years. He was a good and gentle man and I trusted him. I believed our government would protect its citizens from bad doctors and bad drugs. Sure, all FDA approved prescription drugs have side effects—all drugs do—we know that the one person in a million adversely affected will not be us. With respect to Botox, how could anything so easy and so simple be bad for you? I was in perfect health when I walked into that clinic. I respected my body. I exercised regularly. I did not smoke or do drugs. Nothing could have prepared me for the way that day would severely alter my life. How can anyone be prepared for a personal tsunami?

After we finished our tour, Michael, Bonnie and I went upstairs to the medical clinic. Doctors, nurses, assistants and patients were buzzing around everywhere. The holiday season had begun and the practice was overbooked with appointments. We had a long wait ahead of us.

"Why is the clinic so busy?" Michael asked.

"I think everyone here is having a mid-life crisis!" I answered, and continued with my soap-box sermon. "The clinic provides a wide array of services and procedures, many designed to bolster the patient's image and make him or her look and feel younger. Our country's obsession with youth and appearance is the driving force behind the clinic's success. Americans are more concerned with the outward appearance than with what is on the inside. Think about it, if Franklin D. Roosevelt were running for office today, it is doubtful he would be elected president, because we are too shallow a nation to elect a man with polio. We are a superficial society and have placed physical appearance and charisma over character and intellectual capacity. We judge the cover without taking the time to read the book." I was as guilty as anyone else.

Bonnie leaned toward Michael and interupted my sermon. "All I want to do is turn back the clock." Little did we know that we were about to hit the fast-forward button.

Dr. McComb waved to us through the window of the nurses' area. He was a handsome man in good shape. He looked like a young surfer. I turned to my son and said, "Dr. McComb graduated near the top of his class and is always attending seminars to learn more. I respect his thirst for knowledge. He is articulate in every facet of natural health and preventive medicine."

"It looks like his knowledge is paying him well."

"Yes, all he speaks of lately is how well the clinic is doing. He is happier than I have seen him in years."

"Dr. Eric Kaplan?" the nurse called.

"My turn. Are you coming in with me, Michael? You can meet the rest of the staff."

"Sure, why not? You're afraid of needles anyway. You may want me to hold your hand."

I jokingly warned him that I wasn't too old to take him over my knee. We laughed as he followed me to the treatment room. The open area was filled with patients receiving all types of treatments. Two lab technicians were drawing blood and giving IV solutions. Michael was certainly impressed by the facility and the staff. As we were waiting for Dr. McComb, Dr. Shelly, a staff member, came by to chat for a moment. Then, Tom Jr. (Dr. Toia's son) started my IV.

During the half-hour it took to drip the solution into my vein, we casually conversed with patients, doctors and technicians. I was sitting there with a needle in my arm, hoping not to have an anxiety attack. I admitted to Michael, "You are right. I am the ultimate chicken when it comes to doctors and medicine."

A patient, overhearing our banter, could not help but laugh at a doctor being afraid of needles. The patient then reassured me, "There's nothing to be afraid of. I come here often and I feel great."

"Me too," another patient raved. "The doctors have made me feel better than I have felt in years."

It all seemed so innocent, so perfect. Everyone was happy and the staff was very professional.

Upon completion of my vitamin IV, I went to see how my wife was doing. She was still waiting for her turn to have Botox injections. I could tell that she was getting anxious and was concerned with all she had to do to get the Thanksgiving meal ready for our guests tomorrow. We decided to reschedule our appointment for sometime after the holidays. We were literally on our way out the door when Dr. Toia came out and asked us not to leave, because Dr. McComb was ready to see us. One more minute and our lives would not have been drastically altered.

If only we had left. If only Dr. Toia had not come out. If only . . . If only . . . If only. I have always innately believed that God would look out for me. Surely, if I were in any danger that day, God would have warned me. As I lay frozen in my hospital bed, I tried to recall any signs that would have warned me not to go through it. There were none. In fact, there seemed to be only encouragement that I should go through with it. *God, why didn't you let us leave? Please answer me!* There was no response, but my memory tape played on.

We were brought directly to Dr. McComb's office where he injected my wife while I watched. Then he turned to me and said, "Let me do you."

"No, I'm okay."

"Eric, you're looking your age. Let me take some years off your life. You're not scared, are you?"

Yes, I was—not of Botox, but of needles in general. However, as a street-tough kid from New Jersey, I could not back down from a dare. "Oh, alright then," I said.

Later that afternoon while playing golf, I began to feel a little light-headed, almost like I'd had a few glasses of wine. Actually it felt good. At about the ninth hole, Dr. Toia rang my cell phone.

"Eric, how are you feeling?"

"A little light-headed. Why do you ask?"

"Two other patients who received Botox this week report feeling strange since the injections. I've spoken to the Allergan Company and they said that flu-like symptoms are an occasional side-effect."

"I didn't know there were any side-effects with Botox. All the reports indicate that the procedure is safe."

"We've never seen side-effects, so those patients may have the flu. Don't worry about it as long as you are feeling fine."

Bonnie and I continued our day not knowing that botulism, the world's most deadly toxin, was infiltrating and ravaging every cell in our body.

The next day was Thanksgiving. Bonnie and I awoke feeling weak and achy as if we had the flu. However, we had eighteen people coming to our home for the holiday, and we had to get on with our plans. Since Dr. Toia had said to expect flu-like symptoms, we were not worried. Bonnie was a perfectly gracious hostess as she attended our guests, but I could tell she did not feel well. I didn't have my usual pep and energy either. I drank some wine hoping it might help relax my stomach. It did actually relieve some of the queasiness, but by nine o'clock in the evening Bonnie and I were both exhausted. We looked at each other and ran for the bed. We smiled, hugged and kissed, hoping to feel better tomorrow. After all, the doctors told us there was nothing to worry about.

The next day we woke up feeling even worse. I was achy, and Bonnie had back pains. "I feel like someone is sitting on my chest," she said.

That is when I started to get concerned. I had been married to this outstanding woman for twenty-four years and I knew how tough she was. She had beaten colon cancer seven years before. She is normally able to handle pain, but today she was succumbing to illness. And me? Heck, I am a kid from Jersey City. I am not about to let the flu kick my butt. I called the clinic and left a message since neither Dr. Toia nor Dr. McComb were in the office. After not receiving a return call for several hours, I called my good friend, Dr. Dennis Egitto. Dennis is an old-fashioned, Marcus Welby-type doctor, who loves his work and his patients. I have known him for over twenty years. We raised our children together and I knew he would be able to help me. When I got him on the phone, his response was simple. "Eric, I never heard of side-effects from Botox. You may really have the flu. Drink a lot of fluids and get some rest. In the mean time, let me make some phone calls and get back to you."

Bonnie continued to feel rotten, and I was getting weaker by the hour. While waiting for Dr. Egitto to call back, Dr. Toia returned my call. "I spoke to Allergan," he said. "They stated that flu-like symptoms are an occasional side effect of Botox, and the symptoms should be temporary, diminishing in a day or so."

"I researched Botox before I had injections the first time. There was no mention of any side effects," I challenged him.

"They are very uncommon. However, I did speak with the other doctors in our clinic. They suggested I come by and give you and Bonnie some intravenous fluids so you don't get any worse."

"Anything that will help."

"I'll be right over."

"We'll be here. We're not going anywhere." Not going anywhere…not going anywhere…but to HELL!

Chapter Three

False Hope

The toxin was taking over our bodies, and Bonnie and I were in a downward spiral when Dr. Toia arrived at our home with his son, Tom Jr. Bonnie was having pain in her chest and difficulty breathing. I remember saying to Dr. Toia, "If this is the flu, it's the worst case I ever had or heard of."

Dr. Toia reaffirmed, "I spoke with Allergan and the other doctors in my clinic. You are probably just dehydrated. I'm sure you will be fine. Tom and I will start the IV We are putting vitamins in the drip."

"All we want is to get better," Bonnie said. "I feel absolutely horrible."

Dr. Toia and his son scurried around the room. They appeared to be confident about their diagnosis and their work. Soon, my wife and I had received IV drips and were beginning to feel better, so we truly believed we had the flu.

I told Michael, "I hope you will one day be a doctor who does house calls." It was extremely uncommon for doctors to make house calls, but I thought that because I was a peer, Dr. Toia and his son were doing me a favor by coming to my house. Who could have known they were trying to cover their own backsides?

They obviously knew something we didn't. Little did we realize they were only treating the symptoms, not the cause.

Bonnie responded immediately to the IV. Actually, we both felt better, and I remember thinking, "The worst is over now. We're on the road to recovery." How wrong. We were inside the eye of a hurricane on a shortcut to Hell.

When Michael saw how much better we were doing, he went out to dinner leaving us in the care of our younger son, Jason. We napped for a while, but when we awoke, the symptoms had returned with a kick. Bonnie was having severe chest pains and I was having difficulty breathing. My wife was not even able to get up, so I called Dr. Toia again. There was no answer.

Jason came in to check on us. "Are you two feeling better?"

"No. Something is not right. I've called the doctor twice and there's no answer. We are going to the hospital."

My wife is a cancer survivor. She had a terrible distaste for hospitals. "No, I'm not," she responded. "I will be fine right here."

I dragged myself to the kitchen to call Dr. Egitto again. "Dennis, Bonnie and I are in serious trouble," I panted. "Something is terribly wrong. We need to go to the hospital and I can't get in touch with anyone at the clinic."

"Eric," Dennis responded, "I'm on my way to dinner. I have called everyone I could think of, but no one knows what could be the cause. I don't know what to tell you."

"Dennis," I pleaded, "something is really wrong. I wouldn't call you like this for no reason. Bonnie and I need you!"

"Okay, I'll meet you at the emergency room of Palm Beach Medical Center in fifteen minutes."

Jason drove us. It was the longest ten minutes of my life. Bonnie and I were sicker than sick. Unfortunately, our healthcare system is driven by money and doesn't care about individuals. When we got to the emergency room, we were greeted by a woman who hadn't had her cigarette break and wasn't too happy to see us.

"Take a seat and fill out this paperwork." She shoved a clipboard across the countertop.

"My wife and I are deathly ill. We need to see a doctor immediately."

"You will be sent to triage once you have filled out the forms."

I was having trouble breathing. "Help me first, then get your paperwork," I panted.

I received a cold look in return as she slammed the ink pen on the clipboard. I could barely write my name, and my wife was even weaker; she could hardly sit up.

We were trying to fill out the paperwork when Dr. Dennis Egitto walked in, took one look at us and told the orderly, "Bring them back here, now." We were taken to a ward-like room with curtains for walls. There, we were left moaning in pain as we ached all over, much worse than having the flu. Nurses drew blood and checked our vital signs. While waiting for lab results to come back, Dr. Egitto searched the Internet to see what he could find in the medical journals. Our symptoms aligned with botulism, but how we might have contracted the illness was still a mystery. He again called Allergan, but they had no new information to offer. Since none of the staff knew what was wrong, they didn't know what to do besides try to stabilize our vital signs.

My son Michael, my brother Steve, his wife, Gloria, and her daughter Beth, arrived shortly thereafter. Steve began to cry when he saw his usually strong and domineering brother lying there helpless. Gloria was tending to Bonnie, who was much worse than I was at that point. I could hear my wife moaning in pain and gasping for air. I was more worried for her than I was for myself even though I was not well. Her vital signs started falling rapidly. I heard the alarms ringing behind the curtain and instinctively knew that Bonnie's heart had stopped beating. *My wife! My wife! Oh, God! I'm losing my wife! Please let her live!*

In came a rush of nurses and a doctor with defibrillator paddles. A nurse called loudly, "Everybody clear!"

With the pads on Bonnie's chest, the doctor pressed the trigger that delivered 360 joules of electricity to Bonnie's petite body. Michael and Jason peered around the cloth partition and watched in horror as their mother's body reacted to the shock with an involuntary spasm. Her upper torso flounced and landed hard upon the narrow bed. The ten-second wait was unbearable as everyone watched the heart monitor to see if there would be a bleep on the quivering line. Once again a steady bleep was heard and everyone took a breath.

Jason stayed by his mother's side. Michael started crying, "I'm sorry, Dad. I will never forgive myself for being out to dinner when you and Mom needed me. I did not see this coming. You were doing better when I left. How could this have happened?"

I think a part of my soul died at that moment. I wanted to be strong. I wanted to hold Michael and tell him everything would be okay, but I knew I was dying. I took off my Rolex watch, gave it to him and said, "You keep my car, and give your car to your brother.

…I have a watch for each of you.…I'm dying." I slurred. A person knows when he is about to die. I knew it. I felt it.

"Don't be silly, Dad. You are going to be okay." He was trying to be optimistic, but his eyes told me he was petrified.

I was wearing a gold necklace that I had not taken off since the day I got it. I removed it and gave it to him. "Put it on so you don't lose it."

The look on his face melted my heart. Who would have thought a little piece of jewelry could have so much significance? To him, the removal of that necklace meant his dad was really dying.

"I will not take it off until you are well. You must get well. Do you hear me?"

How could I do this to my son? I can't imagine what I am putting him through. I love him so much!

Between labored breaths, I told Michael where my will was located and how I wanted my estate to be handled. This was the last thing he wanted to hear, but all I cared about was making sure he and his brother would be provided for once I passed on.

"I love you, Dad! I need you. Don't leave me, damn it! I am too young to lose you. I'm terrified. I don't know what is wrong with you and Mom. No one does!"

Oh, how I wanted to comfort him, but my breathing was becoming more labored and my strength was failing. At least my brother was there with my sons. I was glad they did not have to face this situation alone. Steve started spooning ice chips into my dry mouth, but I could hardly swallow and most of the melted ice was running down my cheeks. My speech was slow and slurred, and I sounded like a mentally handicapped person trying to speak. I was losing control of my motor skills.

When a nurse came in and hooked me up to an EKG machine, I grabbed Michael's hand and started to cry. I knew I was dying and I didn't want to leave him. In all of his twenty-three years, Michael had never seen me so vulnerable. In my son's eyes, I had always been invincible.

All the tests came back normal, which really confused Dr. Egitto and the other staff members who were attending us. They were only able to treat symptoms until they knew what was really wrong. Once we were stable, the staff moved us upstairs to share a private room. Feeling a false sense of relief, Jason left and Steve took his family home. All I wanted to do was sleep. I kept thinking this situation was temporary—like having a cold. I expected to wake up and feel fine in the morning.

During the night shift in most hospitals, there is a limited staff on call and most doctors are home with their families. The crew on the evening after Thanksgiving was even more sparse. Throughout the night, Michael went back and forth from my bedside to Bonnie's, and then to the nurse's station trying to get answers. He held my hand and kept telling me everything would be all right even though he had no idea whether it was true or not.

"God, help me and Bonnie," I prayed repeatedly, but as the night progressed our condition worsened. It was becoming harder and harder to move. I was hooked up to a machine that monitored my oxygen saturation. Even though the level was below normal, the nurses said I was getting enough oxygen. All I knew was I couldn't breathe.

I awoke in the wee hours of the morning when someone came into my room. "I am a speech pathologist," he said. "I am here to analyze your speech." It occurred to me that perhaps they thought I was having a stroke.

I could not swallow. "I am dying," I gurgled through my saliva. "I need a doctor." My voice rattled with death like an AIDS patient I once saw in a movie. "I'm dying!" I repeated.

A second speech specialist came in. He looked at me and said to his colleague, "You had better get his doctor in here quick."

The head nurse came in, took one look at us and said she would have Dr. Egitto come back to the hospital. Michael called Steve, Gloria, and Jason to let them know things had turned for the worse. They came to the hospital immediately.

The next thing I remember was hearing Dr. Egitto. "Thank God, you're here," I mumbled. "Help me… I'm dying."

"Oh, my God!" he gasped. "Eric, you look awful!" He ran to the door and yelled into the hallway, "I NEED A NURSE NOW!" Three nurses quickly came to my room in response. "Intubate him!" Dr. Egitto then hurried to check on Bonnie. Within minutes Bonnie and I were rushed to the ICU where we were placed on life support. No one was allowed into the ICU until the procedure was finished and our vital signs were again stable. Our family waited in the ICU waiting room for about two hours until Dr. Egitto came out with the news.

"We had a close call. We almost lost them," he explained. "We didn't realize how serious their condition was until we tried to insert tubes into their lungs. Eric's throat was filled with saliva, which spewed everywhere when we tried to insert the tube. He could not swallow due to the closing of his throat. The endotracheal tube will hold his throat open and the ventilator will force air into his lungs."

"What about my mom?" Jason asked.

"Her throat was closed so tightly, we had to use a child-sized tube on her. Both of your parents are going to be on the machines for a while, which is uncomfortable, so we put them on a nerve blocking medication to ease the pain of having a ventilator tube in their throats. It will also keep them from fighting the pain and from trying to pull out the tube. They will likely not remember much about what is going on around them. During this time, they may hallucinate or be in an altered state of consciousness. It could affect their sense of reality, making it seem as if they are dreaming, and vice-versa. If they make progress, we can alter or reduce their medication."

"What is causing them to be so sick?" Steve asked.

"Their neurologist has ordered a spinal tap on both of them to see if they have Guillain-Barre Syndrome—a disorder in which the nerves of the legs, arms, neck, and breathing muscles are paralyzed. I have never seen anything like this before, but I have a feeling it is from the Botox injections they both received last Wednesday. Botox is a diluted version of botulism toxin."

"Toxin?" Steve jumped in. "Are you telling my brother and Bonnie have been poisoned?"

"We do not know for sure what has happened, but if it is an overdose of Botox, we have no set protocol for treating it since there are no cases on file with which to compare. Bonnie and Eric are our only case study, and we will have to learn from them."

"Is there anything I can do?" Michael felt helpless.

"Yes, I want you to meet with me and the team of doctors who are working on your parents' case and brainstorm with us to figure out what could have gone wrong. I'll send for you this afternoon."

"Dr. Egitto," Michael gathered his courage, "I need to know if they are going to be okay."

"I've been a friend of your family for a long time, and I won't lie to you. All we can do is hope they make it. Right now it doesn't look good. They are stable if you want to go in and visit them for a few minutes. However, I must warn you, your parents look worse now than they did a few hours ago. We have put them in a drug-induced coma and we do not know whether or not they are consciously aware of their surroundings. You can talk to them, but I do not know if they can hear you. However, studies show that a person who is in a coma is affected at some level by positive input from friends and family members."

Dennis walked with the family into the ICU. Reality set in quickly. Bonnie and I were connected to tubes leading to machines that were literally keeping us alive. I could hear our loved ones crying as I sunk back into a disillusioned stupor.

"Dennis," Michael was holding back tears as he pleaded, "Mom and Dad are too young to die. I am not ready to lose them."

"Neither am I, son," Dennis replied, "neither am I, but they are in God's hands now."

Chapter Four

The Antitoxin

I have always felt close to God but at my lowest moment, I felt all alone. When I was awake, I tried to pray. *God, I have called on You every day of my life, but today when I need You most, there is no answer. I wonder if You are even real. . . . I'm not sure there is a God.* I was sending God an SOS and I was not getting a response. *God, if you are there, answer me! I'm trapped inside my body. I need Your help to get out. . . Even if I have to die, I want out of this hell.*

Most people think of hell in association with death. I learned that heaven and hell exist here on earth while we are alive. I was living in hell. To the observer, Bonnie and I looked dead as we lay there hooked to every machine imaginable. Hearing all the loving comments made by my family in the room with me assured me that my life had not been wasted. I was scared, but if this was the end, I was leaving Earth a fulfilled man.

Time passed while I swooped in and out of consciousness. I had no concept of time, and therefore I couldn't tell night from day or one day from the next. It was all a harsh blur of confusion and disorder. Being awake was horrible. Every time I awoke, I was in pain and I panicked anew each time I rediscovered I couldn't move my body.

"Dad?" Michael's voice brought me back to the scene in my living hell. "I don't know if you hear me, but I want you to know I am still here with you. Jason is with Mom. We love you." Turning to Dr. Egitto, he said, "He's not moving."

"He's in the same condition as your mother," Dr. Egitto explained to Michael. "Every muscle in his body is completely paralyzed."

"Permanently?" Michael took my hand and held it in his.

"I have no idea. At this point, we know he's slightly conscious, but we don't know if his condition will improve. If we knew exactly what we were dealing with, we might be able to make a better prognosis."

"I've never seen my father like this. He looks like a corpse." Michael gulped back the tears that stung his eyes and throat.

"His health is not much better than he looks. He's fighting for his life. I know it must be frightening for you."

You think you're scared. I'm terrified! I felt like Patrick Swayze in the movie, *Ghost*. People thought I might be dead, but I was very much alive. I just couldn't get anyone to hear me.

Later that day, Michael sat down with the team of doctors to talk about what was going on.

"We assume that we are dealing with botulism but there is no way to test for it here," the hospital administrator told us. "The Centers for Disease Control (CDC) is the only facility that can test for it."

Dr. Egitto picked up the phone and immediately called CDC in Atlanta, but no one answered because it was the Saturday following Thanksgiving and everyone was off work. Together the team must have made a hundred phone calls in about fifteen minutes trying to track down someone at CDC, but they came up

51

empty. Dr. Egitto had an idea. "My brother-in-law is with the FBI. Maybe he can help."

After phoning him, Dr. Egitto received a return phone call from the Director of CDC who explained the antitoxin serum. "There is an antitoxin that can be given in the early stages. It can lessen the severity by neutralizing the toxin that has not yet bound to nerve endings. It is made from a horse serum so there is a risk of side effects."

"Such as?" Dr. Egitto asked.

"Some people may have an unpredictable life-threatening allergic reaction to the serum."

"I don't see how we have a choice. If the symptoms worsen, the Kaplans are not going to make it."

"Please understand that the antitoxin is not a cure. It can only prevent the toxin from spreading and damaging more of their nerves. It cannot undo the damage that has been done."

"I understand. Please send it to us at once."

Time was of the essence. While our condition was getting worse by the minute, CDC sent the antitoxin to the Miami Airport which is over an hour away instead of sending it directly to Palm Beach International, only minutes away. We were losing precious time and Michael was freaking out. He told the doctors he would drive to Miami and get it himself. He was out of the door and in his car when he received a call from Dr. Egitto.

"Michael, you will not be allowed to pick up the serum. It has to be driven by police escort."

"Police escort? And all the while my parents are dying!" He almost lost his temper.

Isn't It Amazing that anyone can buy the botulism toxin by

mail order or on the Internet but it takes a police escort to get the antitoxin? Shouldn't it be the other way around?

After two hours on the phone, and offering to send a helicopter to Miami to pick up the antitoxin, Michael and Steve were politely told that the system works in a certain manner, and that they had to be patient. The Kaplan family waited anxiously in the waiting room for what seemed like an eternity.

While a police officer drove the antitoxin from Miami to Palm Beach Gardens, I heard a doctor's voice among the bleeping machines that were keeping my body alive. I wanted to know what was happening but at the same time, I was fearful of what I might hear.

"At this time, we believe your parents have been poisoned by botulism," the doctor broke the news. "If so, their prognosis is not good. There are no prior documented cases so we don't have statistics on the survival rate. We will have to test their blood to find out if the batch of Botox they received was tainted and what dosage was administered. It appears that the botulism virus has spread throughout their entire bodies. That is why they are totally paralyzed at this point. There is no cure or treatment; however, over a period of time, the paralysis will wear off. Our goal right now is to try and keep them alive."

"It will wear off in time? How much time?" Michael queried.

"Severe cases of botulism are so rare that hardly any doctors have experience treating it. However, the cases of food-borne botulism that we do have on records cause us to believe it will wear off in six to eighteen months. Your parents' case is not normal. We do not know the toxin or the dosage yet. Their muscles will be paralyzed for at least six to eighteen months; we are probably looking at the latter, the full eighteen months. Your dad is in bad shape. He may not open his eyes for six months. The fact that he and your mom are alive is a miracle. We literally have to wait until the toxin wears off. This is going to be a long and difficult road for you and your family."

The antitoxin arrived around seven that evening and was administered immediately by Gardens Hospital under the watchful eye of a proficient team of doctors from CDC, who had flown in. It would have made more sense if the doctors could have brought the antitoxin with them, but the law would not allow it. One of the doctors on the team told the family, "We will have to wait and see if the antitoxin works."

"How long will it take to determine that?" Michael asked.

"We do not know." The doctor was being honest. "This is the first documented case of this kind in the world. Eric and Bonnie Kaplan are 'writing the book' on this situation."

Steve commented, "Eric loves to write books, but I think this is one he would rather have not written."

Chapter Five

Probing Questions

I knew I was alive, but to those around me, I was all but dead because I could not move or respond to them. Nothing made sense but prayer.

God, I do not deserve this . . . Help me. . . I want to live; I need to live. My sons are too young to be on their own. My wife doesn't deserve this. God, hear my prayers, help us... Can anyone up there hear me? Is there a God? God, if You exist, come to me. . . help me. Don't You love me?

I felt as though I had been buried alive as I listened to the dissonance of machines and people around me. I felt pain, confusion, sympathy, depression, avarice and all the chaos in the world. Doctors talked about me as if I was not there.

"What's the report on the Kaplans?" one doctor asked the other.

"We think they may have been poisoned," the expert answered.

"Poisoned? By what?"

"They received wrinkle reducing cosmetic injections less than three days ago. They may have botulism poisoning."

I HEAR YOU! Botulism? How in the world did I get botulism from the injections? What is going on here?

"The problem here," the doctor continued as if he had heard me, "is the amount of toxin they are fighting. We believe they may have received more than 2,000 times the normal dosage."

Great, I am the winner of the Botulism lottery!

"When will you know for sure if Botulism is what we are dealing with?"

"We won't know until the test results come back."

"When will that be?"

"The Centers for Disease Control in Atlanta should phone us with the results in a few days."

"What if it is Botulism poisoning?"

"If they live, they will be in this condition for an indeterminate amount of time."

"What about the antidote?"

"There is no antidote. There's an antitoxin, which we have administered. It will arrest any further damage, but the damage that has been done may be permanent. Right now, we don't even know how Dr. or Mrs. Kaplan have survived thus far. For all we know they may have brain damage."

I'M NOT BRAIN DEAD! I'm as alive as you are! At least I think I'm alive. Yes, I am alive. I can think. I can feel. I have emotions; I can even smell! I just can't move, see, swallow or talk.

The doctors came near my bed. "Watch this," the expert said, "I can stick him with a pin and he doesn't respond."

Stop pricking me!

He lifted my leg and let it fall with a thud. "He doesn't try to resist or catch his leg from falling."

Hey, that's disrespectful! I feel what is going on! How can I show them I'm alive? If only I could move.

He tapped hard on my knee with a rubber tool. "See? No

reflexes."

OUCH! That hurts! HELLO! I'm a person, not a piece of meat!

"Eric?" he was shouting in my ear while pricking me with a sharp object. "ERIC?"

OUCH! That hurts! I'm not deaf!

"Eric, can you move your hand?"

I tried with all my might, but I could not make my hand move. I could not move any part of my body—not even my eyes. I was unable to respond in any manner.

"Since Dr. Kaplan is on total life support," they continued, "we do not know how much brain function he has or if he can hear us. Either way, he cannot respond and he is totally paralyzed. We have given him medication that will help him be comfotable in this state. It is almost a self-induced coma. He will enter a dream state and have difficulty discerning fantasy from reality, but it will allow him to rest until we know what to do next."

Total life support? Paralyzed? Oh, my God. What is happening to me? This is hell! I'm not supposed to be here. Why is this happening to me? God, I'm scared.

The rest of our family and our Rabbi, Joel Levine prayed for us, while Michael talked to the neurologist. Rabbi Levine had become a friend and family confidant over the years. He even talked me into becoming the President of our Temple. He is a sincere loving man who visited us every day while we were in Gardens Hospital. Michael's days were spent talking to our rabbi, praying to God, and going from room to room talking to the lifeless bodies of his parents. As he sat vigil, Michael explained to us what was going on. He wasn't sure we comprehended or even heard him, but he knew I would want an explanation of what was happening if one could be given.

After six long days, we finally received the test results from CDC that confirmed that it was indeed botulism. This was good news and bad news. It was good news because we could stop speculating, but bad news because botulism is a terrible disease that paralyzes the nervous system. He explained that we were dealing with one of the most commonly used drugs in our society and that once the media got hold of the story, things were going to be chaotic. Little did he know how chaotic. While we were fighting for our lives, a careless doctor in the hospital leaked the story to the press the first night we were there, and within minutes, the hospital parking lot was filled with news crews. So much for HIPPA! Nothing was private after that. The news crews did not waste any time identifying us as the victims of this tragedy. The story was on every channel across the U.S. that evening. The next day, the hospital staff moved us to a private wing of the ICU and posted security guards around the clock. They were given a list of names compiled by our family of the people who were allowed in to see us. The first people on the list were our best friends, the Brocks and the Meyers.

Peter Brock is about six feet tall and resembles Richard Gere. Peter is an attractive, well-groomed man that everyone loves to be around. Since he has educated views on most topics, he can be quite serious when he talks business, but then out of the blue, he may come up with a joke that leaves people laughing uncontrollably. Peter's wife, Janice, is a New Jersey girl who looks like Uma Thurman. Janice is a very confident and outgoing red-headed woman who is the life of any party. William and Denise

Meyer are an elegant Ivy League couple with strong family values. William is a stately businessman, tall, handsome, well mannered and very articulate. Like Peter, he makes a statement when he enters a room. Denise is an attractive woman with a strong, matriarchal personality that commands respect. She reminds me of Candace Bergen. Janice, Denise and Bonnie love to go hiking together. They are always involved in helping others.

Both William and Peter are my golf buddies. Both men went to the Wharton School of Business at the University of Pennsylvania, and William went on to the London School of Economics. Bonnie and I have known the Brocks and Meyers for about twenty years, ever since we lived around the block from one another. We raised our kids together. To this day, my younger son, Jason, and Peter's son, Jarret, are good friends. The six of us adults spend every Christmas and New Year's Eve together because we enjoy each other's company so much. Peter and William (Billy, as his close friends call him) have turned out to be my best friends. Janice and Denise are Bonnie's. Michael called the Brocks and the Meyers from the hospital the day we were admitted. They were with our family throughout our hospital stay and assisted my family in all life and death decisions.

Monday morning was the first of what would be many meetings with medical specialists from all over the country. Michael met with every government agency imaginable: the Drug Enforcement Administration, the Department of Health, the Centers for Disease Control, the FBI, and other investigation teams, trying to figure out exactly what we had been given. The two most influential members of the team were Susan M. Turcovski, investigator for the U.S. Food and Drug Administration, and Dr.

Daniel Chertow, CDC EIS (Epidemic Intelligence Service) Officer of the Bureau of Epidemiology. Turcovski was in charge of the investigation and relayed information about where the deadly substance had been purchased and how it had been handled prior to being injected into our bodies. The meetings that took place every morning, via phone and Internet, turned out to be vital to our health. First, they discovered that what we had been given was not real Botox; it was raw botulism toxin. The team of doctors and federal agents analyzed and reviewed the specifics in such detail that there was no room for error. They were proactive in making sure that every government bureau was notified. The team was also great in dealing with the fiasco the media was creating. Everyone wanted an exclusive. When our family refused to speak to the press, the papers published a daily update based on speculation. Every paper was fair except for our local paper, the *Palm Beach Post*. They wanted sensationalism so they lied about our character while we were incapable of defending ourselves.

Our poisonings were the signal for a federal investigation that revealed the sale of the unapproved wrinkle reducing serum knockoff through two companies that had sold over 3,000 vials of the knockoff wrinkle treatment to doctors and clinics nationwide. Arizona-based TRI (Toxin Research International) and List Laboratories of California are responsible for the manufacture and distribution of the unregulated toxin to more than 200 doctors in the U.S. Because it was more profitable than buying FDA-approved Botox from Allergan, the only government-approved manufacturer, more than 1,000 patients were injected by practitioners who purchased the substance from TRI. Drs. Chad Livdahl and Zahra Karim, a husband and wife team who operated

TRI, were found guilty of promoting the poisonous substance for use on humans. The couple made about $1.8 million by selling the unapproved wrinkle reducing serum substitute for $1,250 per 5-dose vial; this is comparable to $2,000 for the FDA approved and legal Botox. The team kept these and many other truths under wrap, which provided security for our family while Bonnie and I received without interruption the care we desperately needed. To this day, I wonder how the FDA could allow any product made from a deadly toxin to be on the market. Isn't it up to our government to protect us? Where is our Homeland Security when we need it?

How could they allow this to happen on American soil? Botulinum toxin puts us all at risk. One gram in a water supply could kill hundreds of thousands of people. How is the most lethal toxin in the world so readily available? Who is monitoring the sales of this toxin? How did the governement not know? These are the questions I ask myself on a daily basis. What happened to us should never happen again. However, with current laws we are all at risk. These toxins should be governed by the governement and a part of homeland security.

Chapter Six

My Mother Visits

Bleep. . . bleep. . . bleep. . . The steady rhythm of the heart monitor was the first thing I heard when I awoke the next morning. I did not remember where I was until I felt a terrible pain in my throat. Then I knew I was in the hospital, but I didn't know how long I had been there. I could feel an IV in one arm; on the other arm a blood pressure cuff inflated itself every so often. I was catheterized, something was stuck to my chest, and a machine was pumping air into my lungs. My body was alive only by the marvels of modern medicine. I had a hard time believing this situation was real. Part of the time I believed I was either dying or already dead. I tried to imagine it was all a bad dream that would go away as soon as I opened my eyes.

Open your eyes. . . I can't. . . Come on, Kaplan, you can do it. . .

I was not dreaming. I could not open my eyes. My back was hurting from lying in one position for so long. *Roll over and get comfortable. . . Come on, move.* My body wouldn't budge. I panicked, fighting the fear of confinement. *I'm trapped in my body! God, help me!* I felt like I was going to cry, but I couldn't even create a tear! *Where is everyone? I need a blanket. I wish I could tell someone I'm cold. Nurse? Michael? Anyone?*

I was in a catatonic state, a dream state. I wanted to dream. I often forced myself to dream. Because of the numerous medications, I often could not tell the difference between a dream and reality. The doctors put me in a drug-induced form of a coma to make my body more comfortable during this difficult time. No one wanted me to suffer. The mental anguish was worse than any physical pain. I enjoyed dreaming because the fantasy was always better then the realtiy. Physically and mentally, I knew what was going on. I was fighting for my life. I wanted to talk, to walk, to tell my family I was going to be okay. Although I could not see anyone, I could hear and feel everyone. I could feel the fear in people's voices, the shock they expressed when they saw me. Even in my drug-induced state I was aware. When I was not dreaming, I was fighting, worrying, praying.

"Eric, wake up."

"Mom?. . Is that you? I thought you were dead."

"Son," my mother lovingly stated, "there is no death. There is only life and afterlife. You have preached that life is a journey, have you not?"

"Yes, but I meant it metaphorically, not literally. Why are you here?"

"A mother brings a child into life and, whenever possible, she brings that soul into the afterlife."

"Afterlife? That must mean I'm dead."

"Like I said, there is no such thing as death."

"I'm sorry, Mom."

"Why are you sorry?"

"I'm sorry I am here. It's my fault. I had cosmetic injections to try to look younger."

"How do you know it is a fault? Perhaps it is your destiny.

Maybe you have served your purpose in life and are ready to bring your skills to the afterlife. Maybe it is your turn to truly grow up and be a man."

"Oh, God. There are lectures in Heaven!"

"I never said you were in Heaven."

"Then where am I?"

"You are here and now," she responded. "There is no past and there is no future in life or in afterlife. There is only now, the present. The present is God's gift of life. Your gift to God is what you do with it."

"I'm confused."

"Then let me explain," she said. "Nothing is ever gained or lost in the universe—only transformed. Wherever there is love or life, there is God. Accept the idea that we are love, and as such, we are God. God never dies. Therefore there is no death; only life."

"And afterlife," I sassed.

"Same thing. The same rules apply there as here. Soon, you will meet two other angels."

"Are you an angel?"

"We are all asked to do the work of God. There are many angels in your life, as well as in the afterlife. An angel is someone who does God's work."

"Am I an angel?" I was curious.

"At times. You could do better, you know?"

"I know Mom. It's good to have you back."

"I have never gone anywhere, son. I have been right by your side. Have you forgotten all I taught you? A mother's love is infinite. I have always been there for you and always will be. You lecture on faith, son. Have you lost yours?"

My mother and I were hovering near the ceiling, looking down on my body as it lay in bed.

"Hey, that's me!" I observed. "I don't look too good,"

"No, you don't."

"Am I going to die?"

"Do you want to die?"

"Not really, but am I going to be okay?"

"That is up to you, son. You have a fight and a struggle on your hands."

"Are saying that I control my destiny?"

"Absolutely. We all control our destiny. Look around you." My mother and I flew into the hallway of the intensive care unit. "There are a lot of sick people here." She led me into the room next door where I was confronted with the sight of my wife.

"Bonnie!" I called. There were machines and tubes everywhere. Michael sat at her bedside, holding her hand. "Mom, Bonnie doesn't look too good either."

"No, she doesn't."

"Is she going to be okay?"

"I don't know son. It is not up to you or me. It is her choice."

"Why did God do this to us?"

"God did not do this to you. God did not tell you to go for wrinkle reducing cosmetic injections." my mother softly stated. "Many people blame God when bad things happen, but I remind you that God doesn't make anyone do anything. He does not drink and drive; therefore, He is not responsible for the car accident that kills another person. People do these things to themselves and to one another. People make choices, and choices are followed by consequences."

"I understand."

"God does not micromanage the lives of humans. He does not sit on a throne waving His royal wand and command, 'Good things for this person. Bad things for that person.' There are three categories of people: angels, messengers, and receptors. Angels are divine beings, but they sometimes appear in human form. They are the people who live their life solely for the benefit of others. All God's children have angelic qualities. The more you emphasize this power, the more evolved you become. Messengers are the second type of beings. These people tell stories through their actions. They may be actors for movies, plays or television; they may be public speakers, comedians, or poets; they may be singers or recording artists; they may use a pen or a typewriter; a canvas and a paintbrush or whatever tool is available, but they are here to convey their message. The stronger and the more purposeful their message, the closer they move to angel status. Thirdly, there are receptors. This is where we all begin. A newborn baby can only receive. As a baby develops physically, he or she may choose to evolve spiritually and give to others. Some people stay in the receptor category forever. They continue to take from others and offer nothing in return."

"Like some people I know."

"Are you judging? Here you are learning your first lesson from the other side of the veil, and you are already going back to your old habits," she scolded.

"You sure sound like my mother." I wondered if I was dreaming or if this was really happening.

"I will always be your mother. Now back to our lesson. The world is full of givers and takers. The more you give of yourself, the more you serve others. Ego is about self. Serving is about others. The more you give, the more you serve. The more you serve, the more you evolve."

"You mean it is my choice whether I go to Heaven or Hell, or whether I become a giver or a taker?"

"Yes, my son. Every day we make choices. We may choose to help, love and give to others. We may choose to ignore their needs and instead strive to accumulate more material possessions. Your choices make you the person you are. You may not be able to control all the things that happen in your life, but you can control your thoughts, emotions, attitudes and feelings. Humans have the ability to read, learn and attain wisdom. You chose to study and become a doctor. God did not take your tests for you. He let you make choices. Every person who walks this earth can change their life at any time by the choices they make. These choices not only affect us, they have an effect on the people around us."

"I didn't know you were so deep, Mom," I laughed.

"Evolved, son, evolved. Life, as well as afterlife, is an evolution. God wants us to evolve continually. The more we evolve, the closer we move to the light—to God. However, that has to do with the Laws of Life. Those will come later. My job is to teach you the Facts of Life."

"But, Mom," I blurted, "why does God let bad things happen? How could this happen to Bonnie and me? What did we do to deserve this? If God is love and life, how can things go wrong?"

"Life is complex. Life comes with choices, and choices come

with consequences."

"Are you saying I chose this?"

"Life consists of two forces. One is positive and the other is negative. They each have intellect and feelings and are endowed with certain qualities. Like plants and animals, they multiply after their own kind. The force you feed the most in your mind becomes the stronger, more dominant force. All people are governed by the force they allow to dominate. Some people make poor choices, which lead to actions that have unpleasant consequences. Eric, you chose to alter your appearance. You and the doctor made a wrong choice. Let's take a look at him."

We were then transported to another room in another hospital.

"Mom! That is Dr. McComb!"

"Yes, it is."

"What is he doing here?"

"His choices not only affected you and Bonnie, they have damaged him as well."

"I don't understand."

"He injected himself with the same drug he used on you and Bonnie. There's one more person you need to see. Come with me," my mother urged.

Soon we entered another room in the Bayonne Hospital in Bayonne New Jersey. How did I get here? Was I hallucinating? I had to be, how else could I explain being on a ventilator one minute in Florida the next in Bayonne, New Jersey?

There, on life support, lay Alma Hall. "Do you know who this is, son?"

"Yes, that is Alma Hall. She is McComb's girlfriend. Why did he do this to her?"

"The answer to that question lies inside of Dr. McComb."

"This is terrible! Is there anyone else?"

"Not here and now. There could be others if greed and medical recklessness continue."

"Now at least Dr. McComb will know what we are going through." I felt angry.

"Yes, he will. His greed has altered the lives of others including yours."

"This has to stop."

"Yes, it does."

"Take me back home, Mom."

"Where is home?"

"Florida. I want to be with my wife. I want to see my sons."

"We have plenty more to learn," she replied as we drifted back to my hospital room. "People choose to defy nature. To defy the laws of nature or medicine is not a wise a choice."

"I see that now."

"You choose your own path—right or wrong, good or bad. Life, Mother Nature, God, whatever anyones belief, has granted every soul the power of choice, but choice should be governed by wisdom. There are laws, which assist us in growth. They are part of the learning and growing process. The law of love is this: with giving love, comes the receiving of love. These universal laws are embedded in nature. When you do not govern yourself by these laws, nature will return a consequence equivalent to the action."

"This is the law of sowing and reaping, isn't it?"

"Exactly. Thus, the need for birth and rebirth."

"And these laws exist even when we pass into the afterlife?"

"Yes, life and afterlife are a cycle of one another. The coming and passing of generations means that new human bodies appear and old ones disappear. The soul that filled the body continues to survive. Your thoughts act as carriers to the brain cells of anyone you have touched, and this energy will never disappear. All that you have done will live on in your family, your sons, your brother, your nieces, nephews and cousins. Your soul, energy and thoughts will live on in the new bodies of the next generation."

"That sounds like reincarnation."

"It is the oneness we all have with our Creator. All souls are considered as one generation because we all are children of God. From the creation of the first human millions of years ago, life continues without end, no matter how many different forms or bodies the soul takes on. Death does not affect the soul because the soul is made of a higher matter. Cutting your hair or nails does not affect your body, and death does not affect the soul. Our task on earth is to remember that we are one with God. Once you realize this, you will want to do good for others. The more good you do, the stronger your spirit and soul become. It is important to bond with others by sharing love and affection. If all people followed their angelic heart and did what is right, there would be no war—only people helping people."

"That sounds profound, yet simple. Giving and loving should be easy. Why aren't we doing it?"

"People must evolve by using their free will to make choices that lead to peace. Whether we choose to do good or bad, we will all eventually reach the same destiny—awareness of our oneness with the universe. It can happen in this lifetime or the next one. Each soul will create the experiences it needs to evolve spiritually.

It can happen through physical suffering, social pressures, natural disasters, economic struggle or any number of things, but sooner or later each one of us will have to accept the idea that we are love, and as such, we are God. This should be our goal and purpose in life. The people who strive for this goal will receive pleasure instead of suffering while they are converging, growing, and evolving with the Creator."

"Mom, I wish everyone knew this."

"Don't worry. They will in due time. Every soul will reach this goal regardless of its chosen path."

"How do we become one with Life, the Universe, God and each other?"

"The goal is to love, honor, and serve all people. We should free ourselves from egotism and envy and develop the feelings of compassion, mutual help and love. Eric, when you surrender your ego, you give yourself to God."

"It sounds simple and easy. Why is it so difficult to be happy? Why do we always want more than we have?"

"Life is for living, loving, laughing and learning. If you choose to live, love, laugh and learn, you will understand the essence of the gifts God has bestowed upon you. If your life is spent living, loving, laughing and learning and not just whining, worrying, wasting and working, you will evolve! It's that simple."

"Mom, I'm scared," I said softly. "Look at us down there. Look at the worried faces of our friends."

"No," my mother interrupted, "be glad you have friends. Look at all the people who love you. Look at all the people who are praying for you. Son, you touched many people and your work on earth is not done. What you have given to others in love and kindness is now coming back to you tenfold. This is nature's way, God's way."

"But, look at my body, Mom. I'm dying and will soon be gone," I defiantly responded.

"Son, THERE IS NO DEATH! There is only life and afterlife."

"I heard you the first time. Why are you lecturing me?"

"Because I am your mother and I can," she laughed.

"That sounds like the old Mom I remember!"

"Nothing is old or new. I am here now and forever. Put your faith in God, who loves you."

Faith, faith is what I lost with the use of my body. Faith was what I needed to survive. I needed to believe that this was real, that God did exist. What I needed was hope. I did not know if I was dreaming or if this was my subconsious taking over, but it passed the idle hours and made me feel good. To be honest, I didn't care, I still don't, all I knew is I wanted more. To be paralyzed and have happy thoughts was a blessing. Dream or no dream. I looked back at my mother,

"I'm still scared," I said softly, "not of dying, but of living in that body."

"I know son, but everything is going to be okay. Remember the prayer that says: 'Lord, give me strength to change the things I can change, courage to accept the things I cannot change, and wisdom to know the difference'?"

"Yes. Perhaps we should remain passive and let things flow— let fate take over."

"Wisdom allows us to make choices and set goals that align

with a higher purpose. Mother Nature doesn't dictate right and wrong. She allows us to make mistakes, both as individuals and collectively. Because she doesn't judge, she does not lead us to grow or evolve; she is simply a 'cause and effect' mechanism."

"That does away with the theory that some people are good and some are bad."

"God loves all people the same and provides each of us the same tools. Sometimes people become disillusioned in their power to change things in life or themselves. Disillusionment is nothing more than an attitude."

"And we control our attitude," I interrupted, "and our attitude is a choice. What you are saying is if I keep my faith and maintain my attitude and make right choices, I will get better."

"You always were a good student when you wanted to be!"

"I love you, Mom."

"And, I love you, son. Draw wisdom from your lessons. Don't let Mother Nature confuse or disorient you. Remember, you have choice."

With that, my mother was gone and I heard people in my room as I awoke. I was terribly confused as to whether or not her visit was real. I knew I was medicated, I heard the doctor say he gave me medication that would induce a dream state. It could have been nothing more than a dream, but it seemed so real—more real that the present condition I was in. I wondered if being paralyzed and in the hospital was just a nightmare from which I would also awaken. Sadly, as I gained my bearings, nothing had changed. My world was still dark and my body was still lifeless. To make matters worse, I heard a doctor talking about me.

"Eric is in bad shape. It appears the botulism has taken over his body. You can expect him to be like this for a year to eighteen months."

"Then what?" I heard Steve ask.

"We don't know," the doctor responded.

"Can he hear me?" Michael asked.

"I believe so," the doctor responded. "We have given him medication to make him comfortable; basically it will keep him in a dream state. It is good to speak to him. Family, friends, music, are all good. How much he hears or understands we don't know at this time. "

Yes, I can hear you! HELP ME! I AM ALIVE. Stop saying bad things about me. Mom, come back! Help me! Please tell me I was not dreaming. I need to know it was really you. God, please let me know my mom's visit was real.

I heard my mother's voice in my head say, "Every thought you think is real."

I fussed with myself, Open your eyes; talk to them. *Do something, damn it! Move your hand! MOVE… YOUR… HAND!* My body would not respond and I thought s*urely I must be dead. No one can live like this.*

I felt guilty and sad as I thought about my mother. She had given me life when she brought me into the world and all she ever wanted was for her sons to have more than she had. I fought with her so much at the end of her life. I wished I could tell her how much I loved her. Just thinking the thought gave me a feeling of peace. My mother's visit may very well have been nothing but a dream. It really doesn't matter. Our interaction was filled with great advice and I trusted that the lessons, insights and memories she shared would help me survive my most critical hour.

Chapter Seven

Groundhog Days

Where am I? Open your eyes...What day is it? I can't move... How long have I been like this?

If you saw the movie *Groundhog Day*, you will have an idea of what it was like being in a drug-induced state. Each day seemed the same as the one before. I slept and awoke, dreamt and fought my internal demons. I had the will to live and I fought the temptation to succumb to my situation; however, fear and doubt are strong opponents. My life consisted of sedated and partially awake moments, some good and some bad. Being unable to move, talk, swallow, or open my eyes, I learned to use the creativity of my mind to survive, but I was still scared and confused.

I was beginning to tell the days from the nights because the days were noisy and I had visitors. Even though I could not see their faces, I could sense the fear of those around me when they came to show how much they loved me. I yearned to tell everyone that I was alive, but I was in a nightmare and couldn't wake up.

The nights were quiet, lonely and scary. I longed for the touch of my son, my wife, my family and my friends. Through my loneliness, I became my own best friend. I might have lost physical strength but as I turned inward to my innate intelligence, I gained powers and insight far superior. This internal power kept me hoping for renewed health while machines kept me alive. These powers exist within all of us, but we rarely access them until a crisis occurs. Then we are forced to ask questions such as: Is there life after death? What is death? Should we fear death? Were we put here on this planet for a purpose?

From my mom's visit, I began to realize we are here on Earth to learn, grow and evolve. There are no mistakes in life—only choices and lessons. I wondered if it was a dream but I was glad I could dream. Dreams were like movies. I was the producer, the director, and the star of the show. This was escapism at its best, but to keep my sanity, I had to dream.

Through my brush with death, I learned the meaning of compassion and thankfulness. I now give thanks for the little things that most people take for granted: breathing, eating, seeing, tasting, smelling, walking, talking, laughing and loving. At my lowest moment, I came to realize that nothing can dissolve my spirit—not terrorism or natural disasters—not even death! The spirit is invisible, as is electricity, yet the spirit is more powerful.

People often ask what I learned from my encounter. I learned that GOD IS REAL. I am not a religious man nor do I consider this a religious book. God means many things to many people. This is why religion and faith go hand in hand. To have religion you must have faith. At this time I needed hope, I needed faith, maybe I was grasping for something, anything. Here is the valuble lesson I learned while alone, scared and lifeless: To believe in **something** is better than **nothing**.

I come from Jewish roots. Throughout my life, I have questioned religion and the physical existence of God. As a boy, I played basketball for St. Aloysius in Jersey City. Father Yanatelli was my father's friend and the President of St. Peter's College. I remember asking him about God and he told me that God is everywhere—in all things. At that time, I didn't understand what he meant. Now, today I did. It does not matter if you are an atheist; when you are paralyzed you will talk to anyone you think will listen. When you can't speak or move, only faith offers any form of hope.

I am now a person of faith, and faith is more than words. Words have subjective meaning. Words create pictures based on our learning, our childhood, our education and our beliefs. Different countries use different words to say the same thing. One country is not more right or wrong than another. For example, the word "Jesus" means one thing to a Christian, another to a Jewish person, another to a Catholic person, another to a Muslim. Love, religion, power, heaven, hell—all these words have different interpretations from different people. While God is interpreted differently by all faiths and cultures, the majority of people believe in a Supreme Being or power—a Universal Intelligence—yet we fight wars trying to convince other people that we are right and they are wrong.

Words are a way to communicate our beliefs. Many times, the only thing that separates us is our vocabulary and terminology. Words are not reality. Saying the word "water" will not quench our thirst. We must look beyond the words and into our heart and soul for the meaning of life, the meaning of spirit, or our belief in God. We must look on the inside and view life through our inner eye. Regardless of your religious beliefs, your house of worship, or your genetics or geography, the presence of God exists in all people. However, our actions speak louder than our words. Our actions may deny the goodness that resides within us.

During my suffering, I prayed to God for a miracle and kept repeating, "I CAN, I WILL, I MUST!" But, every time I awoke and came back to physical reality, I found that nothing had changed. I was still confused and repeatedly wondered where I was, what day it was, and how long I had been in the hospital. At times, I didn't know whether I was awake or asleep.

I didn't need a mirror to know I didn't look good. My visitors confirmed that much in their whispered conversations. They didn't know I was hearing them. I felt sorry for myself but no one would have known it since I was unable to express my thoughts or feelings. Hell, I couldn't even scratch an itch! Daily I battled depression and wanted to give up and just die. I was awake and alone one day when I thought, "Why doesn't God just take me out of this suffering?"

"STOP BEING A BABY!" I heard a voice.

"Who is that?"

"LOOK AT ME!" he barked.

"I can't see."

"You can see *ME*." It was my Uncle Herb wearing a big smile. Boy, did I miss that smile. My Uncle Herb was a special man. The life he and my Aunt Gloria lived was scripted straight out of the *Donna Reed Show*. They had everything and we had very little. As a child, I lived in an apartment in Jersey City. There were no trees except in the park. We did not go out in our yard to barbecue or play catch because there was no yard. My parents loved my brother and me, but our home was not a happy home. In my house on Sunday morning, my father came to breakfast in his boxer shorts and my mother in her tattered nightgown, both with a cigarette dangling from their mouths. My brother and I had cereal for breakfast while Mom and Dad had cigarettes. Uncle Herb and Aunt Gloria lived in

Teaneck, New Jersey and they had everything any child could ever want: a house in the suburbs, country club membership and people who talked to one another at the breakfast table. Breakfast? Wow, they had fresh squeezed orange juice, hot bagels, fresh lox, tuna and eggs. Theirs was the life! I remember Uncle Herb smiling and singing as he did with the family when riding in their car.

"Uncle Herb, is this a dream?

"Define dream," he smirked.

Maybe this was another dream, another way my subconsious passed the time. I didn't care. I welcomed the encounter. I wanted more.

Uncle Herb had died of Parkinson's complicated by dementia and Alzheimer's. At the end of his life, he was not the man I knew as a child. He was only a shadow of himself. During his whole life, he had given to me, but I was not there for him at the end. "I'm sorry, Uncle Herb."

"For what?"

"For not being there for you at the end."

"There is never an end. There is a beginning, a life and an afterlife. Did you ever forget me?"

"No."

"Did you remember the things I taught you?"

"Uncle Herb, you were a great teacher and a great friend. You exemplified all that is good in life. How could I forget that? I modeled my life after you and Aunt Gloria."

"Then you never left me. I always felt your love. Can't you feel the love of your family and friends?"

"Yes."

"There are some things in life you cannot see; you can only sense and feel them. My spirit lives in your body and flows within your veins."

I thought of my loved ones. "Do they know I'm alive? Do they know I can hear them? Do they know I can feel their love?"

"They know," his voice echoed as if he had read my mind.

"Uncle Herb, how can I see you? My eyes won't open. I physically can't see. Wait a minute... You're dead, aren't you? That means ... I'm dead. What's going on?" I cried inside.

"Eric, all those who have loved you, and all those whom you have loved, are here for you. Both now and forever. These are the Facts of Life. Have you seen your mother?"

"Yes, I saw her."

"Did you listen to her?"

"Yes, yes I did."

"Hearing lets you know the music is playing. Listening lets you know what the music is saying."

"Is this one of my lessons?"

"That's why I am here. Your mother taught you the Facts of Life. It is my role to remind you of the Lessons of Life and to teach you more about the power of loving and giving. To love is to give. Do you remember the poem I taught you as a child? A bell is not a bell until it is rung. A song is not a song until it is sung. For love was not put in your heart to stay. For love is not love until you give it away."

"Yes, I use that poem in my lectures."

"You were a good student once."

"What do you mean once?"

"When you are a student, you are a student every day of your life. Recently, you were not as receptive to learning. I know your life has not been easy, but who said it's supposed to be? As we get older, we tend to get colder. Remember the look in your eye as a child?"

"Which look?"

"A child looks at things with an open mind and an open heart. He is in awe of the moment. Eric, you were once the eternal optimist. You used to see only good in all things and in all people. What happened?"

"I guess I was hurt a few times. As I got hurt, I put up a barrier to protect my feelings."

"The wall was becoming too large. You were not letting people in. Your heart was not as filled with love. You need to go back to the basics. You need to become a giver. When you live your life to give, you do not feel stress or anxiety. Those are symptoms or diseases of ego, not the experiences of a selfless person. The lessons of life are simple, but you must apply wisdom. Life consists of growth. There are four stages of growth or evolution: knowledge, wisdom, understanding and love. Knowledge we get from life and education. Wisdom is how we apply our knowledge."

"Who is wise?"

"The answer is simple. A wise person is one who learns from everyone and everything. Even a clock that doesn't work is right twice a day."

"Hey, that's my line!" I shouted.

"Just wanted to see if you were listening." My uncle smiled his grand smile again. "You have learned well, Eric, but lately you have chosen a wrong path. You have forgotten the Lessons of

Life. Let me remind you: You will receive a body. You may love it or hate it, but it will be yours for the entire period of your life. It is the vessel which contains your spirit. If you are good to it, it will be good to you. Secondly, your life is a series of lessons. You are enrolled in a full-time informal school called Life. Each day in this school you will have the opportunity to learn lessons. You may like the lessons or think them irrelevant and stupid; however, all days, all encounters, good or bad, will contain a lesson. There are no mistakes in Life; only lessons. Growth is a process of trial and error through experimentation. The 'failed' experiments are as much a part of the process as the experiment that ultimately works. A lesson in Life is repeated until it is learned. A lesson will be presented to you in various shapes and forms until you have learned it. When you have learned it, you can go on to the next lesson. Learning lessons never ends. There is no part of your day or your life that does not contain lessons. If you are alive, there are lessons to be learned. The wise person learns from his or her lessons."

"I've learned my lesson about cosmetic injections. I will never do that again!" Was I really communicating with my deceased Uncle Herb?

"There are other lessons to learn," he replied. "you've no doubt heard the saying that the grass is not greener on the other side?"

"Yes."

"Being 'there' is no better than 'here.' When 'there' has become 'here,' you will simply obtain another 'there' that will look better than 'here.' The grass is not greener here, so learn to live in the moment."

"In this moment, I am dying, Uncle Herb!" I defended myself. "I'm dying because someone made a mistake. A doctor nearly killed me."

"Others are merely mirrors of you. You cannot love or hate something about another person unless it reflects something you love or hate about yourself. Haven't you ever made a mistake or harmed someone?"

"Well, yes, but…"

"What you make of your life is up to you. You have all the tools and resources you need. What you do with them is up to you. The choice is yours. All of life's questions and answers are inside you. All you need to do is look, listen and trust. You must have faith in your body, your mind, your soul and your spirit. Your inner voice and your innate intelligence will provide you with answers to all questions."

I again challenged my uncle. "How can I find answers inside myself?"

"The secret of life is 'I am.' You harbor the strength and power of the universe within you. When you accept responsibility for your life and your actions, you will learn to harness the power of the universe. Eric, you must embrace life every day and know that it is your attitude that will give you altitude. The brain is like a computer: You must program it. Imagine your brain has two dogs—a white dog and a red dog. The white dog is your good dog and the red dog is your devil dog—the evil twin. The dog you feed the most will become your dominant dog. Which dog were you feeding? Maybe you didn't like the way you look because you were feeding the wrong dog."

"How do I feed the dog?"

"With self-talk and through the power of affirmation. What you think about comes about. Start each day from this day forth with positive self-talk and affirmations."

"Give me some examples."

"Affirm: I am happy, I am healthy, I am terrific. I am empowered by the universe. I am capable of anything. I am smart. I am talented. I am loving. I am a good person. I am a good father. I am in control of my life. I am going to make a difference. I am a child of God. Repeat these affirmations daily. Don't just say the words; believe them. This feeds your white dog—your positive dog. Starve your red dog—your devil dog. For when you do not feed it, it weakens."

"I remember some of those lessons. Aren't some of them from Og Mandino?"

"All words are God's words. There are many people who spread the Universe's message. Og Mandino was one special person."

"He is my favorite author. He is a messenger, isn't he?"

"We all have the capability to be messengers. However, the more evolved we become, the purer our message and our actions."

"Is Og an angel?"

"All people have angelic qualities. We are surrounded by angels. You are not alone on your journey. You will always be surrounded by angels. To give for the sake of giving, and to expect nothing in return is how angels earn their wings."

"And not by the ringing of a bell?" I asked comically.

"That was a good movie, based on a true story."

"Are you kidding?"

"We have no time to joke. You can't stay away from your world forever."

My visit with my uncle came to an abrupt end as Michael and my brother entered the room. "Dad, we're here. Can you hear us?" Michael tapped me on the shoulder.

"Uncle Herb? Uncle Herb, come back!" He was gone.

I wrestled with my thoughts, wondering if my imagination was playing tricks on me or if the drugs I had been given were causing me to hallucinate. Maybe I was dreaming. I wanted to believe I was on the other side with Uncle Herb.

"It's Michael, can you hear me? Dad, I'm scared, I don't want to lose you. I'm too young to be an orphan. If you can hear me, hear this: I need you to get well. I still have so much to learn, so much to share."

I wanted to respond and tell him I was going to be okay. I wanted to tell him about visiting with my mom and Uncle Herb. I wanted to hold my son in my arms. Who would have thought just days ago while playing golf I might never see my son again. *God, I prayed. Help me, help me defeat this. I want to see my son. Can you hear us, God? I am so alone.*

"Alone? You're not alone." My uncle Herb jumped in.

"You're back," I quipped.

"I was never gone," Uncle Herb responded.

"I don't understand, first you were here; then you were gone."

"You must be daydreaming in class, Eric," my uncle stated.

"I was just asking myself if this conversation is real or if I am dreaming."

"What is the difference? Isn't a dream part of life?"

85

"Yes."

"Then a dream is simply a different state of consciousness. Would you agree with that?"

"Yes, I agree."

"Then, which part of consciousness is real and which is a dream?"

"I don't know."

"Yes, you do. Remember your lessons."

"All that I feel, think, do or believe is real; therefore, a dream is real, even if I am in an altered state of reality," I said.

"That's the Eric I know and remember." Herb was proud of me. "Remember what W. Clement Stone once said, 'It's the little things in life that make a big difference. The little thing is attitude. The big difference is whether it is positive or negative.'"

I was aware that I was alive. I remember hearing and feeling the ventilator. Everything Uncle Herb said was so real. I wanted to believe he was really there with me. I needed to believe that I could close my eyes and see anyone on the other side of the veil we call death. When we were children, we did not forget our parents while we were away at school or summer camp. We remembered them and what they had taught us. And so it is when souls pass to the other side. They are still with us in our thoughts and in the lessons they have taught us.

"You're daydreaming again."

"Uncle Herb, I want to believe. I want to know this is real. I want to know whether I am going to get well or not."

"Do you want to get well?" he asked.

"Of course I do."

"What is the tenth lesson of life?"

"I AM."

"Yes, you are," he softly said. "You are in control of what you think and what you believe. What lies ahead of you will not be easy. You can give up, give in or fight back. It's your choice. You choose how quickly you will heal. You must have faith in life and in yourself. I have faith in you. When in doubt, look to your lessons. Do you really want to get better? Are you willing to pay the price and go through the recovery?"

"Yes, I am willing."

"Then, use the power of 'I AM.'"

"I'm learning."

"Yes, you are and you must continue to learn each day for the rest of your life."

"The lessons again?"

"I think you understand. My time here is done. You do not need me. You know what to do; you know where to turn."

"Will I see you again, Uncle Herb?"

"Will I hear you again, Eric?"

"Yes, of course."

"Then you will see me. I will always be with you. Angels surround you and all people at all times. You may close your eyes at anytime and feel their love. You are never alone.

"The principles of life are not for man and man alone. Perfection of the universe is abundant. As with man and woman, so do the animals and plants take great care of their offspring and their next generations. However, after birth, the new life has to start a struggle for survival, and the struggle intensifies as time goes on. This is in stark contrast to the warmth and care of the womb. What we don't realize is that as we leave our mother's womb, we are enveloped in nature's womb. All that is needed is there for us. We must work to eat, survive and continue life, yet all that we need is available to us. We live in an abundant world."

"Then, we are always abundant."

"Exactly! All that you need to heal your body is within you. You must believe and open your heart, soul and spirit. Having created and given us His world, our Creator has given us a task: to meet and converge with the Divine. This should be done through spiritual growth, bonding and uplifting ourselves and one another. All people can grow, love, learn and help others." This is amazing. Uncle Herb is here with me as real as life; the way it used to be and now he's a theologian! I must be dreaming!

"Is this a dream?" I asked yet again.

"Does it feel real?"

"Yes, it does."

"If it feels real, then it is real," Herb confirmed.

"I don't understand."

"Are memories real?"

"I think so."

"Is love real?"

"Yes, I can feel love."

"Dreams, memories, and love: these are all states of consciousness. All that is good, is real. All that is real is the truth. The truth is an extension of God." Uncle Herb paused, "Is God real, Eric?"

"Is He?" I answered with a question.

"You tell me. Do you have faith?"

"Yes."

"If you have faith, you have God."

"But my life is still falling apart!"

"Now you are showing signs of wisdom! Sometimes we have to fall to pieces before we can find peace."

"What defines wisdom, Uncle Herb?"

"One who is truly wise in the ways of God knows that no one individual or one set of beliefs is the only source of legitimate knowledge in our world. Knowledge is like life unto itself; it can be found almost anywhere, even under the most difficult conditions. Lessons are life; they exist in all situations. We experience knowledge with love and like a baby—naturally. The more you exercise knowledge, the stronger it becomes. The knowledge of the afterlife comes from the knowledge we develop in earthly life. The more lessons you learn now, the more powerful you become in the afterlife."

"You said that God is truth," I reminded him. "How is it so many people claim to have the only truth and discredit the knowledge that others know as truth?"

"No one in this world has a monopoly on knowledge or truth. God is the power of the universe. God can be found throughout the world, called by many different names in lands and cultures everywhere. God is in all things. God is love. God is light. God is truth. All that is, is God. The Light of Life is everywhere, but not everyone can recognize God in His many faces. Only the wise know how and where to look. As we grow and evolve, we find and feel the power of life, love, light and truth. It is the love and light of God that emanates from those who are evolved. Eric, for you to return to wholeness, you must evolve. If you want to walk, talk and eat again, you must emit the light of God. God is the power within you that will return life and health to your body if you agree to continue with your studies in life.

"I am willing to keep learning and evolving."

"You are a wise and powerful person who does not make mistakes. There are no mistakes in life—only lessons."

"Wait a minute. What happened to me was a mistake."

"Not if you turn it into a lesson. Remember lesson number one? You will receive a body. You may like it or hate it, but it will be yours for the entire period of this lifetime. Why would you alter the appearance God has given you?"

"I wanted to look younger—better."

"When you alter your appearance, you alter the way people perceive you, but worrying about what people think does not reflect wisdom nor is it in line with nature. Wrinkles are life lines—a map of where you have been. They represent wisdom and character. Everyone is unique in appearance. You must love yourself for who are, not how you look. If you emanate love, then that is what people will see in you."

"This is deep stuff, Uncle Herb."

"Life is full of complexity. Simplicity is the key for unlocking life's secrets and finding true happiness in life. Keep your life simple and stay the way God made you. Trying to change your appearance made things more difficult than they had to be."

"It sounds so...... simple!"

"It is one of the great lessons of life and it is overlooked by most people. We are so busy, we never have enough time to stop and think clearly and enjoy the roses. Therefore, many of the problems we face daily are of our own doing. When life is hard or complicated, we ignore the peace of mind that would allow us to think things through clearly. So what do we do when we are up to our necks in life's quicksand?"

"That's how I feel right now. I'm completely immobilized."

"Remember what you learned about attitude. You are paralyzed. Now what do you do? Do you give up? No, you look into your heart for the wisdom of life. You know how to walk and talk. It is up to you, not the doctors, whether you walk and talk again. You can make this complex or let it be simple. The answers you are seeking are insultingly simple."

"I want it to be simple."

"Then embrace God and enable your mind to do the work for you. Let your heart be full of love, and you will know what to do. The path of God is simple and those who walk the simple path instinctively know what to do. The Laws of Life are written on your heart."

"I've got quite a few lessons left to learn."

"Good or bad, every part of every day is a lesson. I hate what has happened to you, but what are you going to learn from it? What can you give or teach others? You said you had faith. Saying something, and believing it, are two separate things. Now is your chance to prove it as you heal yourself."

Suddenly, I was aware that someone was entering my hospital room and I thought I had been dreaming. Uncle Herb's visit seemed so real! It *had* been so real. At first I struggled with this conflict of what is real and what is imagined. But the reality is that what lies inside of us is real. Feelings are intangible, yet they can alter lives. When one is in a dream state, isn't that a real state of mind? Are dreams real? If dreams are real, then aren't they a part of our reality? Dreams create feelings and emotions, and these emotions, these thoughts are real. Dreams are actually just another dimension of reality. My dreams while I was paralyzed were better then my reality—they were therapeutic. I may not actually remember the conversations verbatim but I do remember the feelings. I remember feeling loved. I remember feeling embraced. It was at this time that I no longer felt alone, and for the first time in my recovery my inner spirit, my faith, was awakened, even if this happened while I was dreaming.

Regardless of whether his visit was real or just a dream, Uncle Herb's advice was good, so I decided to heed it. The chance to put the advice into practice came quickly. I heard one person say, "He is not going to make it," and another say, "If he lives he will be like this for eighteen months." I did not lose hope. Instead, I decided I was going to get well. I knew I would have to rebuild my body from within my mind or I would be without hope, faith or life. I would focus on the lessons of my past to build my future and I would look inside myself to find strength for healing. Uncle Herb's visit gave me hope and I began my quest to recover. I knew who was responsible for my life and my healing: I AM!

Chapter Eight

The Squeeze is On!

I awoke when I heard Jason and Michael talking quietly in my room. Jason had just arrived and Michael was filling him in on the details. "The CDC should return the test results tomorrow, which should determine whether it is definitely botulism poisoning. I called Dr. Tuchman and he is coming this afternoon."

"Dad has made many good friends over the years—some of them are the best doctors in their fields." Jason was curious, "Dr. Tuchman is a neurologist, isn't he?"

"Yes, and I hope he can give us some good news. He should be here any minute now. His flight landed over an hour ago."

"Anybody home?" A man's voice was at the door.

"Dr. Tuchman, thank you for coming. It's good to see you."

"And the two of you as well. So, how are your parents?"

"They are stable for now. That's about all we know."

Looking past Michael and Jason, Dr. Tuchman saw a figure that once resembled his friend, Dr. Eric Kaplan. "I see the invalid over there; just lying around, taking it easy."

It was refreshing to hear his bright banter as Dr. Tuchman approached my bed and patted my hand. He was a compassionate man and was always kind to my family. He touched my arms and legs, pulled open each of my eyes, passed a light over the pupils, and then manually shut them again.

"What do you think, Dr. Tuchman?"

"From what I know about botulism, he's probably going to be like this for a minimum of one year. CDC gave a preliminary diagnosis of botulism, with a significant dosage, far greater than ever encountered. It's a miracle they are even alive."

"Dad has a strong will to live. I believe he will pull through."

I wanted so badly to let everyone know that I was alive and that I was going to be okay. I tried to open my eyes, but I still couldn't make them move. The three men went to check on Bonnie, and I was left to process the news. I heard what they said, but I stubbornly refused to agree with the doctors. I had faith in God and in my body to heal itself. My case was unique and this was in my favor because I had no one else's failure with which to compare. I could write my own success story.

Some people connect the moment they meet. That was what happened between me and Joe Littenburg when we were playing golf together in Las Vegas. I had only recently gotten to know him before being poisoned, but it was as if we had been friends for years. Joe was devastated when he heard about our plight because he had lost his wife of thirty-seven years to cancer and could do nothing to save her. Joe and his girlfriend, Kim, came to visit us while we were unconscious to the world. When he arrived, I was in intensive care, lying on my back, completely immobile. I looked like a corpse. Seeing me in such horrid condition, Joe's inclination was to just leave without saying anything. This thought had hardly formed when somehow, due to the strong connection we had, he believed he could help me. He gathered his courage and sauntered over to my bed. He grabbed my hand in his, bent over and started talking in my ear as if we were still on the golf course. "What kind of person are you? I come all the way from Jersey and not even a 'hello', a cup of coffee, a little danish—nuttin'! You call yourself a host? Your conversation sucks, you are cold and lifeless. You're no fun."

No fun?! I would have loved to come back with some smart-aleck remark. He was enjoying his one-sided conversation a little too much as he continued to razz me. "I know your mudda taught you betta manners. I have had betta conversations with a mannequin!" I was laughing on the inside.

"WOW! Janice, Kim! Did you see that? Eric just moved the right side of his mouth. I think he heard me and he laughed at my jokes. He ain't dead."

"Yeah!" They gave a whispered cheer.

"He will get you for harrassing him like that once he starts talking again!" Janice warned him.

"Bring it on, brother," Joe laughed. "I'll even let you beat me at a game of golf." I regretted that Peter wasn't there to witness my first movement because he and Janice had been with us almost continually since day one helping and encouraging us in our recovery.

Kim and Joe came to visit again the next day before going back to New Jersey. Kim spent most of her time sitting with Bonnie. Joe felt awkward talking with Bonnie because he hardly knew her and he felt she probably did not want a stranger around when she was in such bad shape. I was glad to have Joe continue to entertain me with his verbal antics.

On about day six, Michael came to my room alone. He took my hand and said in a tearful voice, "Dad, I hope you can hear me because I want you to know that I love you. I'm even praying for you."

I tried to let him know that I loved him and appreciated his prayers, but I still couldn't move any part of my body. Michael was gently holding my hand and I had an idea. *Okay, fine, Kaplan. If your eyes won't open, try something else. Move your hand. . . It moved! I moved my hand! It was just a twitch, but it moved!*

"Did you just move your hand? Oh, God! I hope it wasn't just an involuntary twitch. I love you, Dad. Please try again."

I squeezed his hand.

"YES! You did it! You really squeezed my hand. Oh, God, You heard my prayers. Dad, can you hear me?"

I squeezed again.

"If you know where you are, squeeze my hand once for 'yes' and twice for 'no.'"

I squeezed once.

"Do you know why you are in the hospital?"

I squeezed once.

"Now for a 'no' question."

I squeezed twice before he even asked the question.

"I've got to tell Uncle Steve, Jason and the rest of the family! They will be so happy to know you are conscious." Michael rushed out of the room. "He understands!" I heard him shout down the hallway. "Nurse, nurse, get Dr. Egitto. My father is conscious."

I could not smile outwardly but I was aglow inside. After almost a week of worrying that we were in a vegetative state or coma, my family was relieved to know that I was conscious and that I understood what was going on.

Drawing on my spirit, I continued to will my hand to move. I needed to practice so I could communicate with Michael when he came back. He believed in me. He knew I was trying to communicate with him; he knew I had fight. When he was a young boy I told him, "It is not the size of the dog in the fight, but the size of the fight in the dog." I was alive and ready to fight.

A few minutes later, Michael brought Steve and Jason to my room with him. "He squeezed my hand when I asked him a question," Michael enthusiastically explained. "He understands what we are saying. He squeezes once for 'yes' and twice for 'no.' Go ahead. Ask him a question."

"Dad, can you hear me?" Jason asked.

I squeezed once.

"He did it! Dad, I love you. You can beat this."

I again squeezed his hand. My world as I knew it had changed. Squeezing a hand may seem uneventful to some but to me it provided the miracle of communication and it meant all the difference to me and my family. I was still trapped within my own body but I could at least communicate with the outside world again. I thought of the strength of Helen Keller. She was blind, deaf and dumb yet she went on to write numerous books. *I can have a life again. I will beat this!*

Suddenly, I heard my cousin Bruce's voice. *I can't believe Bruce is here. I haven't seen him in years.* "You can beat this, Eric. I know how strong you are." He was encouraging.

"I'm here!" I wanted to tell him. "I am going to beat this."

I was raised with Bruce Garfunkel. His father died at an early age and he learned quickly to take care of himself. He was a tough kid from Jersey City, and as a boy I looked up to him. He had heart and courage and would fight anyone, anywhere. He had such confidence in himself, he lived an exciting life, which made him an exciting person to be around. Bruce had become a successful entrepreneur and businessman, and although we did not speak often, our childhood memories kept us close.

"Man, you've got tubes everywhere, Kaplan." I could tell from his voice he was shaken by what he was seeing, but he was using humor to disguise his emotion. "Here's a tube to feed you. This one here is making you breathe. There's a wire taped to your heart. I hope they're not recording any naughty love scenes! Look, you've got two IVs going in. There's even a tube so you don't have to get up to go to the bathroom! Man, what are they feeding you?" He touched my hand and I moved it ever so slightly. "Eric, I know you hear me. Squeeze my hand once to tell me you're going to beat this."

I squeezed his hand.

"Squeeze my hand twice, if you know that it is me, your cousin, Bruce."

I squeezed twice.

His beautiful wife, Jeanie, was holding back tears as she said, "Don't worry about anything, Eric. We will help you and Bonnie with whatever you need."

I wanted to say, "I am going to be fine. Don't worry about me," but I couldn't speak. At least I could communicate with my hand, and that was more than anyone expected.

Bruce was my cheerleader, "You'll be up and out of here in no time. You've got a lot of fight left in you."

I don't know how long Bruce and Jeanie stayed because I was in and out of drug-induced sleep, but I do know that their words encouraged me to keep fighting to live.

Once they knew I was conscious, everyone else wanted to "talk" to my hand. Peter, Joe, Aunt Gloria, Uncle Buddy, Uncle Jack, Dr. Egitto, and others came to my room to get a squeeze. It was great to have visitors and be able to communicate with my family. I had been like a prisoner in solitary confinement, and this was all I had to hold onto.

I heard my Uncle Buddy telling the people in the room, "Eric is tough. He was a good athlete, and he will beat this."

Yes, I was an athlete. I played both high school and college basketball, but I especially enjoyed playing with the black youths at Audubon Park because they provided a different style of the game. Basketball in Jersey City was comparable to the movie, *White Men Can't Jump.* The blacks were better ball handlers and they went to the basket better. The whites were more involved with fundamentals and were solid shooters. The playground legends at Audubon Park included Harry Laurie, Elnardo Webster, Charles McCalister, Willie Willis, Billy Maynor, and Brian Hurley (the uncle of Duke All-American Bobby Hurley). We played every game as our life depended on winning or losing. If we lost, we sat on the ground, waiting for what seemed like hours for another chance. If we won, we played. It was similar to my current situation. *I will not lose. I will play as if my life depends on it. It does!*

My adopted uncle, Jack Segall, answered Uncle Buddy, "If anyone can beat this he can." Trapped within my body I needed hope to survive. Uncle Buddy came to my bed, took my hand and affirmed, "You can beat this. Right, Eric?"

I squeezed his hand once. I couldn't see him but I felt his smile through the increased pressure of his grip on my hand.

We tend to believe only what we can see. Faith is believing in what you can't see. We cannot see electricity, but we can feel its power. We cannot "see" winter but the cold temperatures demonstrate the change of seasons. Can we see the wind? No, but we can feel its power and see its effects. We believe in the laws of the universe, yet we cannot see the power that governs the universe. We believe that day will follow night, summer will follow winter, and the sun will follow rain. We don't panic when our trees lose their leaves. We believe that Mother Nature will restore them. We all believe in something regardless of whether or not we see it or feel it.

Being blinded by botulism forced me to see with my inner eye. As I looked within, my inner eye took me on a journey back to Jersey City. I was a teenager on the playground with the Hurley brothers—the most famous basketball family in my hometown. Bobby Hurley, who played for Duke University became the most famous, but his uncle, Brian, was a star on the Marist High School team. I attended Snyder High School, and Marist was our competition. Their father, Bob Hurley Sr., is the leading high school basketball coach of all time and he still coaches Saint Anthony's High School team. Brian Hurley was much more talented than I was, so I watched him and played him tough. I may not have been as talented physically but when it came to heart, I was a lion. I would study my opponent and then outwork him. Not bad for someone small, white and Jewish. That's what Coach Bobby Knight said to me at basketball camp one summer.

Coach Knight was a great man, a leader and a motivator. People have a misconception of him. He is a charismatic man who loves kids; he just hates the media. I first met the young Bobby Knight in 1968 when he was an up-and-coming coach for West Point. Prior to my junior year in high school, I attended Five Star Basketball Camp—the ultimate camp for players hoping to play at the college level. During one game, I thought I played well against a top point guard from New York City. I scored eighteen points and had about six assists—a good game by anyone's standards. Coach Knight came to me afterward and asked, "How do you think you played today?"

"I thought I did a good job, Coach."

"How many points did you score?"

"Eighteen."

"How many did your opponent score?"

"I don't know."

"Here's your problem. Son, you're short, white and Jewish and you do not fit the typical NBA profile. You are not talented enough to play on the next level." I was crushed. I thought I had made an athletic statement, and in less than twenty seconds Coach Knight had stolen my dreams. "However," he continued, "if you were to play defense, real defense, you would have twice the game. You can't be 5'8" and just play offense. Defense is about paying the price. I saw heart in you, son. Are you willing to pay the price?"

"Yes."

"Then, be at the court at seven sharp tomorrow morning."

"But, Coach Knight, reveille is not until seven."

"That is your problem. Get an alarm clock."

I was on the court the next morning at ten minutes to seven. Coach Knight took me and three other guys under his wing and taught us the fundamentals of defense. He wanted me to be the best I could be, and I tried with all my might to keep from disappointing him.

Even after being one of the leading scorers on the Junior Varsity the year before, I was still a long way from even making my high school varsity team, much less getting to play. Thanks to the training I had with Coach Knight, I became fundamentally strong in defense. I not only made the team, I became what is called in basketball circles a "stopper." I could stop anyone. I had a very good junior year and contributed to my high school team and its division championship. I was not a star, but I played a good role and I was usually sixth man (the first man off the bench). Coach Knight taught us how to build from within ourselves and ignore the glory. His lessons live in my heart today. Because I could play defense, I was later recruited by many colleges. I chose to play for Fairleigh Dickinson University.

Coach Knight made us work hard. I remember him yelling at me, "Your brain runs your body. Don't give into your body. Push harder." Every day at practice, he was going to pick on someone and try to humiliate him. I worked my tail off so it wouldn't be me. "Kaplan, you don't have to be talented to play defense but you have to have heart. Do you have heart? Show me. Assume the position." I could hear his voice over and over in my head. He pushed me to the limit, and now I had to push myself harder than anyone had ever pushed me. This was no game; I had to defend my life.

Suddenly, I realized I had been dreaming. Those moments when I came back to present reality were tough. One minute I was happily reliving the highlights of my childhood and the next minute I was praying that my present situation was only a dream from which I would awaken. Discovering I was already awake was very disappointing.

I realized there were more people in my room asking me questions.

"Do you feel this?" asked a doctor.

I squeezed once.

"Do you understand what is happening?"

Squeeze.

"Are you in pain?"

Squeeze. My head was hurting, my body felt as though I had a severe case of the flu, my ears ached, and I needed to swallow and couldn't.

The questions were numerous, but through them the doctors and nurses gained a better understanding of what I was experiencing. This became a critical juncture in my recovery. Once they knew I could communicate, they started treating me with respect as a person. No more talking about me as if I wasn't there. No more probing or poking me without informing me of what they were about to do.

After squeezing to what seemed like a hundred questions, the doctors left my room to check on Bonnie and I was alone in my thoughts again. I could answer questions posed to me, but I had no way of asking the many questions I wanted answered. *How is my wife doing? I wish someone would let me know how she is. Bonnie, I love you! I miss you…*

Chapter Nine

Write Back at You

The machines attached to my body confirmed that I was still in critical condition. The days were long and the nights were lonely, but at least I had hope. Hope combined with faith will fuel any spirit. Being able to squeeze a hand may seem trivial to most people, but it had significantly changed my life and gave hope to those around me. With one-way communication, I no longer felt alone or isolated. My family started allowing more visitors at that point. I remember hearing my partner, Dr. Gerry Mattia. The Meyers and the Brocks, Steve Daniels and my cousin Amy Punyon from New York also came to visit, and I squeezed for all of them. I felt like a seal performing in a show, but their presence gave me faith in people, and my response gave them hope that I would one day recover.

Knowing that it was going to be a while before I could attend to my own private and financial affairs, Steve brought in my good friend and attorney Thomas Dougherty, Esq. Thomas asked me if he could draft a document to assign power of attorney to my son and brother. Using the squeeze method of communication, I agreed. Thomas was satisfied that I comprehended what was going on, so he drew up the papers accordingly. Bonnie and I literally turned our lives over to Michael and Steve. Steve went to our banks and had our accounts adjusted for the power of attorney. We trusted them to do what they believed best, but it was no easy task for them to figure out our financial records.

Even though my prognosis was still not good, I wanted to live, and I was beating the odds. I was driven; I knew I was going to get better. I was going to live, walk, talk, breathe, smile and see again. I challenged myself daily: Today I can squeeze my hand; tomorrow I will do more. I spent hours trying to move another part of my body. *I can do this. I must do this. I will do this. I can. I will. I must.* I kept saying this to myself over and over until I believed it and then it happened. My foot moved. I heard my adopted Uncle Jack talking with my Uncle Buddy, my brother Steve, and Michael. "Look at him trying to move. He won't stop. See? There is a twitching in his arm and leg."

The smallest move required a deliberate and strong effort but I was moving and that was more than anyone had expected at this point. The doctors were amazed with my progress. As they stood by my bed and observed my activity, a question arose among them. "Why give nerve blocks to a patient who has little to no nerve function?" one doctor asked. "How would he do if we discontinued the nerve block?"

The neurologist spoke to me, "Dr. Kaplan, since you are able to move this much with the nerve block we've been giving, we believe you should be able to move even more without it. We are going to discontinue the medication." That sounded good to me. No wonder I had been struggling to move.

Eight days had passed and I was fighting mentally and physically. In the solitary confinement of my mind, I fantasized about playing golf, shooting baskets, skiing the Alps (although I have never skied in my life) and going to college reunions. Without the nerve block, my body instinctively responded to what my mind was thinking while I was in a dream-like state of consciousness. My legs would kick spastically when I was running forward to make the basketball goal. My arms would spasm as they tried to imitate a slam-dunk or swing a golf club. I would suddenly hit my leg against the bars of the bed and scare the nurses half to death. I wanted to walk and talk again, so when I was awake, I moved my legs until I was absolutely fatigued. I worked so hard, I was wringing wet with sweat. The nurses got mad and told me to stop.

Excuse me for trying to get well! I don't mean to bother you, but I am fighting for my life here!

I realize that taking care of a paralyzed patient is not easy. The nurses had to change my gown several times per day and I couldn't move enough to help them lift my weight. It usually took two or more nurses to change me, and some were more caring than others were. The ICU nurses came by every night. I looked forward to having them wash me. It felt good to be clean. To be touched was so nurturing. People don't realize how healing the human touch is. I thanked them in my mind, but of course they didn't hear me.

I was moving so much, my doctors were afraid I would pull the ventilator out of my throat, so they strapped my arms to the rails of the bed. Great! Now I am paralyzed, sedated and tied down. I could still move my hands. I didn't have a button to press when I needed to call the nurse, so I starting hitting my hand on the rail to get their attention. They ignored me. It was so frustrating not being able to talk.

Some friends of ours came to visit with Michael one afternoon. They were excited to communicate with me using the squeeze method. When they arrived, Michael took my hand and began talking. "Dad, are you okay today?"

I squeezed his hand once.

"I have a surprise for you." Michael nodded to our guest.

"Hi, Buddy!" It was Peter Brock. "Janice is with Bonnie. I've come to let you squeeze me!" he laughed.

I wish I could see him and talk to him. Peter is a New York executive who reads the *Times,* does crossword puzzles and is well read. Peter is a wine aficionado and Bonnie and I enjoy eating out with him and Janice, especially Italian food. I missed being able to interact with him and the others. *If I can move my hand enough to squeeze, perhaps I can move it enough to write.* I moved my hand from side to side and Michael let go of it to see what I was trying to do. I put my thumb and first finger together as if holding a pencil and began to move my hand as if I were writing.

"Are you writing? You want to write something?" He took my hand and waited for my squeeze of affirmation. "Hold on while I find something for you to write on." I could hear him fumbling around in the room.

"Here, I have a pen." Peter pulled a Montblanc from his pocket.

"I found a pad in the drawer." Michael put the pen in my hand. "I'm putting the pad beside you on the bed." He laid my hand on top of the pad. I was lying flat on my back and could not open my eyes; therefore, I could not see what I was writing. I scribbled a short message.

"I can't read it." He turned to Peter. "Is that a 't'?"

"I think it's an 'i'." Peter picked up my hand. "Is the first letter an 'i'?"

I squeezed his hand twice for no.

"Is it a 't'? Michael asked.

I squeezed Peter's hand twice.

"No," Peter relayed.

I was disappointed but not ready to give up. Michael put my hand back on the paper and said, "Try again."

I gave it my best shot. Michael and Peter both tried, but I was not in control of my motor skills enough to write legibly, so neither of them could read anything I wrote. It was just as well. I had written, "I'm in hell! I hate this!"

"Tell you what," said Michael, "I'll leave the pad here where you can reach it and you can practice later. Maybe Jason or Steve can read it when they get here. Let's do the squeeze for now because I have some good news to tell you. Mom opened one eye with help today!"

I squeezed his hand to let him know I was glad she was doing better. *Hey, if she can do it, so can I. Open your eyes, damn it. My eyes were sealed like an iron gate welded shut. How did Bonnie manage to do it?*

Michael continued, "Mom was using a back scratcher to reach an itch when she got the idea that she would use it to open her eye. Her motions are so spastic, the nurses feared she might scratch her cornea, but Mom is determined to see what is going on around her."

A back scratcher? I was itching all over and would love to have someone help me scratch.

"I brought one for you, too." Michael put the scratcher in my hand, but I wasn't able to control my motor skills enough to use it. Moment by moment I realized how much I missed about being able to move my body at will and do things for myself.

I could hear Michael rustling paper. "I have a stack of letters here for you and Mom. You've been getting emails and letters from people around the world who say they are praying for you. Uncle Steve started a website so your far-away friends could leave a message and check your progress. You sure do have a lot of friends. You must be doing something right! Peter and I will read them to you."

I squeezed a hardy "yes." The reading of those letters became a tradition we continued for the rest of our recovery. So many people cared.

Chapter Ten

The Trach Trick

I had a terrible sinus infection, probably from the head cold I had the week of the seminar. Unable to blow my nose or cough up the phlegm, the condition worsened and I found myself battling a serious case of pneumonia. Even though I was showing signs of improvement, there were still times when I did not want to live. Not in this condition. I was getting depressed and I was tired of fighting against the odds. I soon began to pray that I would die.

"Do you know where you are?" Michael asked me.

Yes, I'm still in hell! Good thing he couldn't hear my thoughts. I felt around for the paper and started writing on top of what I had already written. Michael took the pad and turned to a fresh page where I managed to make a very crude looking "y."

Michael fervently tried to decipher my hieroglyphics. "I'll take that for a yes. Are you still in pain?"

"Y."

"Do you know what happened to you?"

"Y."

I could write "y" and "n" but when I tried to answer questions that couldn't be answered yes or no, my writing was not legible. I was disappointed that I could not write something anyone could read. I wanted to write my own questions, such as "How is

Bonnie?" or "Will I get better?" I was told that Bonnie could write legibly. I have to admit I was jealous!

The ventilator was difficult to bear and I had to be sedated to endure the torture of having a machine pushing air and moisture into my lungs. I actually felt hopeful when the doctors talked with me about having surgery.

"Eric, if you can hear me, squeeze my hand." It was my friend, Dr. Dennis Egitto, the doctor serving as team lead on our case.

I squeezed his hand.

"Good. Ideally, the ventilator tube should be in a patient's throat for no more than fourteen days. We want to remove the ventilator from your throat. Do you understand me?"

One squeeze. Subconsciously, I hoped and prayed this procedure would heal me, allow me to awaken from my lifeless stupor, allow me to sit up, talk and smile.

"I am recommending you have a surgical procedure called a tracheotomy. A tracheotomy is a surgical procedure that makes an incision at the base of the neck allowing a tube to be placed into the trachea. This opening or stoma is called a tracheostomy. Through it, you will be able to breathe and perhaps eat or talk. Do you understand how serious this is? If so, then squeeze my hand once."

Another squeeze.

"Do you agree to have this procedure?"

I squeezed his hand once. I was ready to get the tube out of my mouth and throat, but I had a lot of questions I could not ask: Will this make me feel better? Will I be able to talk? Does this mean I am getting better?

"Bonnie has also agreed to having the tracheotomy," he continued.

So we are both going to have a scar as a memento of our trip to Hell.

"I've scheduled you both for surgery tomorrow morning. I wish you well."

What great news! We will be getting a tracheotomy. That means we are going to get off the ventilator. We're going to be okay.

Before the surgery, I prayed for the ability to see and feel. I prayed for my wife. *God, I love that woman. I need her.* Before this event, I had questioned my faith and wondered if there really was a God. A crisis such as this could bring an atheist closer to God. I can assure you that in your moment of personal crisis, you will look to God. As I did, you will beg a Higher Power to help and heal you. You will realize that if you do not search for something, you will not find anything to get you through the trauma.

As they wheeled me to surgery, I heard people speaking in Spanish. *Why are they taking me to Mexico for this procedure?* I did not know where I was but I knew I was alive and still in serious condition. I wanted to keep believing, but my faith was getting weak. It felt like it had been months since I had the vision of my mother and Uncle Herb, and I still questioned if their visits were real. I wavered between praying to God and wondering whether or not He or She was even real.

I was too sick and too naïve to realize what was happening when I awoke from surgery. *Oh, God. My neck hurts! I feel horrible. How can I let anyone know? Does anyone care that I'm in such pain?*

Little did I know that a tracheotomy is just another room in Hell. Imagine sticking a tube through your neck and into your throat. Now imagine attaching a jumbo blow dryer to this tube. This

112

is what being on a ventilator with a tracheostomy feels like. I did not realize it before the surgery, but it is just another way to utilize the ventilator. My heart went out for the Pope as I know how he suffered at the end of his life. Yet every Sunday he appeared before the masses. The stitches in my neck were painful and something was so tight, I felt like I was suffocating. I could not talk and no one could read my writing, so I was unable to let anyone know I needed help.

God, help me. I can't bear this pain. Please do something. Let them know I need relief from the pain. I am helpless and scared! I am not better; I am worse! What is happening?

When I awakened again, I was back in the Intensive Care Unit. As reality grew stronger, so did the pain in my neck. Seconds seemed like minutes, minutes seemed like hours, hours seemed like days, and days felt like weeks. *What have they done to me? I'm a freak! This hurts. I can't live like this. I don't want to live like this! God, help me!*

"Calm down!" A nurse was stern with me.

I'm in pain. Don't you care? My thoughts were futile. She couldn't hear them.

My poor sons. Michael was twenty-two, and Jason only nineteen. They sat vigil day and night watching their parents connected to life support, not knowing if we were going to live or die. I heard my family in the room and I felt their love surrounding me. They wanted to help but it was apparent that they were shaken by the sight of me. They were still frightened that Bonnie and I might never fully recover. Our friends and family stayed with us every day and I could feel their worry as they each tried to console me in their own way. I wanted to tell them I had seen Uncle Herb.

I guess it was just as well that I couldn't speak. These people were my angels. They didn't need to worry about my sanity.

Steve tried to help me get my bearings as I was coming out of the haze of the anesthesia, "It's been twelve days since you were hospitalized, Eric."

TWELVE DAYS? It felt like forever—one dark abyss.

"You made it through the surgery and you are doing okay. You have a tracheostomy."

I don't feel okay. I hurt so badly, I wish I had died!

I must have blacked out because I awakened suddenly, alarmed that I still could not move or open my eyes. I could feel the apparatus attached to my neck, and I could hear the ventilator pumping air into my lungs. *How could this happen? I was supposed to be off the ventilator.* I hated that machine—no, I despised it—but I knew it was keeping me alive. *Take me, God! Don't leave me like this. Let me die! I hate this! God, I want my life back!* I was worried about my wife. *Did they do the same thing to her?*

I don't remember much about the rest of the day except that I was aware of chaos all around me and alarms ringing in my ears as doctors and nurses scrambled about my room. I had to look inside myself for faith, hope and the will to live. I knew I had to make a choice—life or death. I prayed to God and appealed to all that is good in the universe. I hoped for an answer. In times like these, we learn the power of the force. I knew the force was with me, but I hated being a prisoner in my own body. I continued to question, "What is real?" Friends and family gave me encouragement, and I tried to answer them by writing notes.

All my life I had heard people say, "Savor every moment of your life." The Kabbalah says to live each day as if it were your last. I suppose we all appreciate life, but I doubt many people really treasure it or slow down long enough to savor it. So often, we don't truly appreciate things until we have lost them. We are a near-sighted breed. We look to God for miracles every day while ignoring God's greatest miracle—the simple miracle of life.

My relationship with God prior to this event was more of a business relationship, a give-and-take policy based on negotiation. God, if you give me "X", I will be a better person. If you help me pass this exam, I will study harder next time. God, if you give me this house, I will give more to charity. Like most people, I wanted more and I rarely gave thanks for what I already had. I never gave thanks for the ability to breathe, see, swallow, eat, touch, talk, or to hold my wife or sons. Today, I am grateful for the most simple things, and I never take breathing for granted.

My body was weak but my spirit was strong as my mind raced through all the lessons I had learned over the years. I recalled over and over the messages my mother and Uncle Herb had given me, but I still questioned whether their visits were real. I remembered the other teachers in my life who had influenced me with their wisdom and I drew upon those lessons as I struggled in a state of semi-consciousness. I recalled when I first heard about positive self-talk and affirmations from Dr. Larry Markson, my friend and one of my mentors. I began mentally chanting, "I can, I will, I must. I can, I will, I must. I CAN, I WILL, I MUST!"

I thought of the hundreds of lectures I had given and I could see myself in front of an audience as I reflected back to last year at the Presidents Conference in Arizona. I had spoken to the presidents of McDonalds, Burger King, Wendy's, Coca-Cola,

Pepsi Cola, Land O'Lakes and KFC about health. Every eye was on me and every ear was listening to my exposition.

"The power that created the body has the power to heal the body," I spoke eloquently. "We must understand that there is an intelligence in this universe so great, so powerful that all that lives is within its domain. The human body is perfect. Your heart beats an average of 72 beats per minute, 100,000 times per day, 700,000 times per week. That's over 3 million beats per month and more than 36 million beats per year. It never takes a minute or a day off. Do you ever consciously have to think about making your heart beat? No, you trust the perfection of God or nature to do it automatically." I was on a roll so I continued. "When the body is not at ease, it is at DIS-ease. Drugs do not heal. The power within the body knows how to heal. We call this the 'life force' or energy. The only difference between life and death is energy. A corpse has the same body parts and the same bones, muscle and tissue as a living person. The difference between the two is the energy that travels through the living body. The Chinese have studied this life energy for 5,000 years. They call it 'Chi'. This is what gives our heart the power to beat. It gives the lungs the power to breathe and turn carbon dioxide into oxygen. All this is done daily while the body carries on millions of other functions. We take this power for granted or we do not believe it exists. Have you ever cut yourself shaving? The body knows exactly where the cut is and begins to heal it so we can shave again tomorrow. Have you ever broken a bone? The doctor may set the bone, but the body knows exactly where the break is and how to repair itself. Our body is constantly changing at a rate of two billion cells per day. As a result, we replace ninety-eight percent of all of the atoms and cells in our body in less than a year. Do you think that is amazing? Keep listening. It is estimated that we change our skin every twenty days, our stomach about once per month, our liver about every six weeks, our skeleton every six weeks, and all of our brain cells every year. As a result, who we are today is not who we will be tomorrow. We have the chance to be better, stronger, smarter and healthier.

Regardless of our race, creed, or color, we are all governed by the same powers of nature. A child is born nine months after conception. There is not a separate formula that states seven months gestation for white people, eight for blacks, nine for Hispanics, and ten months for any other ethnicity. Our human genetics are the same. This is the miracle of life."

I had given this lecture many times—but this time it wasn't for an audience. This time, I needed to heed my own advice, trust the power of the universe, and have faith in my body to heal itself.

I wanted to return to the success I had known before this tragedy occurred. My offices were always packed. There were days when we would see in excess of 200 patients per day, but I loved helping people. At times, I had more faith in my patient's body to heal itself than the patient did. I had talked the talk my whole life, but now that I was on life support, I had to live what I had preached for years. The doctors could not give me life. Life comes from within, given to us by the powers of the universe and fueled by our spirit. I prayed for strength to keep fighting. I was still frightened, not by the prospect of dying, but of living my life in this condition.

Dr. Harold Rosen was trained as an ear, eye, nose and throat (ENT) doctor. As his career advanced, he became a prestigious plastic surgeon in New York. I met him through Peter and we had become good friends over the last few years. When Dr. Rosen heard about our plight, he flew to Palm Beach Gardens Medical Center in Florida to check on us. He walked into my room, greeted everyone and then came to my bed. He took one look at my neck and said, "This is all wrong!" Michael moved closer to see what Harold was showing him. "See how tight this trach tie is? This is choking him. He is in terrible pain. We have to loosen this. I am going to find his nurse and get this fixed."

His footsteps faded down the hallway and I cried inside. I was so happy that someone understood and was able to help me. Thank you, God! You heard my prayers! Thank You for sending Harold all the way from New York to Florida just to help me. He's an angel! Angels are in all things that are good. A good quality in a person is an angelic quality.

While I waited for Dr. Rosen to return, I was in and out of consciousness, but the pain was ever present. Once the nurse made some adjustments on the trach, my neck felt much better. This allowed a reduction of some of the hallucinogenic drugs I was being given and I was able to think more clearly about the lessons my mother and Uncle Herb had taught me.

Although better than before, the noose around my neck still hurt badly. Peter talked to me as he sat there rubbing my head. "The stitches will come out in a few days. Just hang in there."

I scribbled, "It hurts."

Peter and my son responded in unison, "We know."

While he was there, Dr. Rosen talked to Michael about relocating Bonnie and me for the rest of our recovery and rehabilitation. "Palm Beach Gardens Medical Center has successfully saved the life of your parents, but this hospital's specialty is not rehabilitation. They might remain in ICU indefinitely if they stay here. I would advise you to find a place that can better assist them in regaining full use of their body."

"What place would you recommend?"

"Shepherd Center in Atlanta is one of the best catastrophic-care hospitals I know of. Their expertise is helping people with neuromuscular illnesses rebuild their lives."

Steve and Michael visited Shepherd Center and came back excited about the possibilities. "Dad, they attach oxygen and your ventilator to your wheelchair so you can go out to the garden or to the gym. This place has everything for the disabled." Yes, I was disabled. What a slap of reality! "Shepherd Center was founded in 1975 in Atlanta Georgia. It is a private, non-profit hospital devoted to the medical care and rehabilitation of people with spinal cord injury and disease, acquired brain injury, multiple sclerosis and other neuromuscular disorders and urological problems. The problem is the center only admits about 850 patients per year."

Michael called Shepherd Center and they flew two of their nurses to visit us at Gardens Hospital. Bonnie was more advanced in her recovery than I was at that time. She was moving her arms close to her body and using a back scratcher to open her eyes. She was writing perfectly. I had a sinus infection and could barely open my eyes. I felt like a high-school boy hoping to get accepted to a college. The two nurses were not optimistic about our recovery and would not approve us for acceptance by Shepherd Center.

My life expectancy was diminished by having the tracheostomy due to the higher risk of infection. Believe it or not, a high concentration of oxygen can be toxic. The gases delivered by a ventilator must be humidified so the oxygen does not dry out the lungs. The moisture may increase mucus production, thus creating more problems. Since I already had pneumonia and a sinus infection, I was extremely congested. I could not swallow or cough so there was no place for the saliva and mucus to go. When the tube filled with mucus, it had to be suctioned out. During the day, my family was there to let the nurses know when I needed assistance. At night, I was on my own. The nights were eerily quiet—especially after Michael, Steven, Jason and Peter left; those were the worst and loneliest times. The machines were noticeably louder and so were the alarms that kept sounding throughout the intensive care unit. I could hear the nurses chatting idly about their love life or gossiping about some coworker. I didn't have a button I could push to call them when I needed help, and there were times when I needed the mucus suctioned from the breathing tube in my neck. One night I was really struggling to breathe. I tried to get their attention by banging my arm on the rails of the bed.

"Stop that!" one of the nurses yelled toward me. "I'll be there when I get there."

I was choking and she couldn't be inconvenienced. *God, I need help! I need someone to suction the mucus out of the trach. I can't breathe.* I felt angry and helpless. I started to panic and banged harder on the rail with my hand. *I'm dying here. I can't breathe!*

No one seemed to care, except Bonnie. My wife could hear me in her room next door and began to cry and pray for me, "God, my husband needs help. Please let the nurses answer him. Please help my husband! Don't let him die! I don't want to live without him!"

Hurry! Help me! I can't breathe. I kept banging. The nurses kept gossiping. My body was fighting infection and I had to fight for attention. I was covered in sweat as I continued to bang on my bed. The line between life and death is so thin. Flanked by the angels, I continued to bang harder.

"Stop banging!"

I was trapped in hell and I could not find the way out. All I wanted was to be myself again. I wanted to laugh, to smile and to talk. I wanted to hug my son. I prayed and prayed. I prayed for life. I prayed for death. *I believe in You, God. Why have You forsaken me? Give me strength. Help me. I'm scared. Is this my day of reckoning?*

"I'm coming!" One of the nurses finally came and cleared my airway.

Recovering from the trauma, I lay there exhausted from the physical exertion. At a defining moment like this, we find out what we are really made of. I thought of Christopher Reeve. In my mind, he was a Superman because he lived his life to show others what is possible. I prayed to have his strength and power.

I remembered the Lessons of Life from Uncle Herb. I AM in control. The doctors could not give me life; they gave me life support. Life comes from within, given to us by the powers of the universe and fueled by our own spirit. My spirit needed a sign. I was losing hope and my faith was slipping. What else did I have? Everything was so difficult. I wanted peace in my body, mind and spirit.

My wife was in the room next door and I was not able to see her. I missed her and longed for her love. I felt so alone. I wanted to cry. *I hope Bonnie isn't having this much trouble. How is my wife? Are we going to be okay? God, help us! Heal us. GOD...CAN YOU HEAR ME?*

Chapter Eleven

Media Mania

Everyone wanted the scoop on the Botox fiasco. The press was everywhere asking questions, begging for a comment and harassing our family. Reporters, cameras and media trucks were waiting outside the hospital and at our home. Reporters were trying to sneak into the hospital; one was caught when he tried to slip into the hospital dressed as a doctor. When our family entered the hospital each day, they had to come through a barrage of cameras and news reporters who ruthlessly shoved microphones in their faces as they passed by. They were waiting for them at home when they returned in the evening. We refused to give comment, so they interviewed our neighbors. Our family refused to answer our home phone or our front door because we knew that no matter what we said, the media would sensationalize the story rather than report only the facts.

The world was curious about us and how the incident had occurred, and the media relentlessly tried to satisfy their viewers' curiosity. They didn't care about us as human beings. All they wanted was to get a story for the evening news. All *we* wanted was to live and get well. We were thus reluctant celebrities as we appeared on the front page of U.S. newspapers and in other papers throughout the world. Michael read articles about our story to his mother and me. The worst coverage was by our local paper, *The Palm Beach Post*. I had practiced in this town for almost twenty years, managed five offices, and had written a highly successful book, which was endorsed by Donald Trump. One day, the local paper stated that Trump didn't even know me, and that I was never in *Who's Who*. All they had to do was go to my office and see the memorabilia, autographed photos, certificates and letters. Instead of being a supportive hometown sensitive to our situation, they attacked me and made me out to be a fraud. I was fighting for my life and now I also had to fight for my reputation. I felt angry about the detrimental attacks on my character by the local newspaper. How could these bullies attack me when I was not even able to speak a word to defend myself? How could they be so harmful to my family? They never interviewed my Rabbi or our congregation or they could have printed something positive. I was president of my temple and had raised over two million dollars to move our temple to a better location. The temple went from being on the brink of bankruptcy to becoming the largest reformed congregation in Palm Beach Gardens. Isn't a good deed newsworthy? The media was yet another virus I would have to overcome. They did not understand the negative effect their lies had upon my ability to recover. I was already struggling to live and they were making me out to be a fake by dishonoring me in my own community. Those who know me, know that the statements printed by the newspaper were not true. We believe that what happened to us could and should have been prevented.

We had made more progress than expected in a short time, but there were many days I did not want to live. After my visits from Mom and Uncle Herb, I did not fear death. I feared having to live the rest of my life in this debilitated condition. I had heard that Heaven is a beautiful place. It had to be better than where I was.

Each day I was surrounded by a cold, helpless silence. The tracheostomy was being suctioned quite often and I felt a sense of panic every time I heard an alarm. One of the nurses finally placed the call button within my reach and told me it was there. Hadn't it occured to anyone before now that I might have needed this simple device? I felt betrayed. I had been lying in bed for two weeks. The buzzer had been there all along but instead of letting me know where it was, they had yelled at me to stop banging.

For two weeks, I had been telling my eyes to open. During the third week, they finally responded to my command and I was able to open them slightly. This may have seemed like a time to celebrate but I was disappointed because I saw everything double. To complicate matters, once I opened my eyes, I could not get them to close. Once I could see, I noticed the look of pity in people's eyes. I am a proud man. I did not want pity. I was coming back to life and I suppose I should have been thankful. I did not want to live my life as a vegetable, yet there was no promise of a full recovery. No one knew what the long-term effects would be. I thought of my visits with my mom and Uncle Herb. They seemed so long ago. A voice inside me nagged, *They were probably just drug-induced dreams. There can't be a God because God would not do this to an enemy, much less to two of His children. I am not as strong or as brave as Christopher Reeve. I am not Superman. Just let me die. I want my day with God.*

I looked forward to Peter coming in and rubbing my head every night. It was a highlight in my day and also a scary time because he and Michael were usually my last visitors. And once they left, I was alone with my memories and mental survival skills. The nights were filled with memories. My spirit would pray and my mind would play. I'm sure the drugs they were giving me assisted my nightly journeys as I relived my life as a founding member of Bear Lakes Country Club. I love my friends and our Saturday game of golf. While I am not a good golfer, I am a competitive one. I played a round of golf in my head one night. I played my best round and won all the money. Collecting will be tough. To me, golf is second only to basketball. *That's what I'll do, I'll go to the park and shoot some hoops...*

Chapter Twelve

Out of Air

A few nights after tracheotomy surgery, it seemed I was getting worse rather than better. In fact, the previous evening I had heard one nurse say, "I don't know if he is going to make it." That is not something you need to hear when you are fighting for your life. Even though I was on a ventilator, I felt as though I was suffocating, so I pressed the button for the night nurse. Thank God, Shelly answered my call for help. She is a nurse who loves her patients and she seemed genuinely concerned for me and Bonnie. I had heard her voice on other occasions, but I had not been able to see her. Now that I was able to open my eyes, she was everything I expected and more. She was indeed an angel. I could see love and kindness radiating from her eyes.

Shelly had not been on staff for a few days and as she entered my room she immediately noticed the progress I was making. "Hey, you opened your eyes! That's great!"

"I am in trouble," I wrote. "I cannot breathe. Please help me."

"Sure, I will help you."

"I'm scared. I feel like I am dying."

She had trouble reading my writing but she responded, "Nothing is going to happen to you while I am here."

"I can't breathe."

She looked at me and knew I was scared. "Let me suction you."

The muscles of the diaphragm allow us to inhale and exhale as they work in conjunction with the lungs. Most people can spit, or swallow or cough up mucus. A paralyzed person cannot voluntarily carry out any of these functions. I had to be suctioned to keep my airways open. Being suctioned is harsh on the body. A plastic or rubber suction catheter is introduced into the lungs to aspirate the secretions. As Shelly suctioned me, she asked if I felt better. I shook my head. She worked diligently, but no matter how hard she tried, nothing helped. I was literally drowning in my own mucus. My body quaked involuntarily and I panicked. HELP ME, GOD. I'm choking! The last thing I wanted on my tombstone was "Dr. Eric Kaplan—he drowned in his own saliva"!

Shelly instilled saline down the trach tube and manually ventilated my lungs, trying to inflate and oxygenate them. The muscles in my body that could respond were spasming so bad, I passed out. The next thing I knew, I was being moved toward a room filled with men and women, many of whom were wearing hats. They were sitting at tables and it looked like they were playing cards. As I got closer, they turned and looked toward me as if to greet me. I recognized my family members—my grandmothers, grandfathers, uncles and aunts. It was not unusual for my family to get together for a game of cards but these family members were DEAD! *Where am I? What is going on?* It dawned on me that I was either dying or already dead. I didn't know what to do, say or think. As I approached the door to their room, it slammed shut right in my face and there stood my father! He was shaking his head "no."

He looked at me as only my father can. On his face was a look of love combined with parental assurance that everything is going to be okay.

"Dad, am I going to be okay? Will you stay with me? Are you my angel?"

He nodded his head "yes" and floated toward me. I was ushered away and the next thing I knew I was on a stage. Not a word was said but I knew I was in the presence of God and it was my turn to speak. "God," I started, "I have been a good man—not perfect—but good. I am not afraid of dying. If you want to take me, that's fine, but please leave my wife and heal her. If I have more to offer the world and it is not my time to die, then I want to live, but if I am to live, heal me quickly. I am not a strong enough to live like this. I can only live if I am whole. Give me a reason for this and show me the way. Allow me to be your messenger." The room went blank. Like a young boy, I called to my father for help.

"Dad, what is happening to me?"

"It's going to be okay," I heard him whisper. "I am here for you. God will have me watch over you."

"Are you my angel?"

"Son, you have many angels, but I am here to teach you about the Laws of Life, right and wrong, good and bad. You must know the difference between right and wrong and choose what is good and right. Behind each decision we make, there are two major forces—good and bad. Even when we choose a good or positive action, the bad side still exists. We must harness the good in order to allow its existence to prosper. Life is about choices, son. Harnessing the good within us gives it energy and power, enabling us to resist and fight bad advice when it's decision time."

"That's what Uncle Herb said."

"We are on earth to grow. In order to evolve, people must know the difference between right and wrong. If a person cannot tell the difference between right and wrong, then that person is not ready to evolve. This is why humans have the ability to learn, share knowledge and grow spiritually. This is how humans differ from all of God's other creatures. You have free will."

"Why did this happen to me? I didn't choose to be poisoned!"

"A selfless man does not worry about his appearance. You chose vanity when you elected to have Botox injections."

"Is that it? We choose to have bad things happen to us?"

"If we all chose to do good and not evil, bad things would not happen. There would be no war in the world—only harmony. In the book of Genesis, didn't Adam take a bite of the apple?"

"Yes."

"God gave Adam (mankind) freedom to choose and offered him his first opportunity to exercise his free will when he told him not to eat the apple. Adam chose to ignore God's request to avoid the fruit. So did you. You knew drugs were not good for you. You even warned people of their harm but you did not heed your own advice."

"So, God did not do this to me?"

"No, son, a doctor did. God does not live our lives for us. He gave us the ability to know the difference between good and evil. People know when they are doing wrong. When they give in to wrong, they feed evil. Once evil is severed from its life support, it will die. However, there is a way to embrace evil by integrating it as part of our life."

"Embrace evil?"

"Even bad things have good components. A positive outcome can come from a bad situation. One day you may tell your survival story and keep this harm from happening to others. By helping others steer clear of the harm you have encountered, you will be turning evil into something good."

"I'd like to help others avoid this hell."

"As you know, I served in World War II," Dad continued. "The war was horrible and many lives were lost, but think of the good that has come from it. The world has healed and grown. The buildings that were destroyed have been rebuilt even better than before. We have better international relationships between countries. Over the last sixty years, as a result of technology released during the war, we now have television, movies on DVD, music on CD, the Internet, better vehicles and easier air travel."

"Easier air travel? You haven't flown in a while, have you?" I joked. "Getting through the terminal is like running through a land mine."

"Oh, you mean 9/11."

"Exactly. Tell me what good has come from that." I was being genuinely sarcastic.

"Nine-eleven has opened the world's eyes. Terrorism and destruction are never good. A few people chose to do wrong and many innocent people were harmed as a result. Our actions carry consequences. During the aftermath, when people's hearts were more open to listen, God moved into compassionate action to comfort those who grieved. God is here to help us heal the wounds of our life and our land."

"Why doesn't God just stop terrorism?"

"He did not stop Adam from disobeying Him back then and He still doesn't interfere with the choices humans make. That would violate our free will. God does not control us like puppets."

"Good point, Dad. Humans are the ones who try to control one another."

It was good to talk to my father again. He had always been a stable and practical force in my life. I had missed him so very much over the years.

"It is good to tend to our own lives and let others do the same. God created the universe and gave humanity the ability to order it as he pleases. When things go wrong, humans tend to blame God. Take global warming for example. God did not create it, man did. Man does not recognize his power or the influence of his choices. That is why most people live their lives trying to define such questions as, 'Who am I? Why am I here? Where did I come from? Where am I going?'"

"I've asked all those questions many times. Especially in the past few weeks."

"Let's talk about that, son. You prayed for God to let you die. Then you prayed for Him to heal you. Which do you prefer?"

"Life, of course."

"Yes, but with certain conditions."

"I don't understand."

"You prayed to live only if you would heal quickly. Those are conditions, are they not?"

"Yes sir."

"You can cocreate and manifest your life as you choose and the Universe will assist in answering your prayers, but when you are wishy-washy and can't decide what you want, you will only manifest chaos. Be direct and consistent about what you want."

"I want to live, but I want to be well. I'd rather die than stay in my present condition. Death can't be that bad. For all I know, I may already be dead. I'm talking to YOU and you are dead."

"Perhaps you are facing the death of your physical body. Death is simply a passing from one dimension of life to another. There is truly nothing to be afraid of regarding this transition. Death is simply a portal to another realm of consciousness, much like the one you passed through as an infant coming into this life through your mother's womb. Our eternal soul is our true identity. It has consciousness and memory that will continue to exist in other realms and dimensions throughout life and afterlife. That's how I'm speaking to you now."

"So, there's no going to hell or heaven after we die?"

"You choose your actions both now and in the afterlife. It is important to make spiritual progress while in the body, but even if you have lived a life that was less than loving on earth, you may continue to evolve in the afterlife. The afterlife is a wonderful place to learn, love, plan and assess your spiritual growth. Free will is a gift from our Creator. It is irrevocable even in the afterlife."

"That's comforting to know. Many religions have made people fearful of the afterlife."

"There is nothing to fear. Now, let's get back to the Laws of Life. God is truth, Eric, but when people do not walk on a spiritual path, truth can be camouflaged. Happiness is found by those who make the effort to safeguard matters of truth. Those who seek truth are seeking to be one with God. It is as simple as right and wrong. To be honest is right. To lie is wrong. I taught you that."

"Yes, you did."

"The truth is, it is normal for the human body to age. God wants us to slow down, respect our body, enjoy our wisdom and pass it on to others. Wisdom is understanding that God is in all things. To alter your appearance is to alter the way God manifests in you."

"Does that mean plastic surgery is not good?"

"God gives doctors the skills to make necessary changes. Someone whose face or body was altered in an accident has the right to heal properly and look normal again. Change in appearance does not bring happiness, but some people need physical change in order to survive."

"And, I elected to have an unnecessary cosmetic procedure."

"You had the world's most powerful toxin injected into your body. Had you needed cosmetic surgery to live and be in good health, you would have been in the hands of a surgeon chosen by God to assist you.

"But Dad, everyone was doing it."

"Look at history and those who killed Jews, enslaved blacks, raped women and pillaged cities. What if they had said to God, 'Everyone is doing it'? Would that justify their actions? We each give an account of our own choices. Being poisoned was not God's will. It is God's will for everyone to live in honest integrity with himself and fellow humans. Money and things do not bring happiness. Happiness comes when the value of truth is recognized and all dishonesty is abandoned. When your passion guides the search, truth will be found, but it may appear in the strangest of places. Damage has been done to your body, but now you must choose the life you want. It's time to make a decision and move forward. Your faith and spirit will drive you. Look at all the people who are helping you: Dr. Egitto, Dr. Price, Dr. Kerner, Dr. Ooh, the Centers for Disease Control, therapists, lab technicians and all the nurses—even the cranky ones. They don't want to lose you."

"I see them and appreciate all they are doing to help me." It was good to see my Dad. Being in his presence was comforting and it felt so real. Having him by my side gave me hope. I was eager to hear what more he had to say.

"You must find a purpose if you are to continue to live in your body."

"I want to walk with my wife. I want to hold my sons, and I want to pet my dog. Without the ability to feel, I cannot be happy."

"Are you giving God conditions again?"

"Yes and no." I knew he was right, but like the prodigal son, I wanted my way.

"Which is it?" It had been so long since my dad had lectured me. "Truth is light. I see the light in your heart. Can you see it?

"No, Dad. I can barely open my eyes."

"You don't need your eyes to see the Light."

"I don't understand."

"The future of your life is in your vision."

"But, I can't see!"

"Not being able to see with your physical eyes does not mean you have no vision. Son, if seeing is believing, then visualizing is realizing. Don't look at your body as it is now. Instead, see yourself as you want to be. Can you see yourself getting well? Can you see yourself walking?"

"I want to see and walk and talk just like before. I want to be happy again."

"Were you truly happy before this incident?"

"I don't know."

"You always know the truth. Your truth is in your beliefs. Passion will guide you to the truth in your heart, soul, and spirit. Have faith in God and you will happily stand with vigor and devotion. You will see with spiritual eyes that God is always with you. When one has walked in the ways of God, knowledge of right and wrong becomes intuitive. He or she will do what is right and honorable on every occasion. You don't need a Bible, a doctrine, dogma or a list of rules to know what is good and what harms others. The Laws of Truth and Love are written on your heart, but not all of God's children follow His path."

"Why is that?"

"Haven't you ever gone astray? Have you always been perfect? Even then, God is with you waiting for you to return and be guided by wisdom."

"Does this mean God is with me in this situation?"

"If you believe in God, God is here to heal you and your wife. Angels are all around you. Remember your lessons."

"Dad? DAD!"

My father was gone. I came back to present reality, and there beside me stood Shelly. "Are you okay?" she asked sincerely.

I nodded my head "yes," thankful that I was able to breathe again.

"You scared me for a moment," she said kindly. "I thought we were losing you."

I motioned for the pad and wrote, "What happened?"

"You passed out." Shelly explained. "Your blood pressure and oxygen level dropped really low."

"You are my angel," I tried to write.

"Just go to sleep and stop scaring me." She was clearly shaken by what had happened. So was I. Going to that room and seeing my deceased loved ones was eerie. I had given ultimatums to God! I knew it was not a dream. Unlike with the other encounters, I was no longer in a drug-induced state. I was conscious of everything. I am convinced that the encounter with my father was real. To this day I often have questioned if the other angelic visitors were drug-induced. But not this one: My father's visit was real. It was as real to me as the words you read on this page. Through it, I learned the most valuable lessons of my life: God is real, I have the power to choose, and I am never alone. I lay in bed that night remembering my father and the lessons he taught me. It had been years since my father died, but I always believed if one person could return from beyond it was my father. My father was one of my angels.

Chapter Thirteen

Give Me Three Steps, Mister

I awoke early the next morning drenched with sweat. I pressed the call button and Shelly came in. "You're soaking wet," my angel nurse replied. "It looks like you are breaking your fever." I knew something significant was happening in my body.

I had been afraid to let my friends know about the angelic visits and lessons from my mother and Uncle Herb because I was worried about what people would think. They might say I was hallucinating or dreaming, and I was already doubting whether the encounters were real. However, after my father's visit, I resolved to tell my story. My father would have wanted everyone to know he was alive and helping me. Even with my newfound hope, the red dog of self-pity started to nag me. *Look at me. I have a ventilator attached to my throat. I can hardly move; someone has to close my eyes once I finally get them open. I can't breathe on my own and I look like death warmed over. Some might say that the encounter with my Dad was probably just a dream or wishful thinking, but to me his visit was as real as life itself. His visit gave me continued hope and faith, thoughts I needed to survive..* All I knew to do, all I could do was pray, "God, please let the visitations be real and not a dream."

The white dog within me arose to combat the negativity. "You prayed to God and He came to your aid. Are you going to discount it as a dream? You must have faith."

Regardless of whether my encounters were real, I knew I had to make a choice to live and recover. *I choose to live. I choose to get well. I can. I will. I must.* I was scared, yet determined because I knew I was not alone. My angels were with me, and God is real. Bonnie and I were both surrounded by angels. I could feel them the way one feels the wind. Even when I felt negative and wanted to give up, I could sense their power and strength urging me onward. Proof of their presence began to manifest as miracles that were impossible to discount. It had been approximately fourteen days since our poisoning. After my dad's visit, I started getting better by the minute. The pneumonia I had been battling since before the tracheotomy began to clear up overnight, which absolutely amazed the doctors.

I started taking control of my health and my medical treatment. I asked for 3,000 milligrams of vitamin C in my IV. Heck, if Norman Cousins could do it (in his book, *Anatomy of an Illness as Perceived by the Patient*), I could. The staff also complied when I asked them to cut back on my medication. From that point on, I began to work harder than ever. I moved my arms and legs throughout the day. Some of the nurses would get mad because I would kick off the covers and set off the alarms. They would just have to deal with it. I was going to get well and get out of there!

A few days after my angelic encounter with Dad, the physical therapist came in to examine me. "I hear you are kicking up a storm. I want to see what you can do." I performed my disco dance in bed and he was impressed. "Today we will try to walk with a walker."

That surprised me. For three weeks, I had been paralyzed, and now only a few days after my interlude with God and my father, my therapist was going to have me try to walk. There is a Chinese proverb that says, "The journey of a thousand miles begins with one step." I was ready to take my first step.

Getting me up was no simple task since I was "all hooked up." I was attached to a feeding tube, a ventilator, a catheter, an IV, an EKG machine, and a spirometer used to determine oxygenation content. I could not move my neck, and most of my body was still paralyzed. It took a physical therapist, an aide, and a nurse to pull my body into an upright and sitting position. It was the first time in three weeks that I had sat up. I wanted to smile but my face was frozen. After getting all my medical gear tucked up and pinned out of the way, the others helped me stand to my feet. I was extremely wobbly and uncoordinated. My hands gripped the walker as if my life depended on it. With a rush of elation, I spastically, but happily took my first steps. I can imagine how the astronauts must have felt the first time they walked on the moon. My heart rate and blood pressure elevated quickly so I was only allowed to take a few steps. Still, my faith was renewed. I looked up and gave thanks to God. I was beating the odds.

"Tomorrow we will try again," the physical therapist said.

...and I will walk to the next room and see my wife!

Chapter Fourteen

Dog Days

If every dog year is equal to seven years in a human life, I was living a dog's life. Everything was seven times harder to do and it took seven times more energy just to move about in bed. Every time I got myself comfortable, the nurses would come in to move me so I wouldn't get bedsores.

Botox is a form of botulism that paralyzes the muscles. When a small amount of Botox is injected into a facial line, the muscle underneath can no longer contract. Therefore, frown lines and crow's feet disappear. This works until the botulism wears off in approximately one year. Natural botulism can develop in canned food when inadequate canning procedures are used. Research showed one woman who had botulism from food, who recovered in seven months. However, Bonnie and I received 2,000 or more times the normal dosage. No one in history had ever received the amount we did. We were originally told that Bonnie and I would not be able to open our eyes for six months. We opened them in two weeks. We were also told that we would not walk for a year. I was walking during the third week of recovery. We were not expected to live, much less recuperate so quickly.

I had a limited amount of voluntary muscle activity and the harder I worked, the more muscle control I gained. I was writing legibly enough that Michael could interpret it. I could move my neck backward, but not forward. I could use my right leg and left arm better than my left leg and right arm. It was the anterior (frontal) muscles that were not responding. This affected my ability to read, see, breathe and talk. Also, my face and tongue were frozen, so I could not eat, talk, swallow or smile. I hated life as I knew it, but at least I had hope for recovery.

Having a feeding tube is very unpleasant, but useful for giving nourishment when a person cannot take food through their mouth. It also allowed one of our IV lines to be removed. The feeding tube with a plastic balloon catheter was inserted into my stomach and protruded externally just below my ribcage. I was chugging four to six cans of enteral nutrition a day. My peg site (short for percutaneous endoscopic gastrostomy) was always red and sore. When I complained that it might be infected, one of the doctors told me my white count numbers were not high enough to put me on antibiotics. Doctors try to reduce the indiscriminate use of antibiotics a person receives, because pathogenic bacteria may build resistance to antibiotics, thus causing antibiotics to become ineffective.

One day when my partner, Dr. Gerry Mattia, and his wife, Paulette, came to visit me, the peg site was so sore I wanted to pull that dang hose out of my body. Gerry and Paulette were pleased to see me walking, but on the way back to my room Gerry pointed to my stomach and asked, "Are you bleeding? That looks like blood."

Sure enough, blood was coming from my abdomen where the feeding tube was inserted. This scared both of us so we called the nurse to come and take a look. He examined the area and decided that it did look infected.

When the gastrointestinal doctor came by, my peg site was reddened and inflamed.

"I need antibiotics," I wrote.

"Yes, you do," he agreed. Within a few days of treatment, the peg site was much more comfortable.

Daily I was visited by Steve and his wife, Gloria; my cousin Steve Daniels; my adopted Uncle Jack; my Uncle Buddy, my mother's sister, Aunt Gloria; my friends the Meyers, Doughertys, Zweckers and Brocks; and my Rabbi, Joel Levine. Others wanted to visit, but the ICU was highly restricted due to the media's disrespect of our need to heal without being bombarded with questions. It was impossible to think of everyone who might possibly come visit us; however, if a person's name was not on the list we gave the security team, the person would not be allowed in. Of the friends and family who were allowed to visit us, I could see the fear in their eyes. I had once been so vitally healthy. Now attached to all kinds of machinery, I was scary looking. Everyone was happy I was alive, and I wanted so much to give them hope that I would pull through. What hurt me most was having my sons see me so helpless. They helped me shave, wash my face and hair, and even tried to brush my teeth. I could not spit out the paste. I had to lean forward and let it fall out. After I had taken my first steps, I decided to try to do more on my own. My body was recovering as if it were being born again. Like a baby new to the world, I had to re-learn to walk, move, smile, swallow, and breathe. I even had to learn to go to the bathroom on my own. Such things we take for granted.

All my life, people had told me I shouldn't do this, couldn't do that, or wouldn't be able to do whatever. Those negative and limiting words fueled my spirit, and I was out to prove them all wrong. I was told that I was too short to play high school basketball, yet I led freshmen team and Junior Varsity in scoring and was soon brought up to the Varsity. In no time I was being recruited to play basketball at Division one Universities.. I was told I was too small to play college basketball, yet I had a solid career. As an athlete, I was told that pre-med was impossible due to the time and travel required to play college basketball. Some said I was not smart enough to be a doctor. I went on to prove them all wrong. Even today, Michael read more unfair and untrue stories published by the media. I was determined to show them who I am and what I am made of.

We are all given the will to grow, to change ourselves and our destiny. Too often, our human nature is lazy. While it is natural to desire maximum benefit through minimal effort, we sometimes perform thoughtless and ineffective actions. Often we act as if everything is pre-programmed or pre-ordained; therefore, we are passive, often reacting to life rather than taking the initiative to make things happen. We sit and wait for something good to fall into our laps, not exerting the energy to get up and open the door when opportunity knocks. The course of events in our lives can be changed, no matter what others may say. We must have faith. Not just in God, but in ourselves as well. We are responsible for transforming our lives. We must become decision makers and risk takers and let the power of life flow through our veins. Sometimes that means knowing the difference between what we can change and what we cannot. We cannot change other people, but we can change ourselves. I was determined to take control of my life. I would push myself as much as it took to get well.

I longed for the visits of my father, Uncle Herb and my mom, but that phase was over. I had to move forward and apply the lessons I had already learned. After God parted the Red Sea for him, Moses didn't say to God, "That was cool, but I need another miracle. Can you do that again today?" Eventually, we have to build our own bridge. That bridge is our awareness and thankfulness of daily miracles—simple tasks and pleasures such as being able to see, smile, talk, eat, wave hello, love and be loved. Those simple things we take for granted in life are the miracles.

My father used to say, "Your best friend is the person who brings out the best in you." Peter Brock is one of my best friends. Peter came to visit me nearly every evening.

"You are going to be okay." Peter would rub my head as he spoke, "You are a tough guy. You can beat this." Knowing there are healing powers in our hands, I find it amazing how little we are touched in a hospital. I therefore looked forward to Peter's visits and his pep talks each evening. As I started to regain my bodily functions, he became my coach. "What did you accomplish today? How much can you raise your arms?" No matter what I had done that day, he expected more from me the next. The day I took three steps was special and I couldn't wait to tell Peter.

"I walked three steps today," I wrote on the pad.

Peter responded, "Tomorrow, I want you to walk six steps."

Even with limited function of my body, I felt free. It was apparent how the love of my friends and family was inspiring and influencing me, but I also realized I had given them hope. Nature often puts us in a compromising position between pain and pleasure. A marathon runner feels the pain of fatigue, sore muscles and a longing for air. A hungry dieter will endure mental and physical anguish in order to achieve weight loss. Being able to see the goal of a healthy body in the distance, I was willing to endure a certain amount of suffering while anticipating future compensation.

Sometimes our personal pain gives pleasure to others. I don't mean that to sound sadistic, but I endured pain in order to bring pleasure and hope to my friends and family. I saw pleasure in their eyes as I was able to accomplish more and more. Often a novel will make you cry before it makes you smile. Yesterday, I saw tears in the eyes of my friend Bill Meyer. Today, I saw him smile. When we see others endure unusual anguish, we say it is a heroic feat. I was in no way a hero, but my effort was heroic in the eyes of the people who loved me, and their love fueled my spirit. My friends and family were by far my best medicine.

Steve, Michael, Janice and Peter were optimistic because of the progress Bonnie and I were making. Together with the Meyers and Steven Daniels, they started looking for a rehab center for us. Dr. Egitto and Peter wanted me out of the Gardens Hospital because they felt I needed more sophisticated rehabilitative care. My attorney recommended a place in Florida, but when Michael and Steve went to visit they came back depressed. "There is no way I am going to let you go there, Dad. The place is filled with old people waiting and hoping to die."

Dr. Harold Rosen was still pushing for Shepherd Center because it was a place of hope. People whose lives have been dramatically changed are introduced to a different way of living that is fulfilling. Shepherd denied our application the first time they evaluated us because they didn't feel they could help us. My family and friends were persistent, however. They felt Shepherd was the place for us, so Michael and Steve began a marketing campaign to have them accept us. I continued to work hard. I was going for botulism valedictorian.

Chapter Fifteen

My Eyes Adored Her

I awoke determined to see my wife. I had missed her so much and I was no longer going to let my disability keep us apart. All I had to go by was second-hand reports about her progress. I wanted—rather, needed—to see for myself how she was doing. I was feeling guilty that somehow I might be responsible for her condition.

Bonnie's life had not been easy. She was an orphan raised by the State of New Jersey but in spite of her difficult upbringing, she remained truly thankful for everything. She and I went to the same college, yet we never met while we were there. I would always tease her that I didn't have enough money to allure her back then. Seven years prior to our current hospitalization, Bonnie had survived colon cancer. After a year of chemotherapy and managing her life with a colostomy, she understood pain and personal suffering. Once the colostomy was reversed, she went back to her job as the principal of Batt Private School in Juno Beach, Florida. She did not have to work; she chose to work because she loved those children. Having won the battle with cancer, Saint Bonnie was again fighting for her life.

I was as nervous as a thirteen-year-old boy on his first date. I washed my face but my arms were incapable of reaching to the top of my head to brush my hair. I did the best I could to make myself presentable. After shaving, I was exhausted. It felt like I had ran twelve miles. Around eleven o'clock, the physical therapist came by and my adventure began. Getting all the tubes ready to travel was an ordeal, but soon I was on my way. Clinging to my aluminum walker, my heart pounding with both fatigue and excitement, I slowly shuffled with my entourage to the room next door. I was about to see my wife for the first time since our ordeal had begun.

As I turned the corner into her room, I stopped short at the doorway. Seeing my beautiful wife lying there helpless and shattered grieved my heart. I loved her more at that moment than I ever had before. Oh, how I ached to hold her in my arms again. Although she was unable to make a facial expression, her eyes communicated her surprise to see me and I could tell she was smiling on the inside. With the help of my physical therapist and nurses, I slowly made what seemed like a million-mile journey to the chair next to her bed. I sat down without taking my eyes off my beloved wife. I took the pad and pen, which were next to her and wrote with a shaking hand, "I love you."

Bonnie feebly wrote, "I love you. I hate this."

I knew exactly what she meant. Our once serene lives were now chaotic with no certainty of ever returning to normal. We were apart from each other and completely dependent on someone else to take care of us. Visions of endearing memories we had shared washed over me. Unable to blink because my eyelids were frozen, I felt the sting of tears welling up. We had a long way to go before being well, but at this moment, I was thankful to be alive and in her presence.

"You are going to be okay," I wrote.

She shook her head "no." She did not believe me.

I touched her hand and became overwhelmed by the emotion of the moment. God, why my wife? She is such a good woman. Continue to help us. Please continue to heal us. With all the effort I could manage, I pulled her hand to my face. I missed her touch. I wanted to hold her, kiss her, and be with her. The thoughts of our love, our life, and our memories swept over me in those seconds. I vowed then and there to get well so we could experience our love again and make more sweet memories together.

Several of our nurses stopped by to witness the two of us together again. The raw emotion that I experienced was clearly felt and much too sacred for some to bear. Those too touched by the scene turned quickly as if they suddenly had other patients to attend. We were a broken man and woman. We seemed to have so little going for us, yet we had so much because we had each other. Bonnie and I ached for things to be as they were before this fiasco ruined our lives. Words, if we could have spoken them, would not have adequately expressed the sadness and love we felt—sadness for having such a tragedy in our lives and love that only increased in the shadow of death.

With unmoving faces, our souls stared through eyes that would not open or close at will. Our bodies spasmodically moved only with extreme physical exertion while our hearts beat passionately with the miracle of life. Time stood still as we danced in our Cinderella fairy tale knowing that midnight would soon toll my return to my own cell in ICU where I would be locked away from my princess again. Our trance was broken when Michael walked in and saw us. He wept at the sight of his parents together again. I don't know if those were tears of joy that I was able to walk to his mother's room or if he was saddened that we were in such a pitiful condition. Probably both. He couldn't possibly have understood what he had just witnessed.

My journey to Bonnie's room drained me. The simple act of sitting upright fatigued me and every muscle in my body ached. I did not want to leave but I needed to go back to my room and lie down. As I struggled to rise, I placed the communication tools beside my wife and tapped the pad to reiterate, "I love you."

I had begun my climb up the mountain of wholeness. I had done what no one thought possible, and I knew in my heart that tomorrow I would do more. I remembered what Dr. Egitto had told me, "Eric, there is no history of survival here. You received 2,000 or more times the normal dosage of Botulinum toxin A. In most medical cases, doctors just follow the book on procedures. In this case, there is no book. You are literally writing the book for us. Make history. Show us the way."

The next day I was visited by my pulmonologist, Dr. Ooh. "If you are able to walk, then perhaps you can also breathe on your own. I want to take you off the ventilator to see how well you do."

Sweet music to my ears! I was ready to get rid of that air-puffing dragon. However, when they turned the machine off, I felt like a drowning swimmer gasping for air. It was the scariest moment of my life and I knew just how far from true health I was. The doctor and respiratory therapist stood by my side as I forced my atrophied diaphragm to move and breathe. Every few minutes, they would turn the ventilator on or off. I was able to do this for five to ten minutes before I felt like I would collapse. It was a long way from being off the machine 24/7 but it was a good start. Just wait until I tell Peter! Just wait until I show Billy!

Over the next few days, they all wanted more from their star performer. I have to admit that the attention drove me harder. The therapist suggested I try to walk without being attached to the ventilator. They promised to follow me with an oxygen tank, just in case I had trouble. After a half hour of preparation, I was on my feet, taking slow, uncoordinated steps while holding to my walker. The nurses stood in awe.

I huffed and puffed to Bonnie's room and sat next to her. I was gasping for air but I was breathing on my own. I grabbed her pen and pad and wrote, "Look, honey. I am breathing on my own. I am walking. If I can do this, so can you."

She squeezed my hand and wrote, "I will try."

I wrote, "Soon we will be at our home in Big Canoe. We will walk the mountains again."

"I wish I could believe you," she wrote. I could tell she was ready to give up. I could not let her do that after all we had been through.

"I had a visitor a few nights ago."

"Who?"

"My father."

She drew a question mark on the pad.

"Yes, he is with us and we will get better."

Bonnie turned her head away from me. I nudged her hand. When she returned her tearful gaze to me, she had a faraway look in her eyes. Clearly, she was losing hope.

"We have to have faith that God will take care of us."

She turned her head away again. She was in such emotional turmoil from the ordeal. We were always each other's main support but I was not physically able to tend to her as I wanted. I felt helpless, but I would not let her give up the will to live.

Later that night Peter returned. As he rubbed my head, I wrote all about my day. He smiled as he read my gibberish. But like my old coach, Bobby Knight, Peter was not going to let me rest on my laurels. "Tomorrow, I want you off the vent for an hour."

"God willing," I wrote.

The next day, I stayed off the ventilator for two hours and made it one time around the nurse's station without it. I was as proud as an Olympian running a victory lap. My friend Bill walked with me each step. I could tell he was afraid that I might fall as I wobbled along, but he constantly gave me verbal praise and confidence. "That's great, Eric. You are doing better than we ever expected. I'm so proud of you."

Bonnie also had family and friends who encouraged her. Denise Meyer, Janice Brock, Penny Beers, Karen Zwecker, and Barbara Egitto would visit Bonnie whenever their husbands came to visit me. Gloria, Steve's wife, came every day and stayed by Bonnie's side. Aunt Gloria, Uncle Herb's wife, is one of the most inspirational people in my life. She was there the morning the staff got Bonnie up to walk for the first time. Gloria walked behind Bonnie and her medical regalia. I filed in line behind Gloria. Aunt Gloria cried as she witnessed the miracle. We must have looked like a wrecked train in slow motion.

I had made tremendous strides in only a few days—more than I could have hoped for and certainly more than the doctors expected. When I heard that Shelly was my nurse that night, I was excited. Although it had been only three days since I last saw her, it felt like months. I wanted to show off my newly found skills of breathing and walking. I had it prearranged with the staff that I would walk for her. I could not wait to show her how much I had progressed since that night with her, my father and God.

When she entered my room, I wrote, "You are my angel, Shelly." She smiled warmly. When she smiled, the whole room lit up. "I have a surprise for you."

The therapist helped me out of bed. The staff detached most of the wires and unhooked me from the ventilator. I walked holding to the walker. I looked like a young toddler, weak, wobbly and unstable but it was nevertheless a walk of faith. Only days earlier, I was in bed unable to breathe on my own. Tonight, I was walking and breathing. Shelly was like a parent watching her baby taking his first steps. Her eyes welled with tears of pride.

Sharmella was my nurse in the day. She was tough and she pushed me hard. She and Peter were two of a kind. Together, they were like drill sergeants, always pushing me to reach my potential out of a sincere desire to see me well. If I was off the vent for one hour, they wanted two hours. If I walked one lap around the nurse's station, they wanted two. If I did two laps, they wanted four. Thank God for Bill and my cousin Steve Daniels, who showed compassion to balance Sharmella and Peter's toughness. Like good cop and bad cop, one team pushed me and the other praised and encouraged me.

Even though we were making great strides, we were still mere shadows of our former selves. It was extremely difficult and sad for our two boys to see their parents in this condition. Our roles were now reversed, and our children had become our caretakers.

They literally put their lives on hold for us. Michael dropped out of college so he and Steve could handle the day-to-day financial aspects of my consulting business. Because Jason was often left out of the loop of what was going on in our day to day recovery as he attended college at Saint Leo's University in Tampa, he transferred to Palm Beach Community College to be closer to home. Being the youngest son in my family, I understood how he felt. However, Jason never showed any signs of weakness or jealously. Instead, he grew stronger every day and became an exceptional young man. When he would visit each night, he would take lotion and massage my legs. I never knew my young son had such good hands, or that he was so loving and compassionate. I literally felt his love in his hands.

"You have healing hands," I wrote. "You should consider a healing profession that uses hands-on therapy."

He chuckled. "Maybe I will follow in your footsteps and go to chiropractic school."

"No cosmetic prodecures!" I wrote.

"Dad, I think you just smiled!"

"Yes, I did." I continued to write a more serious note. "I'm sorry, son."

"For what? Smiling?"

"No, look at me."

"Yeah, you look terrible. What's your point? If you hadn't been so concerned about your looks, this never would have happened."

"I know. That is what I feel terrible about!"

"Did you learn anything from this?"

"Yes, I did."

"What did you learn?"

"I learned that there is more to life than what we perceive. I learned that life is far more beautiful than I originally imagined. I now know there are angels everywhere and God loves each of us."

"It sounds like you learned a lot, Dad. I figure if you learned anything from this experience then it is a lesson, not a mistake. You are going to get better."

"How do you know?"

"What are your other choices?" My son's wisdom astounded me. I was enrolled in the University of Life and here he was performing his role as my teacher. "If you say you believe you will get well, then you must believe it with all your heart."

"Are you lecturing me?"

"Yes. How do I sound?"

"You sound just like me!" I laughed inside.

"I learned everything I know from you. You are my hero."

"Even now?"

"Even more so now. I see how hard you work every day. I watch you take care of yourself, watch over Mom and still lead your family. Dad, I always knew you were strong and I always loved you, but I have never been prouder of you than I am today. I need you to get well. There is so much more you can teach me."

"I will, son. I promise."

"I am holding you to that promise."

Never is a moment of our life wasted. I had spent years trying to teach this boy and direct his path to success. I even sent him to military school! In today's class, Jason was my teacher and I was never prouder. He was becoming a leader. My life had value. How else could my son have turned out so wise?

Chapter Sixteen

You Talkin' to Me?

During the latter part of the third week of our stay at Gardens Hospital, our pulmonary specialist, Dr. Ooh, came in with a speech pathologist. Now that I was breathing without the ventilator for a few hours at a time, they thought I would be a good candidate for an apparatus called a Passy-Muir valve. The valve is a plastic cap, about the size of a small spool of sewing thread, that is attached to the outside of the tracheostomy. The cap opens to allow inhalation, then closes upon exhalation, thus forcing the patient to release air through the nose, or through the vocal cords, enabling speech. My speech pathologist proceeded to teach me how to use this small but powerful device. Then he inserted the valve and asked me to give it a try reminding me, "Your voice may sound strange, so don't be alarmed by that."

I took in a deep breath ready to deliver my first post-Botox sermon. I closed the valve and tried to speak. My diaphragm muscles were weak so no sound came out. The pressure on my trachea was uncomfortable, so I let the air out through my nose and took in another breath. I still could not speak. The mechanics of the process felt awkward and unfamiliar.

"Keep trying." The speech pathologist was confident I could learn to speak through this valve in my neck.

I took in another breath and still could not make a sound. Additionally, I could not breathe and I began to panic. The pathologist removed the valve. "You will improve with practice. We will try again tomorrow. In the meanwhile, I want you to work on moving your tongue, lips and facial muscles."

My face was tight and frozen. I could barely move my tongue. I wondered if my speech would be understandable if I could get a word out. I truly wanted to talk and I was willing to keep trying. But I still hated the limitations my body imposed on me. I wanted my old life back.

Once the team left, I sat there and cried inside. In some ways, I was so strong and in other ways, I was so weak. I wanted results now. I had to learn that God's delays do not mean denials. I remembered the lessons my father gave me, "All of life's questions and answers are inside you. All you need to do is look, listen and trust. You must have faith in your body, mind, spirit and soul. Your inner voice and your innate intelligence will provide you with answers to all your questions." I had plenty of questions I wanted to ask.

My days were consumed with rehab, but even the simplest task was difficult to manage. I felt frustrated with my body. I wanted to be strong but my body was weak. Mentally I was constantly fighting demons of negativity. I suppose we all battle discouraging thoughts, but my demons represented a choice between death and destruction and life and wellness. Friends and family were helpful in providing faith and comfort. Through their daily visits I learned the importance of giving and receiving love.

Although I could not do them consecutively, I was walking several sets of laps around the nurse's station every day. I was now off the ventilator for several hours a day. Each day the speech pathologist came in and had me do facial and tongue exercises. In my solitude, I would work my tongue muscles. I fantasized about kissing my wife while affirming to myself, "I will be whole again. I will kiss my wife again." I kept trying to speak through the Passy-Muir valve, which is a lot more difficult to manage than you might think. I had to put the valve on to speak, then take it off to breathe again. I finally got the hang of it and uttered my first "hello." The strange reverberation that came from my neck sounded like Mickey Mouse playing a kazoo. Michael, Steve and Gloria came by later that day and I put the valve in and buzzed a greeting. I could only say a word at a time, but we were excited about my progress. Being able to talk was a milestone in my recovery.

The next day Dr. Ooh set a new goal. I had to talk for five minutes straight. I wasn't able to do that until the third day and I got laryngitis as a result. I was exhausted by the effort, but I was happy to have conquered a major hurdle. Quick to burst my bubble, however, Dr. Ooh said, "Eric, when you can stay off the ventilator for ten hours straight we will be ready to take you off permanently."

My cousin, Steve Daniels, was there at the time. I looked at him when Dr. Ooh left the room. "Ten hours?" I started to cry. "That's IMPOSSIBLE!" I didn't think it could be done and I was really discouraged. "I thought I had climbed a mountain but I still have so far to go."

My cousin gave me good advice: "You breathed without the vent before the poisoning; you can do it again. Don't focus on ten hours. Just focus on one hour at a time."

That became my goal. I would try for one more hour off the vent each day. In the meantime, I decided to utilize the Passy-Muir valve to have some fun. Dr. Warren Zwecker is a dermatologist, and healthy skin is his specialty. Dr. Zwecker is a good-looking light-complexioned, red-headed man whom I consider gentle for his robust 6'4" stature. He and his wife, Karen, are good friends of ours. They regularly came to visit Bonnie and me in the hospital and would bring dermatology creams and smooth them on our dry, chapped cheeks. When Dr. Zwecker came in, I used my Bugs Bunny voice and asked, "What's up, Doc?" It blew him away that I was able to speak. When Janice came by that afternoon, I startled her with my Austin Powers voice, "Hey, Baby!"

Speaking was hard, but communication was so important to recovery. The ability to talk made me feel almost whole. The staff would soon regret my fortitude and perseverance because once I started speaking, I never stopped. As they came in to check on me, I talked their ears off.

If seeing is believing, visualizing is realizing. I visualized myself getting better and I pushed myself hard to make progress. At night, I reflected on the progress I had made that day. I cherished every victory—especially when the catheter was removed! It was one less bag to carry around with me on my walks. We possess so much power and strength when we believe in ourselves. Through my ordeal, I was learning a lot about myself and how tough and strong I could be. I knew I had angels with me and I knew God was with me. How else could my healing have been so quick? As my body healed, my spirit became stronger. I wanted to live, love, laugh and learn. I wanted to walk and talk unassisted. I wanted to eat, to hold my wife, make love to her. Still, I was doing better than Bonnie. Not only was she unable to walk, talk or eat, she was having trouble hearing. She was unable to swallow, and fluid was backing up on her eardrums. She agreed to have surgery to put tubes in her ears. They wanted to do the surgery on me, but I decided to take my chances without it. I wasn't about to risk a setback in the forward motion I had made in my recovery.

Healing is a time of reflection. I began to answer for myself the age old questions such as Who am I? Why am I here? Where did I come from? Where am I going? Can we know ourselves and not know the universe? Why does man suffer? Is it possible to avoid suffering? How can one find peace, satisfaction, and good luck? How can we attain tranquility, fulfillment, and happiness? Why do people seem so lost? Why are we still a world at war? Why do we continue to try to defy nature? I attempted to answer all of these questions during my time of solitude. My angels were diligent in their teaching. I understood the Facts of Life that my mother taught me. I believed the Lessons of Life that my Uncle Herb taught me. I clung to the Laws of Life that my father taught me. Still, I continued to look into my own heart for more. Without these lessons and my inward self-talk, I would have succumbed to the depression that loomed at every corner and I doubt I would have lived to tell this miraculous story.

Super-Eric

From Peter I gained more than wisdom and confidence; I gained strength. No matter how hard it was to breathe I knew I could not go back on the ventilator until Peter left. I didn't want to—no, I was afraid to— disappoint him. One evening when he came by I was exhausted and battling fear. He noticed immediately.

"What's the matter, Eric?"

"Look at me," I wrote.

"You look better than you did a week ago," he encouraged.

"But how am I going to look a week from now, or a month from now?" I whined on.

"I don't know."

"Peter, I don't want to live like this." I was struggling to breathe while talking through a Passy-Muir valve.

"Are we having a pity party tonight?" he asked.

"Yes."

"Then I'm leaving! The Eric I know does not attend those sort of functions."

I didn't want him to leave, yet I wanted sympathy. "I'm ill. My business is going under, and my wife is getting worse instead of better. What kind of life do I have?"

"A good life. You have family and friends that love you. I have heard you lecture before large audiences. Do you not believe your own message?"

"Yes, but..." Surprised that he didn't interrupt, I continued, "yes, but I was well then and things were easy."

"Then now is not the time to give up. Now is the time to fight. Now is the time to lead. And now is the time to prove to the world who you are."

"You sound like my son."

"I was hoping you would say I sound like your father."

"I saw my father," I reminded him.

"I know. You told me and I believe you. Doesn't that tell you something?"

"What?"

"Doesn't that mean God is real and God loves you?"

161

"What if it was all a dream, Peter?"

"Was it?"

"No, it had to be real."

"Then it is real. Eric, I have learned about life from you. I have admired who you are, not what you have. I have watched you work a room; lecturing and teaching are your gifts."

"But who would listen to me now? I am concerned that I will never be able to earn a living again. I may lose my house before all this is over!"

"What about Christopher Reeve?"

"Hell, Peter, he is Superman!"

"Then you are Super-Eric!"

I smiled. There was no way he was going to let me give in to self-pity, and I appreciated him for it. I made a commitment that night. I would walk the walk, not just talk the talk. I would be Super-Eric.

Chapter Seventeen

A Christmas Miracle

I may be Jewish, but Christmas is my favorite time of year. In our house, we celebrate Chrismakah. In spite of my progress, I was depressed about being stuck in the hospital and still on life support as the holiday approached. Bonnie was not doing well. She was not able to speak with the Passy-Muir valve nor was she able to be off the ventilator at all. The struggle of trying to breathe without the vent even for a short while caused her chest to ache and her heart to start racing.

On Christmas Eve, as Jason was rubbing my legs he asked, "What's wrong, Dad?"

"I hate this. I've been watching *A Miracle on 34th Street* on TV and I want a miracle. I want out of here."

"Dad, you're alive," he responded. "That is a miracle!"

"How could this happen to us?"

"My whole life you have taught me that everything happens for a reason and that good always follows bad."

"I LIED!" Jason was surprised at my outburst of emotion. "Son, look at me. Look at your mom. What reason is there for this? What good will come of it?"

"You will make good of it. You will find a reason. That is who you are Dad. I love you." My youngest son put me back on track. Maybe I did do something right in raising my sons.

Later that day, Peter came to visit me and challenged me as usual. "How many laps did you walk today?"

"Twenty," I said proudly.

"I expect twenty-one laps tomorrow. How many hours off the vent today?"

"Ten." I didn't suppose he would praise me.

"I expect eleven tomorrow."

"Peter, give me a break. Tomorrow is Christmas."

"Good! God will be with you then," he smiled.

Once he left the hospital, I was lonely, angry and depressed. It was Christmas Eve and I wanted to be home holding my wife in my arms. When would I ever be able to walk with her, hold her hand, take her out to dinner, sit by the fire and watch a movie, or drink a glass of wine? I wanted to do all those things we take for granted such as eating, drinking, laughing, smiling, swallowing, and breathing. Yet, I was alone in one room and my wife was alone in the room next door. This was the most difficult night of all. The life support equipment hummed and pumped while alarms went off all over ICU. I watched Christmas specials on television and prayed for another miracle. Then I cried myself to sleep.

I was already in Bonnie's room when my sons arrived early on Christmas Day. We opened gifts together as a family and gave our best performance at being happy in spite of our circumstances. It was an emotional time. Bonnie wrote, "I am thankful to be with my family today. I didn't expect to see Christmas." This was our twenty-fifth Christmas together and we had wanted it to be the best. We didn't know it would be our worst. The Grinch stole more than Christmas from us.

My wife is a special woman. She is loving and generous. Even in her illness, she was thinking of others before herself. She would not let there be a Christmas without presents for the Kaplan family. She had our friends do her shopping for our sons.

Michael wrapped and brought in the gold watch I had bought for Bonnie prior to our illness. She loved the watch but the look in her eye told me she didn't think she would ever be able to wear it.

"We will get well, honey," I tried to comfort her. "I have had visions and appeared before God. We will be okay. This is my gift to you. I make you a promise. We will walk again together." She squeezed my hand. "This is Christmas, and Christmas is about miracles. It is a miracle that we are alive." Jason looked straight at me and smiled.

This might have been the worst Christmas we'd ever known, but we were blessed with the greatest gifts—friends and family who loved us. The Meyers, Brocks, Doughertys, Daniels, Zweckers, Egittos and the Beers dropped by to wish us well on Christmas day. Aunt Gloria, Uncle Jack, Uncle Buddy, Steve and Gloria also came by. We were blessed to have such a good and loyal family. Bill's wife, Denise, gave us each a children's magnetic sketch pad so we wouldn't have to write on paper. Bonnie was elated with her new communication tool and didn't put it down all day. For a fleeting moment, I felt lucky until I realized we were unable to eat Christmas dinner. I don't think turkey and dressing would be the same through a feeding tube anyway.

Soon our friends and family were gone and we were back to our sad reality. I sat next to Bonnie's bed, holding her hand and reflecting on our day. "I never knew so many people cared for us," I told her. "Steven put his life on hold and is running my every affair." She squeezed in agreement. "And so many people took time from their own family gatherings to visit us today. This is a Christmas I would never want to repeat, but it sure is good to know that people care about us."

Bonnie wrote on her magnetic pad, "I am thankful."

Bad News for Bonnie

During the first week of the new year, Bonnie started having terrible abdominal pain. The doctor gave her morphine and altered her nutrition through the feeding tube, but nothing relieved the hurting. I prayed for her to get better. Unfortunately, she got worse. A CAT scan revealed an obstruction in her bowel due to her colon cancer surgery seven years earlier. What made matters worse was they also found a tumor on her bladder. They would have to operate.

How quickly in times of distress we forget our lessons and all we have learned. I began to question God, "How can you do this to my wife? How can you continue to make us suffer? I want my wife back!" Bonnie had been so strong before the injections and she was doing pretty well in her recovery until now. I needed to regain my faith. I was reminded of the lessons from my angels: God does not micromanage. There are no mistakes in life, only lessons.

I spoke with the surgeon to coordinate Bonnie's surgery to open her colon. Dr. Vazquez was a New Yorker raised in the Bronx, with a Harvard education. He had to be tough and smart to get to where he was. He exuded confidence and I could tell he genuinely cared about people. After her first colon surgery, Bonnie had a temporary colostomy, which was later reversed. Her mantra on colostomy bags was, "Never again." Dr. Vazquez could not promise that she would not have another colostomy but he assured me, "I will do my best to avoid it, but it is really up to God." I instantly knew I liked this man.

When they wheeled her down to surgery, she didn't look so good. She only weighed about ninety pounds. She was on a ventilator as well as a feeding tube, and now there were IV lines not only in her arms, but also in her neck. I was afraid of losing my wife. What if she died? I wouldn't even be able to attend her funeral. I waited and prayed, battling anger and depression. An hour into the surgery the doctor called me. He told me Bonnie was going to be okay and would not need a colostomy. "Thank God for miracles!" I prayed.

The first night was touch and go. When Peter, Steve, Billy and my sons left that evening, I sat with Bonnie as she slept. I asked her angels to be with her and teach her the Facts of Life, the Lessons of Life, and the Laws of Life as they had taught me. I loved this woman and didn't want to lose her. I wanted to see her smile again, but I realized that it was up to her to survive. It was her choice, not mine.

Usually crisis hits only one spouse in a marriage, but Bonnie and I were both struck down and neither of us was able to fully fend for ourselves or watch out for one another. I wanted to stay with my wife all night, but when I was in her room, I was off all monitors. The nurses had to come find me and manually check my vital signs and oxygen saturation. Besides that, I was weak and could not sit for very long before my muscles started aching terribly. After exhausting all my strength during the day, I still needed the ventilator to work for me at night so my body could rest. Once

I was put back on the ventilator, I could not speak through the Passy-Muir valve and I was stuck lying flat on my back for the rest of the night. I was weary and struggling for air that night, but I didn't want to be hooked up. What if Bonnie needed me in her weakened condition?

I shuffled slowly back to my room. I was so glad to see that Shelly was assigned to care for us that first night after Bonnie's surgery. Shelly came in to check on me. "Is everything okay in here?"

"I'm tired but I'm more concerned for my wife tonight. How is Bonnie?"

"She had a rough day but her vital signs are good."

"Will she be okay?"

"So far, someone's been watching over you two. Hopefully it will continue."

"That someone is you, Shelly. You are my angel."

"Eric, you have more than one nurse." I think she was uncomfortable with my sincere gratitude for her help.

"When the therapist puts me on the ventilator tonight will you stay with me?"

"Yes."

"I hate that thing."

"I know, but it is keeping you alive," she said as she put the cuff on my arm.

"Your blood pressure is a little high tonight."

"I'm worried about my wife."

"Eric, I will not lie to you. Bonnie is weak. Her body cannot take much more. Maybe your angels will visit her."

"So you don't think I am crazy?"

"Of course not. I'm going to check on Bonnie. I'll be back soon."

A new respiratory therapist came in a few minutes later. "Are you ready to get back on the vent?" she asked.

"I don't suppose I have a choice. I held out for nine hours today but my body and mind are weak."

"What are your settings?" she asked me.

"I don't know. What does my chart say?"

"I can't read it."

I pushed the nurse's call button and a voice answered, "Yes?"

"I want Shelly in my room."

After a few moments, Shelly came in. "What's up, Doc?" She asked smiling.

"The therapist doesn't know the vent settings."

"Did you look at his chart?" she asked the respiratory therapist.

"I can't read the writing," she answered.

"Now, you see why I want you here, Shelly?" I buzzed out the words through my neck.

Shelly took the chart and reviewed it. "It is right here," she said, pointing to the numbers on the chart.

"Oh, I see."

"You have my life in your hands," I told them. "I'm having a little trouble trusting anyone but Shelly."

Shelly looked at me as only she could. "Everything is going to be okay, I promise." I felt like a little boy trusting his mother to feed, protect and nurture him.

The therapist connected the vent and turned on the air full speed. Even though my response to the machine was normal, the initial start up was difficult. My stomach rose like a balloon; then as it should, the air stopped to allow my diaphragm to deflate. However, I couldn't breathe and thought she must have hooked up something wrong. With the vent inserted into the trach tube, I could not speak. I waved my arms up and down signaling for help. With the Passy-Muir valve put away, I was not able to speak so I grabbed my pad and wrote, "I can't breathe. No air."

"Check the setting!" Shelly yelled.

"They are exact," she responded.

I felt like I was going to have a heart attack. I was turning blue and the respiratory tech, who was new on the job, panicked. Shelly jumped up and pulled the inner cannula out of the trach tube in my neck, and much needed air came pouring in.

"What happened?" I wrote.

"You had a mucus plug. Let me clean out the tube," Shelly comforted.

Soon I was on the ventilator again, this time breathing normally. I knew someone was watching over me, but I needed to know that someone was watching over my wife as well.

"Eric, I promise Bonnie will be okay. You need to sleep. I will awaken you if there is any problem whatsoever. I'm giving you your sleep medication."

Once I was reconnected to the ventilator, I was lonely and sad. Yet I knew I was not alone. I remembered the visions of my mother, my father and my uncle. It dawned on me that events occurring to us are messages from our Creator. Our Creator influences us through the people in our lives and in every situation we face, although we may not feel the presence of our Creator because many of our thoughts and attitudes.

Every night the Hallmark channel ran *M.A.S.H.* episodes for two hours. This show represented the funny side of health care. Alan Alda and company became my friends. Hawkeye might have been crazy but he cared and his patients always got well. Soon I was asleep.

When I awoke the next morning, I buzzed for the nurse. Shelly was gone but the morning nurse came in. "Take me off the vent," I told her. "I want to visit my wife."

"Your wife is doing fine," she consoled me.

"I want to see her."

It took about half an hour but soon I was soon disconnected from the equipment. I made an attempt to wash and get dressed, then ambled over to Bonnie with my walker. She looked extremely weak. "How are you, baby?"

"I'm tired."

"No colostomy," I told her.

"Thank God. My stomach hurts."

"That is normal," I told her. "Shelly was with you all night."

"I love Shelly," she wrote.

"So do I."

"Eric, I'm scared," Bonnie scribbled weakly. "What if this is our life from now on? What if this is as good as it gets? What if we don't get any better than this?

"Honey, I saw my father."

"I know. You told me, but maybe it was just a dream."

"Maybe it wasn't."

"There is a big difference," Bonnie was discouraged.

"Either way, my father represents hope. If we give up on hope, we give up on life."

"I won't give up," she wrote.

"You'd better not." I clumsily brushed her hair away from her face. "Bonnie, I could not live without you. I don't want to live without you."

A tear fell from her eye and ran down her face toward her ear. "Look at me," she wrote.

"Look at *me*," I rasped back.

"Why did this happen to us?"

"I don't know, but we are getting better."

"No! *We're* not. You are."

"Honey we are alive. We can write and open our eyes. I can walk. If I can, so can you."

"I love you," she wrote.

"I need you to get better."

"I will," she promised.

I went for a walk around the nurse's station. When I saw a doctor moving toward my wife's room, I stopped him and asked, "What are you doing?"

He introduced himself and explained, "We are going to do a biopsy on her bladder today and operate tomorrow."

"No, you're NOT," I stated. "I will not allow you to operate on my wife. Look at her. She is barely alive. She's too weak to survive another surgery. Let her recover from this before you go in again." I was more concerned with the botulism than I was with cancer. I had to win one battle at a time if I was to win this war.

"You are not her doctor," he replied curtly.

"No, but I am her husband and I will not allow any more procedures on my wife until she gets stronger."

"Take your time and think about it," he said, then walked away.

There was nothing to think about. I had already decided that I would not approve any more procedures to be done on my wife.

I went back to Bonnie's room. I knew she had seen or overheard part of the conversation.

"What is going on?" Bonnie wrote.

"They wanted to do a biopsy on you. I know it is ultimately your decision, but I told them it would have to wait."

"No more surgery!" Bonnie wrote emphatically.

"We have angels on our side. You will be fine," I encouraged her. I had a deeper faith since my angelic meetings.

The next few days were tough on Bonnie. Her entire abdomen had been opened during surgery. Besides having a diaphragm that didn't work she had an abdomen that hurt like hell and a husband who continually pushed her to exercise. "Honey, you have to walk," I told her.

"Why?"

"Don't give up on me, Bo-Bo!"

"I won't, but it hurts so bad."

"You need to exercise to get your strength back." She looked at me like I was crazy so I tried to explain. "Honey, the more I'm off the ventilator, the more endurance I have. You have to get up and move around so you don't get bed sores."

The next day, we managed to walk together around the nurse's station as they smiled and cheered us on. "Soon we will be walking in the mountains of Big Canoe," I encouraged her.

"Your mouth to God's ears," she wrote on the sketch pad that never left her side. "I hope He hears our prayers."

"He does, honey. Look, you are up and walking with me. I am so proud of you."

After one lap, Bonnie's blood pressure was elevated and the nurses wanted her to stop. They helped her get back to bed. She was so frustrated and disappointed. "I want out of here! I hate this! I hate my life!" she pounded the stylo on the magnetic pad.

"Bonnie, you are getting better. We are getting better."

"I'm ready for Georgia. Will they accept us?"

"I don't know—we have to show them we are fighters. We have to make them believe we will get well."

"I will walk two times around tomorrow," she wrote. Then she grabbed my hand and kissed it. It was the first kiss she had given me in days. She was regaining hope and faith and she was healing from her surgery.

I was continuing to make progress as I waited for Bonnie to begin her recovery anew. I was still very spastic and uncoordinated. I did tongue exercises: do, re, mi, fa, sol, la, ti, do. The physical therapist recommended to the doctors that I be allowed to walk whenever I wanted. I would walk, then rest and then walk a little more. I did the same with the ventilator. I would stay off it until I was gasping for air and about to die before asking to be put back on it.

Health care is not always black and white. We must learn to trust our instincts. I spoke with all our doctors, my family and my friends, and not everyone was happy with my decision to put off Bonnie's bladder surgery. The decision was not easy but I knew it was the right one. God would eventually prove me right.

Chapter Eighteen
Blue Cross No Shield

Blue Cross Blue Shield is a corrupt power. Initially, they paid all the doctors, but once they knew the severity of our claim, they wanted nothing more to do with us. They even started asking our doctors to return the money they had paid them. They found a loophole they could use to substantiate not paying our medical bills. Our policy had a clause that stated the company did not have to pay for cosmetic procedures or any side effects thereof. Hell, I did not have a cosmetic procedure. I was poisoned with raw botulism; there is nothing cosmetic about that! What if I went to the doctor for a nose job but instead he decided to shoot me ? Would a gunshot wound be considered a side effect of cosmetic surgery? I don't think so.

Blue Cross Blue Shield wanted to send us to a nursing home. We would never have recovered there. In my opinion, the state and Blue Cross were rooting for our death. After all, dead people can't defend themselves. Our only recourse was to seek legal retribution for bodily harm and the damages caused by medical malpractice. We retained an attorney named Stuart Grossman. I don't care what you have heard about personal injury attorneys. This man was different. He cared about people and I needed him. I needed a warrior on my side—someone to go into the arena and protect us in our weakened condition. This man was our gladiator, our protector. You could see tears in his eyes when he first met us and heard our story. He was an angel in an arena of devils. We not only wanted his help, we needed it. All Bonnie and I wanted was to have our lives the way they were before this incident.

My days were filled with rehabilitation exercises and I continued to make progress. I was using a walker to travel twenty-five to thirty times around the nurse's station in the course of a day. I could wash and dress myself. I could speak with a Passy-Muir valve, but I could not eat, and was still on a ventilator part of the day and all night. Gardens Medical Center sent an occupational therapist to me for half an hour a day. That was it. My friends and family admired my fight and wanted a more aggressive rehabilitation for me. They wanted me in the Shepherd Center in Atlanta, but there were three problems. One, Shepherd did not accept us. Two, if Shepherd were to accept us, they would require $200,000 down and another $100,000 in thirty days, and our insurance refused to pay for it. Michael and Steve offered the Shepherd Center $100,000 to take us but they rejected it. Three, I would not leave my wife alone at Gardens Medical Center. She needed me to protect her, inspire her, support her and love her. She had taken care of me my whole life. I was staying at Gardens until she was able to move with me.

Bonnie could barely walk to the nurse's station. One time around was her daily maximum. She could only stay off the ventilator for half an hour per day. I worried that she was giving up. I needed to work hard to inspire her and encourage her to keep moving. Each day I would go into her room and give her pep talks. As I was a motivational speaker, you would think I could motivate my own wife, but she was still very weak from all she had been through and she wanted to give up in the fight. I knew if I didn't get her out of the hospital in Florida she would die.

Everyone was convinced that Shepherd was the place but I was out of work and feared the worst financially. I was worried about how I would keep my family and homes afloat while I recovered. It would take everything we had to pay what we owed to doctors and Gardens Hospital for two rooms in ICU for six weeks. Once the hospital knew that our insurance wasn't going to pay, they wanted us out of there, but we had no place to go. Many of my clients and companies who employed my consulting services dropped me like a hot potato when they heard what had happened. LPG, a French company, was the only company that remained loyal to me. LPG is the founder and patent holder of Endermologie®—a noninvasive way to remove cellulite. They offer a wonderful and safe product, which is number one in Europe but new to our culture. It's a sad truth that Americans look for ways to avoid paying their debts. I will never let anyone criticize the French. They were there for me and continued to pay me when other clients selfishly and unprofessionally ran for the hills. I felt lost and rejected.

One night on his routine visit, my friend Peter Brock said to me, "How much would you pay to walk again? To breathe again? How much would you pay to get your life back?"

I got the message. There is no way to put a price tag on health and life. "Well, there goes my retirement," I said to myself. I told Steve and Michael to sell my stocks. Twenty-five years of working and saving would be spent on something greater than retirement. I would be paying to stay alive. Dr. Egitto called Shepherd Center and they agreed to review my medical progress. Once they saw what I was capable of doing, they figured Bonnie would eventually follow. My family and our friends the Brocks, Meyers, Garfunkels and Punyons offered to loan us the money to go. I know there are other people who are in dire need of the help offered by Shepherd. I was lucky to have a retirement plan to borrow from. Others don't. That's why a percentage of the money made from the sales of this book is going to Shepherd Center. Maybe I can save at least one life.

My whole life long, I had been a control freak and now I had no control. This made me totally dependent upon God's provisions. I made a heartfelt demand of God to bring us nearer to our eternal connection with Him. It follows then, that all the rejections we experienced actually resulted in bringing my family closer. God was showing me the good in people. He was showing me that people cared—that there are good people in this world. All the love I had given my entire life was being returned tenfold. To hell with Blue Cross Blue Shield. My wife is alive. I am alive and we have friends and family who love us. I knew and felt something few people ever come to feel or know in their lifetime: GOD IS REAL.

Chapter Nineteen

The Lord and His Shepherd

After six weeks in Palm Beach Gardens Medical Center, we were accepted at Shepherd Center. We were elated, but getting us there would not be easy. There was plenty of preparation to be done before sending two patients on life support to a hospital in another state. As we made ready for our trip to Atlanta, Georgia, my doctor was worried that my eardrums would burst during the flight. He suggested I have tubes placed in my ears as Bonnie had earlier. I chose not to have the surgery. Hell, I was used to pain by then, how much worse could it get? I would rather deal with deafness than have surgery that might jeopardize my recovery.

I was again reminded of how blessed we are with good friends—I now call them angels. John Preston offered to transport us in his private plane but because Bonnie and I were still on ventilators and feeding tubes, the trip posed too high a risk for us to go it alone. We needed so much care and equipment, one private plane could not take us both together with our medical entourage. We needed two medical planes at approximately $7,000 each. Of course they were not covered by our insurance.

The Gardens Medical Center saved our lives, and we are indeed thankful. Bonnie and I were equally grateful that we would leave before incurring any more expenses for which we couldn't pay. In one way, it was sad to be leaving our angel friends at Gardens Medical Center. Sharmella, Shelly and Julio were my favorites. Nurses work harder than people realize.

There were so many times I wanted to give up in my recovery and let fate take its course. I learned that persistence pays. When you feel like giving up, remember that Walt Disney was fired by a newspaper editor for lack of ideas and went bankrupt several times before he reached his goals; Michael Jordan, one of the greatest basketball players of all time, was cut from his high school basketball team; Beethoven, one of the greatest composers in musical history, was told by his teachers he was too stupid to learn anything; after his first screen test from the testing director of MGM, Fred Astaire received this glum studio report: "Can't act! Slightly bald! Can dance a little!"

I did not have a big-eared mouse in my pocket. I could not jump. I could not dance even a little, and I have never written a song but I was walking much sooner than anyone thought possible. This was the greatest success I could have known.

It was a rainy day in January when the teams from medical transport arrived at Gardens Medical Center. They loaded us in two separate ambulances and we headed for Palm Beach International Airport. I wanted to prove to the world I would fully recover. Driven by perseverance and persistence, I made a personal decision while riding in the ambulance. I was going to walk onto the plane.

Our attorney warned us it was going to be a media circus. He was right. All the television networks and newspapers were waiting for us at the airport. The airport provided a separate area for us to load while the media remained behind a fenced area. We were like freaks at a freak show. Ringling Brothers would have loved our act. My wife, attached to a ventilator, was carried to the plane on a stretcher. With the help of a walker, I ambled onto the plane. I even climbed the steps. The world had been following our progress. The fact that I walked to the plane stunned them. I was not alone; my angels were with me. It felt as if my father were holding me up. No one knew how lonely we were and how the system had betrayed us; however, there were many people there whose love and prayers we felt.

My brother flew with me in one plane, and Michael flew with Bonnie in the other. Although I have flown all over the country as a speaker, I have never enjoyed flying. I often felt anxious about it and had trouble breathing on a plane even under normal conditions. Here I was breathing with the assistance of a ventilator through a tracheostomy on a tiny plane cramped with medical personnel and life-saving equipment. My mind was racing so I decided not to focus on the flight. Instead, I reflected on the teachings, facts and lessons taught to me by my father, mother and uncle. The secret of life is "I am." You harbor the strength and power of the universe. When you accept responsibility for your life and your actions, you will learn to harness the power of the universe. God has given you the ability to think, learn, live and love. You must take responsibility for your life. It was time to implement what I had learned. Once again, I began to affirm: *I can, I will, I must. I AM responsible. I AM going to get better.*

I knew I was not alone. None of us are. The powers of the universe, the Force, God, or whatever you call it is with all of us. I knew God and my angels were with me. I felt closer to the light and more connected with my spirit as I flew on the wings of angels. I opened my eyes and my heart to the light, which strengthened my belief in God, the power of nature and my body's ability to heal. All that we need to heal and grow exists in the universe. Nothing is ever lost or gained in our universe, it is only transformed. A house may have been a tree, a forest, a stone, a rock. Cut down and reengineered, it becomes a home. Infections have existed throughout centuries but we did not have antibiotics till the 1940s. We had bread for thousands of years yet penicillin, discovered in moldy bread, has been around for less than a hundred years. It existed, but we didn't realize the healing qualities it contained.

Things are always changing. Look at our growth over the last 100 years. Things you plug into an electrical outlet were not available then. The materials that make up our new modern homes, the fireplace, the marble, the TV, DVD, existed a thousand years ago in a different shape or form. All we did was utilize our resources and transform what the universe gave us. Imagine if you could go back in time and bring a DVD player with you. Would this technology be considered a miracle or witchcraft? What about a cigarette lighter? A car? Our world is filled with miracles. Is not flying from one continent to the other as great a miracle as parting the Red Sea? Here I was flying in an airplane on life support.

I was thankful to be out of the hospital even if it was only for a few hours. I was scared yet excited as I looked forward to what was ahead for me. My goal at Shepherd was to be able to breathe again on my own. To some, this may seem a simple task. To me, it would be a miracle. I believe in miracles. My angels taught me that difficulties provide the perfect platform for miracles to occur. Life is difficult for many people, yet none of us is alone. We are here for a purpose—to learn and help one another. I remembered Uncle Herb and his teachings: We are all enrolled in the University of Life. When the time is right, the student will further his studies under the guidance of qualified teachers—angels in our past, present or future. Help will be there when we need it, if we all help one another.

I knew my life was about to change. Now removed from my home and family, heading to an innovative treatment center in an unfamiliar city, I was apprehensive. What if something goes wrong? What if I stop breathing? What about Bonnie? How was she making the flight? What if my eardrums burst? As I looked out the small window onto the clouds below, I saw a flash of light. For a split second I saw my father! I looked to Steve and said, "Did you see that?"

"See what?" he asked. I looked again and my father was gone.

"Oh, nothing." It was bad enough that I was sick. I didn't want everyone to think I was sick *and* crazy. Or was I? People have reported seeing angels for thousands of years. Here I was in the sky thousands of feet above the earth. What better place to see angels? They appear to people of all religions, and even those who claim no religion at all. The Bible speaks of angels being sent by God to bring warning or comfort to people in critical situations. My situation would qualify as critical. Perhaps I should have expected an angelic escort.

The term for "angel" in the Hebrew language is "mal'ak" or "messenger." So far in my recovery, I had seen three angels, and each had given me messages to help me live and recover. I'm sure there had been angels before that I didn't see. As a young child, I had sensed their presence and found it comforting to know that I had angels watching over me. Many people say that angels have the task of protecting humans. They were certainly protecting Bonnie and me and showing us the way in our time of distress. We were flying on the wings of angels and I would simply have to trust them to get us there safely.

Humans tend to get freaky when an angel shows up. Some people quiver in fear or fall down in worship. Most people usually find themselves responding instantly with some amount of trust, comfort, or awe when they encounter an angelic presence. Some people do not believe in angels, and may choose to invalidate my claim. Others who understand first-hand what I am talking about feel comfortable placing their faith in this inexplicable spiritual mystery. I accept angels as part of a team to guide me on my path to spiritual growth. On the plane that day, I knew I would someday share with others the messages I had received.

We were soon cleared to land. I didn't realize until later that I was about to meet a new flock of angels. As our planes touched down in Atlanta, two ambulances awaited us in a private jet hanger. While the medical transport team loaded my wife by stretcher, I walked to the ambulance. It was an hour-long ride from the airport to Shepherd Center, but I stayed off the ventilator the entire time. I wanted to show the Shepherd people that they had not made a mistake by taking a gamble on us. We soon arrived in Buckhead, Georgia, and again faced the media. We were in the spotlight with cameras shooting in a frenzy. Everyone wanted our picture and our story. In spite of the media frenzy we arrived at Shepherd Center quietly and safely and were ushered to the intensive care unit. Bonnie was tired and weak and had literally given up on her recovery by the time we arrived. When asked which was tougher, botulism or cancer, my wife responded "Botulism is a thousand times more difficult than having cancer." For someone who had battled colon cancer, a colostomy, endured multiple surgeries and one year of chemotherapy, this was some statement. She needed hope, and Shepherd immediately started to restore it. The moment we arrived, I could feel that something spiritual had transpired. My spirit felt something special in the air. My wife and I needed help and a miracle was waiting for us at Shepherd.

That entire afternoon, we were visited constantly by someone from Shepherd: pulmonary specialists, physical therapists, speech therapists, occupational therapists, x-ray and lab technicians, and nurses and doctors galore. Shepherd Center employs 980 employees and I think we saw all of them the first day. I was exhausted by the time I was hooked up to the ventilator. I tried to sleep, but the unfamiliar sounds of our new surroundings were distracting and there was little rest to be had that night.

Shepherd Center has a thirty-year history of providing care and hope in a time of crisis. I found it reassuring to know that the Shepherds had been in our shoes. While bodysurfing in 1973, James Shepherd nearly drowned when a wave slammed his body against the ocean floor. James, who was twenty-two at the time, was instantly paralyzed from the neck down and required immediate medical attention and months of rehabilitation therapy. Through that family's personal crisis, Shepherd Center was born. I soon learned what a special man James was, what a wonderful mother he had, and the vision this family gives the world.

My own family wanted back the old arrogant, boisterous, athletic Eric they had grown to love. I wanted to be that Eric again. Michael no longer looked to me as he did before my illness. He was becoming the father in our relationship as he was taking care of me. I had been his hero, and now he was mine. Daily, I watched him grow into a young man any father would be proud of. He and my brother rented an apartment in Atlanta to help care for Bonnie and me. I promised myself that they would see me walk out of here soon.

Upon initial evaluation, Dr. Brock Bowman, a rehabilitation specialist overseeing our care at Shepherd told the newspapers, "We are shooting for a full recovery. We don't know if we are going to get that." He thought it might take Bonnie six months to recover enough to leave the Center. They estimated four months for me. I knew I had to push Bonnie, for I did not want to leave there without her. I loved my wife and needed her. She is my soul mate. We have been through so much together. Now we had the fight of our lives. In this fight, I wanted her not in my corner, but by my side. I had to teach her what my angels had taught me. She had to learn of the greatest power God gives us: the power to choose. She had to choose to get well.

In facing trauma, there are lessons to be learned about the spirit and the will to survive. The spirit is resiliently powered by forces greater than the natural eye can see. The mind has so much to do with the body's ability to recover. I had to remain positive and hopeful in my thoughts in order to succeed in my recovery. I share my Thoughts for Success with you here:

• You can never change your outer world without first changing your inner thoughts.

• Don't wish for things to *get* better in your life, but actively work to *make* things better in your life.

• Be solution conscious. Focus 10% on the problem and 90% on the solution.

• The future is your tree; plant it today. The choices you make today will shape your tomorrow.

• Build a reputation on delivering more than you promised. It comes back to you tenfold.

• No one can stop you from reaching your goals unless you give them permission to do so.

These phrases were the same ones I used during my many lectures before we were poisoned. Now I had to live by the advice I had given others. I began by changing my inner world. I grew happier and more spiritual. The more active I became, the more I inspired the people around me. I was making choices and planting seeds. I was committed to getting well and going home. I started to share my philosophies of life and heard my Uncle whisper in my ear, "There are no mistakes in life, only lessons." I was living and learning. No one was going to stop me from reaching my goals. I would walk the mountains of Northern Georgia holding hands with my beautiful wife.

Chapter Twenty

Progress at Shepherd Center

The staff at Shepherd went right to work. They planned to move me out of intensive care the next day. Dr. Rosen was never happy with the trach tube I had been given at Gardens Hospital and neither was the staff at Shepherd. I was brought to my own room and a smaller tracheostomy tube was put in. It had a button that closed off the airway when I was not on the ventilator. This allowed me to talk better and improved my lung function. I had only been there for one day and I was already making progress.

Dr. Leslie was our internist. He was a very good-looking man who showed compassion to all his patients. He helped oversee our case, but Dr. Bowman was in charge. There was rarely a day at Shepherd when we didn't see Dr. Bowman at least twice. This Duke- and Johns Hopkins-educated physiatrist was a special man. He had done his homework on botulism poisoning and was prepared to treat us when we arrived. He and his team set up a recovery schedule with daily goals he wanted us to aim for. There was no sympathy at Shepherd but there was plenty of encouragement. Whenever I told them I was tired, they pushed me to work a little more. During these moments of fatigue I had to decide whether to give up or push on. I thought of marathon runners and the pain they endure to reach their goals. I thought of my hero, Lance

Armstrong—the king of endurance—and I pushed onward. I remembered my lessons from Coach Knight, "The mind controls the body, not vice versa."

Every day when I awakened, my lungs were filled with mucus and my muscles ached from the day before. After being suctioned, I felt sick and physically weak. Although Bonnie and I could open our eyes, we could not always close them, so our eyes were red and dry. I still had poor range of motion in my arms and could not touch the top of my head. Every task took so much effort and was so much more difficult than in normal life! It took me an hour just to shave, wash my face and get dressed.

My days were spent following my rehab schedule and visiting my wife. Bonnie had given up confidence in recovery while in Florida. Now that she was supported by a wonderful caring staff of doctors and nurses, I saw hope in her eyes again. Aunt Gloria's daughter, Ellen, flew in from Seattle to help. Ellen was good for Bonnie, as she often massaged her feet and encouraged her when she wanted to give up hope. Bonnie was soon released from intensive care and we were the first couple to my knowledge to share a room at Shepherd Center. Still recovering from the surgeries she had been through in the past two weeks, she was confined to her bed and could not talk.

As a former athlete, I drew on my past experience at training camp. My college coach, Paul Lizzo, worked us hard before he went on to coach the Philadelphia Seventy-Sixers. He taught us to work through pain in order to conquer it. Bonnie never had the advantage of being coached so I took it upon myself to keep her inspired. I kept telling her, "Honey, if I can do it, so can you." She wanted so much to believe me, but everything was so difficult and took such tremendous effort. I tried to share with her Lesson Number 8 from Uncle Herb's teaching: What you make of your life is up to you. You have all the tools and resources you need. What you do with them is up to you. God's gift to us is life. Our gift to God is what we do with our life. The choice is yours. Bonnie had to make the choice of life. She was alive, but she was not living. She had to choose to live again.

The nights were lonely once Gloria, Steve and Michael left. I practically had to throw them out because they would have stayed forever. I felt guilty for consuming so much of their time and attention. Our recovery had become their life. If only I could get off the ventilator, I could do more for myself and Bonnie. The ventilator looked like Darth Vader and I, The Force, knew I had to defeat it. I would sit and stare at it, hating it so much I wanted to destroy it and everything it represented. But I needed it to live. I also needed encouragement to keep pressing onward. No longer in my hometown surrounded by my support team of friends and family, I had to give myself my own pep talks.

My first Sunday at Shepherd, I walked about a hundred yards to the church services they offered on-site. Almost everyone attending was in a wheelchair. There is an old proverb that states, "In the kingdom of the blind, the one-eyed man is king."

"I can't breathe on my own, but I can walk," I said to myself. "I guess that makes me king." What an epiphany! This was the first time in my recovery that I actually felt lucky. It had been easy to feel sorry for myself at Gardens Medical Center while I constantly prayed for a miracle. Here, I was surrounded by tragedy. I was hurting physically, mentally and emotionally. I was drained from my walk to the make-shift church where I had gone to pray for yet another miracle. I had found one. I just didn't know it yet.

On weekends we were visited by members of the Punyon, Garfunkel, Zwecker, Brock, Bard, Beers, Beechler, Fox, Braile, Harmon,Gutstein and Alfonso families. We were so grateful to have their company. We never knew we had touched so many people, or that we were so loved. Every night, Steve would share messages our friends and family had written on our web site. We reveled in their encouragement. Steve kept the site visitors informed of our progress. Friends and family were receiving hope by seeing or reading about our progress. It didn't seem to me as though I was making much progress, because things were not getting any easier. Each day, I felt the same and was able to do about as much as the day before. I wanted to see my angels again but knew this would not be possible. However, I could relive their teachings at anytime. In the activity of my mind, I could part the Red Sea over and over again. All I had to do was hit the rewind button. The joy from those times is still living in my heart.

My first night alone in my new room at Shepherd was my most difficult and most rewarding. Exhausted, I lay in bed strapped to the ventilator feeling sorry for myself. I was asking God, "Why me?"

There was a man in the next room named John Rice. John was a Vietnam veteran and former Marine. Around Christmas, he had been on his way home when he lost control of his car. He did not receive a single cut or scratch. The only bone broken was one in his neck, which rendered him a quadraplegic—paralyzed from the neck down. He was not expected to move any part of his body again. I overheard John's brother ask him, "Are you mad at God?"

"No," John replied, "God loves me. God kept me alive. He allowed me to be here today with you and my wife and daughter. God is here. I feel Him and I love Him. God hurts no one, but He works to heal everyone."

I was shocked. This man was not able to move a muscle and he was giving thanks. Thanks for what? He was giving thanks for living after such a horrible accident. I knew my angels sent John to remind me of the gifts I already had.

The next day I walked to the room next door and met John and his wife, Becky. We talked together and instantly became good friends. He reaffirmed that God loves me. "God loves everyone," he said. "The greatest miracle in life, is life itself. Talking, walking and eating are just gifts to help us further enjoy our life." His message was profound. "The magic of the moment *is* the moment, and we must cherish each moment every day. We cannot hold on to any moment, for as soon as you know it is here, it is gone. What you can do, though, is live each moment fully so its value will always be with you. A memory is a moment trapped in time and stored in your superconsciousness forever."

John and I visited one another every day thereafter. He became more than my friend; he became my spiritual brother. We were both in sad shape so we began to pray together on a regular basis. We began to witness healing miracles. John was in my room one night, thankful that he was then able to move his right hand and arm. Bonnie, Michael and I prayed for John to be able to also move his left hand and arm. Soon after our prayer ended, he moved his left arm. The room was silent as we stared in awe at the miracle we had just witnessed. We all cried and gave thanks. He prayed for me to get off the ventilator and for my wife to walk and talk again.

When we first arrived at Shepherd the prognosis for our recovery was not hopeful. In our original team conference with Dr. Bowman, we were told it would be at least eighteen months before we got our lives back and that would be with some restrictions. There was talk of selling our Georgia home because they didn't think we would be able to navigate the terrain, and because they didn't think the house could be made wheelchair accessible. Wheelchair accessible? There was no way I was coming out of this ordeal in a wheelchair. I refused to accept even a mental picture of myself in a wheelchair. After all, if I could walk with a walker, why should I sit and allow my leg muscles to continue to deteriorate? I wanted to build my muscles and my confidence.

My refusal to use a wheelchair created a commotion at Shepherd. The staff did not want me walking without supervision for fear that I might fall and injure myself. The physical therapists called a meeting and gave me at least twenty reasons why I needed to be in a wheelchair. I gave them one reason why I should not be: "I DON'T WANT TO!"

"Then we will take you to the gym for a test." One of them was willing to take a chance on me, or perhaps she wanted to prove me wrong. This therapist pushed me hard and made me try things I actually did not think I was capable of doing. It felt like trying out for my high school basketball team. She did not know I had spent two grueling summers with basketball Coach Bobbie Knight and years with my obcessive college coach, Paul Lizzo. As she pushed me with difficult requests, I heard my former coach say, "Your brain controls your body; push it. Don't listen to your body. Make your body listen to your brain."

She was sure she would break me when she took me to the stairwell and made me walk stairs. "Just try to make it to the next landing." She didn't know how I felt about being dared! I went up two flights and the tryout ended. No wheelchair for Dr. Kaplan.

"Okay, we are convinced you are able to walk with a walker. We won't force the wheelchair issue."

"I don't even need a walker. All I need is a cane," I told them. I was going to stay ahead of their expectations. I never used the walker after that day.

On my way back to my room, I stopped to talk to John Rice and his new roommate, another paraplegic. I was proud of my progress as I told them, "I just walked three flights of stairs."

John's roommate said, "I wish I could walk like you."

I responded, "I wish I could breathe like you."

John was in the worst physical condition of all three of us but he was the most spiritually evolved. He looked at me, and then at his roommate, and said, "You will breathe, and you will walk. Just keep the faith. God put us here to heal and we are doing just that."

"I love this man," I thought as I went back to my room.

Sundays were supposedly a day of rest at Shepherd, yet I continued to work. I would sneak into the stairway where I would walk one flight, then rest and do another. The staff would have been mad if they had known I was doing this unsupervised, but I needed stamina to get off the ventilator and breathe on my own again. I also used Sundays to reconnect with myself and my higher power. I became distinctly aware of both my physical and spiritual side. The physical side wanted to surrender and give up. The spiritual side wanted me to push on. I needed to focus on my spirit and not think of the physical pain in my muscles. I heeded the voice inside me as I walked the stairs repeating, "No pain, no gain. I can. I will. I must!" My muscles ached but my body and mind yearned for life, and my spirit was getting stronger by the day. We each have an internal voice—it is part of having innate intelligence. This intelligence, combined with our physical and spiritual knowledge, guides our lives. The stronger we develop our spirit, the stronger the voice becomes. The more we trust in that voice, the more whole we become.

Bonnie and I had just bought our home in the Appalachian Mountains of Big Canoe, Georgia, the summer before. We had only used it once but we loved it. After proving to my therapists that I could walk, I knew my wife and I would again hike the mountains one day. If seeing is believing, then visualizing is realizing. I sent my son Michael to the house, where he took panoramic pictures of our home. We posted those photos in our room at Shepherd and visualized ourselves being there every day. I sat by Bonnie on her bed and told her, "We will walk these hills again. We will hold hands and give thanks to God."

The media could not get enough of our story. ABC's *Primetime Live* contacted us and wanted to do a story to give the world an update on our progress. I was ready to prove the power of my spirit and show everyone that we were beating the odds. Our attorney, Stuart Grossman, did a wonderful job of protecting us, but Bonnie and I agreed to be interviewed at Shepherd Center by the *Primetime* team. We did not want the publicity because we did not want the world to see us so disfigured. But we were on a mission to prevent what had happened to us from happening to anyone else.

Chris Cuomo is the son of former New York Governor Mario Cuomo, one of the most articulate politicians in the last few decades. Chris Cuomo and Diane Sawyer are the co-anchors of *Primetime Live*. The day he came to Shepherd Center with his news team and camera crew, they closed down our floor and we spent the entire day doing interviews. Bonnie still could not speak and I spoke with the help of the Passy-Muir valve attached to my neck. My voice was raspy, which made it hard to distinguish my words. At one time during the interview one of the camera and sound people asked me if I could speak more clearly. Mr. Cuomo, with a tear in his eye, responded to this person, "Can't you see he has a tracheostomy?" With sincerity and concern Chris turned to me and said, "Eric I know this is not easy, I'm sorry."

To which I replied, "All I can remember is the person I used to be. I want to be that man again. Do you see the way people look at me and talk to me?"

"Yes, I do and I am proud of you. You will get better," he affirmed. "Eric, what do you miss most?"

"I miss eating."

"What would you like to eat?"

"Pizza. Rays Pizza."

"When you get well, I want you to come to New York and I will take you to get the best pizza you have ever eaten."

"Is that a promise?" I quizzed him.

"Only if you promise to get well!"

"I promise."

"And so do I. Now let's get back to work. We have a story to tell."

As the day progressed, the team followed Bonnie and me to rehab to watch us as we were learning to walk, breathe, swallow, talk, and move. I worked hard that day to impress the reporters, but nothing about our bodies worked at 100 percent capacity. Chris could see how hard we were working to get well. He knew how difficult and painful our life had become.

Mr. Cuomo asked Bonnie, "What would you tell anyone who is considering getting Botox injections?"

She wrote in response, "Think twice!"

"What message would you share with the viewers?"

"Take time to smell the roses." I sat by her bedside, so proud of her. We looked twice our age. Bonnie wore a hat because she did not want anyone to see her face. Still, we felt we had to share our story in order to expose the insanity of the age-defying cosmetic treatment market.

Our case was receiving international recognition as it unfolded. The more the investigators uncovered, the uglier it became. During the interview, they revealed information about the ongoing investigation. The Botox we thought we had received was not really Botox. It was pure botulism toxin sent to Dr. McComb's office by a company in California called List Biologicals. This company produces some of the most deadly toxins in the world including anthrax and botulinum toxin. People who are not medical doctors can purchase these lethal substances intended only for animal research. A company named TRI (Toxic Research International) bought botulism in large quantities from the List Group and was teaching doctors how to dilute and use it on humans. The botulinum toxin McComb injected into Bonnie and me was bought from List. The Government arrested everyone at TRI and closed the operation, but they never approached the List group. My attorney, Stuart Grossman, wanted to know why.

Stuart had become a close family friend by then. My brother and son became very attached to Stuart because he was genuine. Michael especially looked up to Stuart because he helped him through the crisis by offering guidance and hope that justice would be served in our case. He is a charismatic man and wanted the story to represent us in a sincere light; therefore, he came to Atlanta for our filming with *Primetime Live*.

Chris Cuomo gave me hope. *Primetime* did an excellent job with the editing and I was proud of the outcome. Shepherd Center was graciously accommodating to our visitors. The nurses and other patients thought I was a celebrity, although this was not the way I intended to become famous. The night the show aired was the first time I had seen myself in such poor condition. I looked old, worn, sickly and weak. I resolved to regain my strength and put back on the weight I had lost. That might be a challenge. I would have to be able to swallow again before I could eat.

Primetime showed our story to the world; now I had to begin their next story on the Kaplans. I wanted this to be one of the greatest comeback stories of all time. To do that, I knew I had to get off the ventilator and I knew I had to do it soon. Peter was coming next week and the last thing I wanted to do was let him down.

Chapter Twenty-one

The Vent Nazi

Karen was a physician's assistant who specialized in pulmonary care. She was one tough woman and I had to learn to trust her. "You're off the machine by Wednesday," she said.

"I hope so," I replied softly and without confidence.

"I KNOW so!" she shot back at me with a look that pierced my soul. I was afraid of her and didn't think she understood my condition, but she would hear none of my excuses. "The ventilator is not called life support for no reason. You can't be on it forever!"

Karen taught me to rise above my beliefs. She had more faith in me than I had in myself. I had become so dependent upon the ventilator that I did not think I could live without it. Each day when they took me off the ventilator, I would gasp for air for nearly an hour. This was the most difficult time of the day. Either the pulmonologist or Karen would come back to check my progress.

"Dr. Bowman feels that when you can do the stair-step machine nonstop for fifteen minutes you will be ready to permanently stay off the ventilator," Karen told me that Friday. "You can start today."

"I'll try it." I have to admit my faith was weak.

"Ann, your physical therapist, will take you to the gym." Karen had it all arranged.

I went with Ann to physical therapy that afternoon and we commenced our trial run. I did two minutes and could go no farther. I felt like I had run twenty miles. My heart was beating so fast I thought it would crash right through my chest. "How will I ever do fifteen minutes?"

"We will try again tomorrow. Karen says you are to be off the vent by the end of next week. I hope you can do it." Ann tried to console me.

Later that day, Dr. Bowman's assistant, Dr. Gutay, came in. I told him, "Karen expects me off the vent in five days, I don't know if I'm ready. That woman is the Vent Nazi."

Dr. Gutay laughed. "Yes, but she knows her stuff. You can trust her."

It was hard to get out of bed the next day, but I went to the gym as planned. I did four minutes on the Stair Stepper as I repeated my mantra over and over to myself, "I can. I will. I must!" After four minutes, I was soaking wet. It was eleven in the morning and I was done for the day. I was exhausted and did not leave my bed the rest of the weekend. No stairs that Sunday. My body told me it needed rest, and I listened. I lay in bed and stared at my wife through the mirror. "Hi Bo-Bo." I called her by the affectionate nickname I had given her. She waved back. "The Vent Nazi is wearing me out over here."

An athlete gets a pre-game meal and a cold drink after exercise, but I still could not swallow. My mouth was very dry. After many attempts with the Passy-Muir valve, Bonnie still could not speak at all. She was very weak and fragile. She could walk to the nurse's station, but upon exertion her heart rate would soar and they would have to take her back to her room in a wheelchair. Miraculously, though, she could swallow and was able to eat. I sat and watched her in the mirror when they brought her lunch. What is wrong with me? Why can't I swallow? I was afraid that I might never be able swallow or eat again.

My brother Steven is the gadget king. He brought in a mega vibrator he purchased at Brookstone. In the evenings, he would spend hours massaging my legs and back. It was the highlight of my day, which shows you how bad things were! The massaging not only helped relieve my muscle aches and anxiety, it also helped break up mucus in my chest. Jason flew in every other weekend. We had him leave Saint Leo's University in Tampa and enroll in Palm Beach Community College to care for the house and our dog. Watching my sons grow gave me pride and great comfort. At a time when the world thought we had so little, I knew we had so much. I was alive. I was with my family and I was getting well. I may not have been the luckiest man in the world, but I sure as hell knew I was lucky.

The next Monday, after a day of complete rest, Ann took me to the gym for another tryout. I was able to go sixteen minutes on the Stair Stepper. The physical therapists and doctors were stunned by my progress. With my trusty cane in hand I wobbled back to my room where I was greeted by Karen and Dr. Bowman

"Wednesday is your big day!" Karen said.

Dr. Bowman reaffirmed her statement. "You will stay off the ventilator all night on Wednesday."

While off the ventilator during the day, I had to concentrate and make a conscious effort to breathe. How would I do that if I were asleep? I couldn't even take a nap without the vent because was afraid I would stop breathing and not be able to wake up and call for help. This time, I would have to trust in my body's innate ability to know what to do. I knew God and my angels were with me.

"We have this down to a science," Dr. Bowman explained. "We will bring you to the Intensive Care Unit and hook you up to a several machines that let us know how you are doing. We will have someone monitoring you all night."

"This is my job and I am tough, but so are you. I am positive you can do this, Eric," Karen said with confidence and authority. "I wouldn't put you to the test if I didn't think you are ready. If anything goes wrong, we will help you. The Vent Nazi will not let you die!"

Oh God! How did she know I called her that? Dr. Gutay must have told her. I knew I could trust Karen. I also knew I could trust my body, God and my angels. I agreed to give it a try come Wednesday.

It is amazing what we do to impress and inspire others. My wife, son and brother wanted me so to succeed and I wanted to please them. And then there was Peter. Hell, if I failed, I would be letting him down. He wanted me back and I wanted to be back. Everyone stopped in. "Tonight's the night!" they would say. I had entered my own personal health world series.

I knew I would not completely recover unless I was able to breathe without the vent, yet all day Wednesday I tried to come up with a reason why I could not or did not want to go through with the plan to stay off the vent all night. Fear is often much more destructive than that which is feared, and anxiety can often be far more harmful than those things which cause us to be anxious. Avoiding my situation would only make it more difficult to deal with later. Therefore, I had to confront my present situation and not fear my future. When fear popped into my head, all I had to do was stare at the vent. I hated that thing, but like a heroin user, I was addicted to it and didn't believe I could live without it. It was my biggest obstacle to freedom. "You are my enemy," I told it. "This battle belongs to ME!"

Wednesday night, I was taken to the Intensive Care Unit. As promised, I was hooked up to all kinds of monitors. My son and brother couldn't stay with me but they left me in good hands. The nurses at Shepherd went out of their way to provide an extra measure of patient care. Several of them came by to offer me words of encouragement that night. One even massaged my back before I went to bed. I trusted in God and the doctors he chose to assist me in my journey back to wellness. My angels were rooting for me. God had given me the tools I needed. My angels had provided me with courage. Now I had to show them my faith.

I watched *M.A.S.H.* on TV until I could no longer hold my eyes open. I went to sleep praying and was still praying when I woke up at four o'clock the next morning. My first thought was, "I'm alive! I can do this!" I looked at the vent and said, "I beat you.

I will never use you again!" I smiled and went back to sleep. I had slain the dragon.

The next morning, everyone stopped by to congratulate me. Dr Bowman, Dr. Leslie and Dr. Gutay were thrilled, and I felt excited about showing everyone that I was alive and well.

I was gaining confidence with each visitor, but Karen knew how to push my buttons. When she and the team came in to check on me she said, "Good job! We're taking out the tracheostomy tube either today or tomorrow." TAKE THE TRACH OUT? Yikes! That's like taking the net from under a tightrope walker at the circus. Yet there would be no nets for Dr. Karen. "You're on your way home!" she smiled. Her confidence meant so much to me.

Karen removed the trach tube from my neck the next morning. It looked like Baby Alien. In one moment, the six-inch-long apparatus that had been surgically implanted in my neck was gone and I conquered my first two goals: get off the ventilator and have the tracheostomy removed. My next goal was to eat.

I walked from ICU to see my wife in the room we shared. I could tell how proud she was to see me, and this was only the beginning. Each day my muscles got stronger and I doubled my exercise routine. I was making such progress some of the nurses starting calling me "Rocky." I was ahead of Bonnie. I could walk, talk, and now breathe without the ventilator, yet I could not swallow. Bonnie on the other hand, could not walk or talk, and was still on the ventilator, but she could swallow. I knew I could never get out of Shepherd if I couldn't eat. I was being given eight cans of liquid each day through a feeding tube to sustain my nutritional needs. I was concerned, but I was also sure Shepherd had a plan to recover my ability to eat and bring back those muscles.

Soon they started me on biofeedback. I went to x-ray and watched myself try to swallow. Electrodes were attached to my neck. As I tried to swallow, an electrical current would stimulate the muscles to contract. This was uncomfortable, but I really wanted to eat —especially when they brought pasta to my wife on her dinner tray. I love pasta and I was so hungry even the hospital food smelled good. I toddled over to Bonnie where she sat with her banquet before her. I picked up her fork and put a curly noodle to my lips. I closed my eyes and I visualized myself swallowing it. My body reacted to the vision as if it were reality. I actually swallowed for the first time in seven weeks. Time for a celebration. I couldn't wait to tell the world. I couldn't wait to see and tell my doctors. The next day, a new x-ray confirmed I was ready to eat!

It took me three to five tries for each successful swallow and I found it easier to swallow thick liquids than thin ones. For example, ice cream was easier to swallow than water. The hospital freezer had numerous brands of ice cream, so I began a Häagen-Dazs diet. Once I could swallow, Steve and my friend George Fox brought me frozen treats from Steak n Shake. Ellen brought us healthy smoothies every day. I was having fun: I was breathing on my own, I was walking, and I was eating ice cream! This may not seem like much to some but to me it was everything. I was reborn!

Each day I worked harder, ate and drank more, and appreciated everything. I was like a boy with a new toy. I looked a hundred and twenty years old but I only felt ninety. Soon, Shepherd started talking about letting me go home. I was both excited and scared. How would I fare on my own without the medical staff around me for support? The news upset Bonnie because she was behind me in her recovery. But not for long. Karen came in that same day and told Bonnie, "You are off the ventilator tonight."

I looked at Michael and Steve. They looked back at me, and then we all looked at Bonnie. She was so weak and frail.

Dr. Bowman agreed, "Tonight is the night."

"Is she ready?" I asked.

"Karen thinks so."

"I know, but she is the Vent Nazi!"

"Yes, and she was right about you," Dr. Bowman replied.

Knowing it was useless to argue with the Vent Nazi, Bonnie agreed. Besides, Bonnie saw me having Häagen-Dazs parties, and heard about me leaving Shepherd and she was planning on going with me.

That night Jason phoned. I missed him rubbing my legs, but we needed him to be tending to things at our home in Florida. After Jason wished his mother good luck on her solo flight without the vent, Michael and I walked Bonnie to ICU. Then I went back to my room with my Häagen-Dazs!

The next morning I went to check on Bonnie. Miracles are abundant for those who believe and have faith. Not only had

Bonnie made it through the night without the vent, the staff had already taken out her tracheostomy tube.

"You did it, Bo-Bo!" I was so pleased with Bonnie's progress. "I didn't think you could do it, but Karen was right."

"Neither did I," she smiled, neither did I." I had not heard my wife speak in eight and a half weeks. My heart fluttered when she looked at me and whispered, "I love you. I am so proud of you. You are my hero." She was beginning to believe it was our destiny to get well.

It seemed that she would take two steps forward and one giant one backward. But not today. Today, she began to only move forward. The wind of our recovery had changed and was blowing us the direction of restored health. Each day as we climbed our mountain of recovery we learned to cherish every moment. Each meal became a banquet. My rehabilitation now included walks outside the hospital, which frightened me because my legs and body were still weak and the ground was often covered with ice. Like an elderly person, I feared falling.

Bonnie was scared and rightfully so. Infections in hospitals are common and Bonnie became sick again. She couldn't keep any food down and we feared there might be another problem with her bowel or complications from surgery, but it turned out it was just a hospital-borne infection. However, with the infection came a loss of strength and added depression. Bonnie and my mother had been best friends and they loved one another dearly. I thought it might encourage Bonnie to know that I had been visited by my mom, so I shared with her the Facts of Life my mother shared with me. Life is for living, loving, laughing and learning. Life begins with love, and God is love. Accept the idea that we are love, and as such, we are God. We have the power of choice, but choice should be governed by wisdom. Nothing is ever gained or lost in the universe—only transformed. Whether we choose to do good or bad, we will all eventually reach the same destiny—awareness of our oneness with God. THERE IS NO DEATH! There is only life and afterlife. I'm not sure Bonnie was ready to be preached to, but I desperately wanted to help her gain strength both physically and spiritually because the lessons had been so valuable to me in my recovery.

I have been strong, confident and even arrogant my whole life. Only my friend Richard Palladino could talk more crap than I could. I missed him and my other golf buddies Rich Kaufman, Rich Lubin, Harvey Golden, Keith Hammond, Sandy Meyers, Bill Meyers, Andy Brock, Warren Zwecker and Boom Boom Shalhoub, Rich K, called and said he and the boys wanted to visit us at Shepherd. I told him, "Be patient. I am coming home sooner than anyone thinks."

That same day, Ross Mandel, the CEO of Sky Capital, called. "Kaplan, I have a job for you when you get finished lying around having people feel sorry for you."

"Really? What kind of job?"

"I want you to be involved as a consultant in a company I am starting."

It was as if the Universe knew I was coming back. Everyone was calling that day. My former clinic director, Dr. Donald Gutstein, is one of my mentors. He is a brilliant man who reminds me of House, a character in the hit television series on FOX. He called to cheer me up. "Dummy, (not his actual word) you were never so good-looking to begin with. What were you thinking having Botox injections? You've earned your wrinkles. I'm coming to see you on Sunday."

"I can't wait to see you, Dummy!" (Not my actual word choice either.)

What a day! All my friends were calling, Bonnie and I were both off the ventilator, and I was almost ready to leave Shepherd Center. Still, the highlight of the day was seeing my wife smile again. It had been a long time coming. As with the angels, you cannot see hope, but you can feel it. Hope was abundant.

Sleeping without the ventilator was still scary. I kept waking up to make sure I was still breathing. It was hard to believe that my body remembered how to breathe on its own. Every night I repeated my affirmation, "The power that created the body heals the body." I had developed faith in God and Mother Nature. I was learning to live fully in each moment.

Though life is constantly and relentlessly changing, the goodness we experience is never left behind or forgotten. Good times continue to live in our heart and we can relive those fond memories in our minds. We can express the joy from those times again and again in new and creative ways. The joys we have in life came because we opened ourselves up to life's goodness. These joys are still with us even though many things may have changed. There were countless times in my recovery that I was scared and fearful. By living in the "now," I was able to overcome my fears.

You have heard it said many times, "Live in the moment. Live for today, not for tomorrow. You may plan for the future, but all we have is today." It sounds good, but what does it really mean? It means being focused on the task at hand without dragging baggage from the past with us and without worrying about the future. Our mind allows us to visualize and create our future by guarding what we think and attract to ourselves. Although many people thought I would be in a wheelchair for a year, I never visualized myself in that situation. I only saw myself walking and running again. I had to learn to walk, talk, swallow, smile and breathe again. I tried never to see myself as I was, but rather how I wanted to be. I was learning not to fear the future or the unknown, by mentally tossing out any memory that did not serve my road to recovery. I focused only on the memories that were worth reliving.

The time I spent at Shepherd Center was like competing in my own personal Olympics. Daily I was challenging my body, battling my mind, and overcoming obstacles. As I was preparing to leave Shepherd, I was stepping to the platform to receive my gold metal.

Yet Bonnie was still so weak and frail. Every night I would sit at her bedside and tell her about my angelic visits and remind her that angels are with her. One night she looked at me with tears in her eyes and whispered in her new raspy voice, "I don't want you to leave here without me. I am going to get better."

We hugged and held each other as we cried tears of hope and happiness. We knew we were getting better and we knew we were not alone on our journey.

Chapter Twenty-two

Prison Break

There are angels painted on the ceilings everywhere at Shepherd Center. These are more than paintings: They are reminders of the fact that angels are around us always, both seen and unseen. Angels, dressed as humans, work at Shepherd Center. These dedicated doctors, nurses and staff made a difference in our lives. Shepherd Center is a place of miracles, and we are living proof of that. I arrived there incapable of caring for myself and within thirty days I was capable of caring for my body as well as my spirit.

Surrounded by my angels, I was pushed to new limits and levels of success every day. The difference between success and failure lies in making right and wrong choices. My days at Shepherd were filled with choice. I had to stop talking about success and start getting it done. I had to stop seeing every obstacle or fear as an excuse and instead start seeing obstacles as a pathway to my goals. There was no quick and easy shortcut; I had to take the high road. It did no good to complain about how things were, so I started making the most of what I had to work with. Instead of using my words and thoughts to put myself down, I used my mental power to lift myself up. I gave my recovery effort a hundred and ten percent, always expecting the best. Now I know that I AM indeed fully capable of anything.

The staff at Shepherd decided to push my schedule ahead. I did not want to leave my wife, but I was not given a choice. I awoke one morning and was told they were discharging me that day. I signed myself out but continued to stay with Bonnie as long as I could. That night, Michael, Steve and his wife Gloria took me to the apartment they had rented for the next three months. Escorted by my human and spiritual angels, I walked out feeling like a man released from prison. I was still weak, but I had reached my goals. I could breathe, eat, swallow, talk and walk. I had not been in the outside world in more than ten weeks and here I was in an unfamiliar city in a strange apartment and sleeping alone. I always thought my wife and I would leave Shepherd Center together. I missed her so much. Without the nurses and staff constantly near me, I realized how weak and vulnerable I was.

Gloria and Steve could not have been nicer. Michael set up my DVD so I could watch *M.A.S.H.* The fridge was filled with Häagen-Dazs, but that night had to be the loneliest night of my life. Lying in bed, I was scared. What if my breathing stops? What if I get a mucus plug? I was too proud to ask for help from my caretakers. They needed to rest. Instead, I looked to my angels and my lessons. I remembered my Uncle Herb telling me, "Eric, you must embrace life every day and know that it is your attitude that will give you altitude. Are you going to feed the white dog or the red dog?" I fed the dog of hope and faith and soon fell asleep.

I went to visit Bonnie the next day. I looked at her lying in bed and started crying. How long before she gets out of here? Did she feel as sad as I did? Hell, no, she was mad at me! I had escaped from prison and hadn't taken her with me. Fortunately, this motivated her to work twice as hard on her recovery. Exercise was essential to getting our life back, so it was off to the gym for both of us. Afterward, I walked across the street to a restaurant called Mama Fu's to pick up lunch. I bought enough to share and took it back to Bonnie's room.

"Bo-Bo?" I pushed open her door. "I brought you something."

"I smell food. What is it?"

"Lo mien."

"Lo mien?"

"It's easy to swallow."

Not that swallowing was easy. With almost each swallow, it felt like I would choke. We took very small bites, did lots of chewing and made several attempts to get each bite down, but we were enjoying the taste of food after weeks of not eating. While we ate, I told Bonnie how much I missed her and wanted her out of Shepherd.

"I miss you too," she said. "It's lonely here without you."

"It's lonely in that apartment without you, but it won't be much longer before they release you. Just keep up the good work. Speaking of work. I'm exhausted and I don't have a bed here anymore. I guess I'll go back to the apartment and rest until time for evening visiting hours."

"Traitor!" she snapped in a teasing whisper.

One night, my son and I went to Ted Turner's Restaurant in Buckhead. I decided to call Dr. Dennis Egitto while we were there.

"Dennis? Guess who this is." I wanted to surprise him.

"Eric? . . . You're able to talk!"

"I'm out of Shepherd and I'm eating a bison burger."

No answer.

"Dennis?"

He was speechless.

"Are you there?"

"Uh . . you're. . . out . . . a bison burger. . . really?" He chuckled in amazement.

"Bonnie and I are both off the ventilator and working to regain our strength. She's still at Shepherd and boy, does she want out."

"I am so glad to hear the good news. When do they think Bonnie will be released?"

"The problem is she is not eating enough for them to remove the feeding tube. She only weighs ninety-eight pounds. She looks like she's been in a concentration camp, but she is a survivor."

"God bless her. I am so thankful to hear your voice and know that you are progressing so well."

"We'll be home before you know it. It is so good to chat with you, Dennis. You saved our lives and we will be forever grateful that you took us seriously when we called you that Friday night."

As Bonnie started to eat, she developed more stamina. After nearly a week at Shepherd on her own, Dr. Bowman soon gave us the news: Bonnie gets out Monday.

Often we realize how much something means to us only after it is taken away. Never again would I take my health and the simple pleasures of life for granted. I had learned my lesson. I would appreciate and seek health and spiritual well-being every day. Unless it has happened to you, it is hard to imagine what it is like to be paralyzed, unable to open your eyes or communicate with the outside world, to be unable to eat or drink, walk or talk.

It's like sitting at a 50-foot-long banquet table on which there are delicious main courses, desserts and drinks—all your favorites—and not be able to partake of them. Slowly, you are able to take a sip, then a bite or two. Bonnie and I began to appreciate food like never before.

It is easy to take food for granted when there is so much in front of you every day and you are allowed to enjoy it, knowing there will always be more. This example can be transferred to many things in life. It is difficult for most young people to appreciate every day they have because they seem to have so many days left. What good is it to think that today might be our last day? Because it teaches us to be truly appreciative and to make the most of what we have.

As my mentor, Dr. Gutstein made me the doctor I am today. He was not only a good teacher, he was also a great person, because he turned men and women into doctors. No one, with the exception of my father, had more influence on me than Dr. Gutstein. He was a brilliant professor and clinic director of New York Chiropractic College of Brookeville, New York. He demanded that his students be their best and meet their potential. When I entered my last year of chiropractic school, I was talented and cocky. I was also rough around the edges, having grown up in Jersey City. On my first day in his class I showed up in a pair of jeans and a leather coat. My hair was long and since his class was at 8 A.M., I was also unshaven. I sat in the back of the room. Dr. G., as some students referred to him, asked the class, "What is the cause of venereal disease?"

The correct answer would have the genus and species of the bacteria involved. However, I challenged this mean and tough doctor, I stood up and said, "Women!"

215

The class went into an uproar. Dr. G. waited for the laughing to subside, then liked a trained actor he ripped into me, "What is your name?"

"Eric Kaplan," I answered.

"Are your parents alive, Mr. Kaplan?"

"Yes, sir." I no longer found this funny.

"Call and tell them you just flunked out of chiropractic school."

"Excuse me?" I asked.

He replied, "You will never pass my class. I am failing you. Go pack your bags. There is no room or time for comedy in my class. There is no need for comedians in medicine. You failed. Now get out!"

I was devastated. I went home and I studied hard for the next class. I cut my hair, shaved my face and put on a jacket and tie. I sat front and center of Dr. Gutstein's class and waited nervously. He walked in, took one look at me and said, "Who are you? You look like Mr. Kaplan."

"I am Mr. Kaplan," I replied.

"No, son. Mr. Kaplan flunked my class; I sent him home."

"Sir, I know this material. I deserve a second chance."

He drilled me for thirty minutes, asking me question after question as I stood in front of the class. Then he finally smiled (which was rare) and said, "Okay, Kaplan. I see you put in a lot of time and serious effort. I will give you a second chance but there will NOT be a third. For you, anything less than an A in my class means failure. If you keep up this pace and keep this attitude, I'll allow you back."

I had a new attitude and a new work ethic while I finished school. He reminded me of Coach Knight. In every class, I knew Dr. G was going to pick on someone, and I didn't want it to be me. He would not tolerate less than 100% effort; many young men and women were sent home that year. He would not allow anyone to become a doctor if they didn't earn it and represent our profession to the highest standard.

It had been twenty-five years since I graduated chiropractic school and I was excited about seeing him. I got dressed and thought I looked pretty good when he and his wife came to visit me.

"Schmuck!" he yelled sternly as he entered. "Pure schmuck!" Now he was smiling. "Kaplan, you were never that good-looking to begin with. If you wanted to have work done on your appearance, you should have done more than Botox!"

"Well, I missed you, too!" I smiled.

"You seem to have forgotten all I taught you as a student."

"What do you mean?"

"If you focused your life on giving to others, you wouldn't be looking in the mirror so much."

"But I was getting old," I protested.

"We all are. Such is life."

"But I wanted to look better!"

"Do you think you look better?"

"No, of course not!" I felt like I was in class again being drilled for a test.

"Was it worth the risk?" he asked.

"No way."

"Life is not about what people say or what they think of you. Life is not about how you *look* to others, but how you *see* others."

"I hear a lecture coming. Tell me more." It took botulism to reacquaint me with my teacher.

"Everything we sense is given to us by our Creator. As surely as our sensations are subjective, the perspective we build is also subjective. We need to see the invisible in order to do the impossible. In your case, you needed to see yourself getting well in order to get well. Scientists try to expand the limits of our senses with microscopes, telescopes and all kinds of sensors. I should know; I'm a teacher." He was in full classroom-instructor mode and there was no stopping him. "But all these aids do not change our perception. It is as if we are imprisoned by our sensory organs. All incoming information penetrates our five senses: visual, auditory, tactual, gustatory and olfactory."

"Of which, most of mine do not work properly!" Here I was in class taking on my role as class clown.

"Eric, are you listening? Pay attention before I come over there and smack your head!"

"Yes, sir!" Oh, how I loved and respected this man. My uncle was so right. We are enrolled full-time in the University of Life, and here I was again learning lessons from a man whom I had never seen as an angel before now.

"We receive messages every day. We sense love, anxiety, fear and hatred. We sense emotion, but we cannot see it. We need to focus on bringing only positive data to our senses even at our lowest of moments. For once the received information undergoes processing inside a person, it is assessed by one algorithm: whether it is better or worse for me." The professor turned to his wife and asked, "How many senses do you have?"

"I know this is a trick question, but I have to say at least five," she replied.

My lecturer was proud to have added a student to his roster. "We are given the ability to create a sixth sense."

"I saw that movie!" I joked.

"Again, you are talking when you should be listening," he teased. "This sixth sense is acquired with a belief in the perfection of life. In his seminars, Anthony Robbins teaches that man's pursuits are either of pain or pleasure. Many scholars of religion teach that the only thing created is the desire to have pleasure and delight. Our brain is aimed only at the development of this sensation, measuring it correctly. The brain is an auxiliary appliance, nothing more. The heart is perceived to react to man's inner reactions even though it is simply a pump."

I looked at this bearded man with his beloved wife. He was happy to be teaching again. I was alive and happy to be learning.

"Eric, what are you feeling?'

"What do you mean?"

"What are you feeling right now? What are you sensing?"

"Now it's time for show and tell, eh?" We all laughed. "I am sensing love and guidance. Is that a good answer?"

"There is no right or wrong answer when it comes to what you are sensing. In fact, our sensations and feelings are purely spiritual. The various organs that enable us to experience them are also of a spiritual nature. The heart simply reacts to sensations. It's primary function is to pump blood through the body."

I raised my hand like Vinnie on *Welcome Back, Kotter*. "Dr. G? I think I understand what you are saying. When our physical state is altered, we must look inside to find direction to the light of our true soul. My family loves me but they could not understand what I have been feeling. It was my belief that I am not alone, that there is order to the universe that gave me strength far greater than any doctor could have dreamed. My beliefs caused my body to recognize and respond to its power to heal itself."

"How did you know this?"

"I sensed it internally."

"Exactly, and this is something that science still does not grasp."

"I saw angels."

"Did you see them or did you sense them?"

"Both."

"Our sixth sense tells us God is real. When we begin to perceive or believe in a higher force, we empower ourselves with hope. Hope was your savior. I'm sure most people at one time or another have hoped or prayed for God's intervention. Regardless of whether or not such a power exists, our belief in the ability and willingness of a higher power to respond to us gives us reason to pray. Without this belief, there is no reason to pray."

"That makes sense."

"When a person begins to evaluate his own deeds in accordance to what he thinks the Creator expects, he begins to criticize his own actions and reactions. This is our conscious at work. The Laws of Life teach us right from wrong and how to follow the path of right. When a man increasingly performs good deeds more light enters him. This inner light is God."

"It seems like I've heard this somewhere before."

"Eric I taught you this years ago. The more you serve others, the more resources you will have. This also gives you more responsibility. You chose to be a doctor, not a magazine model. You chose to serve others. I expect you will get well and serve again, but this time with purpose and meaning."

"I survived botulism but the lessons of life will never end." I had been lectured by three angels and now by my professor. Obviously, I still had much to learn.

"Eric you must grow from this. If you don't grow, then you have lost the lesson intended. Help others and prevent this from happening to anyone else. Tell your story."

I had to get well. I had a mission to accomplish.

Chapter Twenty-three

Big Canoe and the Kaplans Too

While Bonnie was happy to be getting out of Shepherd Center, she was also afraid of being on her own without the support of a medical staff and equipment nearby. What if there was a relapse or she quit breathing? Those were the fears she had to give to God as she and I faced life with our bodies still not up to par.

Bonnie and I decided to go to our home in Big Canoe, Georgia, to regain our strength before making our way back to Florida. Driving into Big Canoe through scenery that resembled a national park was a majestic experience. Undaunted by commercialization and industry, Mother Nature silently stretched her naked tree branches to welcome us to her paradise. God's peaceful presence beckoned to us from the lakes and mountains. The small development of homes nestled in the foothills of the Appalachian Mountains seemed to embrace the spirit of the Cherokee Indians, who cherished this sacred area. Our yard was a play area and feeding ground for deer and other wildlife. The spirit of life was in the air—air we could now breathe. It was the perfect place to rest and heal.

There was nothing in the house to eat when we arrived, so Michael and I went shopping for groceries. We are both stubborn and determined men and it was not easy to give in to him when he would not let me drive the car. It was awkward having my oldest son so protective of me. I wanted to be whole and show him I was again the man of the family. Yet I am indebted to his love. When we came home with the food, Bonnie had dressed, fixed her hair and put on her makeup, but she was crying.

"What happened?" I thought she must have been afraid of being alone in unfamiliar surroundings. After all, it was the first time in eleven weeks she had been totally alone.

"Everything is so hard to do," she cried.

"I know." I held her close.

"It takes ten times more effort to do a simple task than it did before. I don't think I can do this every day," she continued to cry. "I'm not ready."

"I completely understand."

"I don't think you do," Bonnie was frustrated with me. "You refuse to recognize our disabilities. I want to use a cane so I don't fall, but you push me to walk without one. As a woman, I do not have the physical strength that you do. Besides that, I have had two surgeries while battling botulism; you haven't!" She was right. Even though I considered myself weak at that point, I was physically much stronger than she was. Bonnie continued to weep as I held her. "I no longer feel like the beautiful woman I once was. What if I don't get any better than this? I don't want to be disabled. I want my life back!" She weighed around ninety-nine pounds and looked like a concentration camp survivor, but I certainly didn't look much better. Our lives and appearance were altered but our love for each other remained constant.

I had another advantage that Bonnie didn't; I was spiritually strong. On my quest for spiritual enlightenment and personal healing,

I had had to give myself to God. But I also had the advantage of three supernatural visits from my angels; Bonnie didn't have that. Her days in semi-consciousness at Gardens Hospital had been absolute hell. She had been terrorized by nightmares and haunted day and night by horrible mental scenes and unpleasant memories. Internally, she had wondered, "Will I ever feel like a woman again? Will I be capable of making love to my husband again? What if Eric leaves me?" I knew there were powers in the universe working for us, but that wasn't a reality to Bonnie. No matter how much I wanted to give her peace of mind, she needed her own faith to pull her through. I had to give her time and be patient.

Our days were spent talking and rekindling our love. Our first night in Big Canoe was the first night in eleven weeks that we had slept in a bed together. It felt like a lifetime. We were as awkward as two honeymooners, not because of sex—we were not ready for that—but because we were so weak. Lifting the blanket was a chore. Moving the pillow was a task and getting out of bed in the morning was a major feat. But, once we were up, we spent our days doing rehab at the fitness center in our community. They offered water aerobics and I was the only man in the class. I was probably the youngest too, but I looked and felt much older. I still had a long way to go.

Big Canoe is a small community covering approximately 6,000 acres. Let me tell you, Southern hospitality is alive and well there! Big Canoe Chapel is a non-denominational church on the property, and Lamar Helms is the Christian minister. When he heard about our plight on the news and in *Smoke Signals,* the Big Canoe Newspaper, he made it a point to drive to Atlanta every week to visit us at Shepherd Center. Once we arrived at Big Canoe, the warm and compassionate neighbors, developer, and church groups embraced us as part of the family.

Although we were of different religious persuasions, his congregation worked together in harmony to help Bonnie and me. Every night someone brought a meal to our house. This is how the world should be, people helping people regardless of race, creed or color. The beauty in people of any faith is their belief in a supreme power that governs the universe, and that is what unites us.

I wanted to do everything at once, to walk the property, visit with neighbors, drive through the area, or do simple chores. I was able to walk without the aid of a cane, but fatigue would set in quickly and I would have to rest before I could get up and try again. Bonnie was still very frail and weak and continued to use a cane to steady herself.

After one month of convalescing in Georgia, we were not yet emotionally ready to go home and face our friends, but we felt guilty about having Michael be our nursemaid. I wanted him to move on with his life. Bonnie and I needed to go home so he could go back to college and finish his senior year.

Homeward Bound

A team of angels was coming to take us home. Michael had his car to drive back, but we were not up to traveling in a car the distance from North Georgia to Southern Florida, so Steve and Gloria flew to Georgia to help us manage the flight.

The flight was difficult and tiring, but returning home was worse. Our room was exactly as we left it. Although we had a housekeeping service to assist our younger son Jason, they never touched our room. The atmosphere still held the feel of death.

The room was cold and empty, void of life. It reminded me of my parents' house when my father died. Sorrow clung to every fiber and fabric. Panic and sickness laughed at us as we entered what had once been our safe haven. It took weeks to shift the energy to where we felt comfortable in that room again.

My partner, Dr. Gerald Mattia, had heart surgery a few months after we were home. The surgeons had to open Gerry's chest, take out his heart, put him on a heart and lung machine while his heart was literally out of his body, put in a new valve, then do two bypasses. The fact that a dysfunctional heart valve can be replaced with a bovine valve shows we are one with the universe and that there is no difference between any person regardless of his or her religion, race, creed, or origin. Gerry was off the ventilator in one day and walked out of the hospital in four days. I, on the other hand, went for a few injections in my forehead and was on a ventilator for eight and a half weeks. It goes to show you that taking drugs can be more dangerous than having surgery. Surgeons provide compassion—a human component. Drugs have no conscience, memory or thoughts. Michael and I went to see Gerry in the hospital right after his surgery. His children were there. I was touched when I saw them crying. Gerry looked bad. Michael said, "Dad, you looked worse!" And, I looked like that for months. At least Gerry looked better the next day.

A few months later, on November 10, 2005, Dr. Bach McComb pleaded guilty of providing fake anti-wrinkle shots containing botulism toxin to patients who thought they were getting FDA-approved Botox. He accepted a plea bargain in order to avoid a trial and possible long-term imprisonment, but he still doesn't think he did anything wrong. A hearing was set for January

2006 to let a judge decide who was responsible and who would have to pay for our condition.

Allergan, the FDA-approved and -licensed distributor of Botox, recorded $564 million in Botox sales last year. Allergan said they were working with the FDA and the government, and that they were not to blame for our poisoning. The toxin injected into Bonnie and me came from List. Allergan may not have been to blame for our poisoning, but the fact that animals suffer and die in the potency testing of Botox is undeniable. Nature protests against any form of enslavement. Being paralyzed and stuck inside my own body was torturous, yet I can only imagine what animals suffer in captivity as research victims. Why should animals die so humans can smooth out a few wrinkles? I have learned so much on this horrific toxin. Was I naïve? Yes. Was I ignorant of the facts? Yes. Did I think it was safe? Yes Do I now know the truth? You bet I do but the world needs to know that this drug is harmfull, potentially addicting and possilby lethal. I learned the hard way hopefully you won't have to.

Almost one year later, Bonnie and I still spend our days continuing our rehabilitation and giving thanks. The good news is another miracle has occurred: the tumor on Bonnie's bladder has vanished. The bad news is our faces remain partially paralyzed, our muscles overtire easily, our energy is depleted quickly, and Bonnie's mobility is impaired due to the collapse of three vertebrae affected by the botulinum toxin. Bonnie can't close her eyes all the way or move her eyebrows. If I sneeze, my eyes will close, but they won't open again right away. I need glasses now, but at least I can see. Bonnie has lost part of her hearing and will always have to wear hearing aids in both ears. I still have fluid in my ears but I refuse to have surgery. We're already facing a million dollars in medical bills and the government has merely slapped the hand of those responsible for our medical condition. But, we have not lost hope or our desire to help others. Our next project is already underway. Bonnie and I are working with Yvonne Perry, the editor of this book, to write children's books on health and body/mind/spirit wellness. We feel that children need to know how to appreciate and accept their body and understand the spiritual component that is so vital to being whole and in good health. Other projects we are undertaking include a revision of *Dr. Kaplan's Lifestyles of the Fit and Famous* to be reissued as *Beyond Atkins* and a new book entitled *The Five-Minute Motivator*, a book intended to be a quick read geared to motivate and inspire. By simply reading any chapter in the book, you can alter your existence, transform your dreams into realities and have your realities create dreams for other people. The book will offer a series of vignettes, motivational techniques, and stories that will teach the secrets of success.

Good things can come from bad situations. Because they almost lost their parents, our sons have both decided to become doctors. In massaging my legs and caring for his mother and me during our worst nightmare, Jason discovered his life's calling. He wants to use his healing gift to help others. Now twenty years old, he is living in Marietta, Georgia, and attending Life Chiropractic College. Following in his dad's footsteps, he plans to be a chiropractor. Michael is a sensitive young man who is committed to saving and restoring lives. He has graduated from the University of Central Florida and is applying to medical schools in hopes of becoming a physiatrist, specializing in physical medicine and rehabilitation like Dr. Bowman. Before our incident, Michael had never heard of an air ambulance. Recently, he passed his paramedic test and took his first career flight to New Jersey as a medical escort on a critical care aircraft. His first flight, of all places, was to the Shepherd Center, a young girl was injured in a car accident. If this isn't destiny, what is?

John Rice called me on Thanksgiving Day. He is at home and continuing his rehabilitation. He can move both arms and is able to stand in a swimming pool. His doctors are saying that he may one day walk again. Miracles continue to occur.

I will never be the same as I was before the incident; I am better. Maybe not physically, but mentally, emotionally and spiritually, I am a changed man. I have faced death, been to hell, and escaped a destiny that many thought would be mine. We are not prisoners of life and we do not have to be prisoners in hell. I found a way to escape through the power of my mind and my spirit. Still, our tragedy could have been avoided. There were agencies that did not want the public to know they had failed. With the help of my attorney, more than two hundred other doctors throughout the country were found buying this product. The government reacted and recalled all products from TRI and put them out of business, yet they never went after List Biologicals or changed the law on this toxin. Therefore, Americans are still at risk. Something has to be done and someone has to do it. Maybe that someone is me. Our goal is to shut down List.

Chapter Twenty-four

The Sentencing

On Wednesday, January 25, 2006, my wife and I awoke at 5 A.M. We were anxious and could not sleep, as we anticipated being at the Federal Courthouse in Fort Lauderdale, Florida by 9 A.M. We knew this day would be difficult. We were to serve as witnesses in the federal hearing for Dr. Bach McComb as he appeared before U.S. District Judge James Cohn. I will not lie. There were times I thought of hurting McComb in revenge for what he had done to us, but I would have to trust our justice system.

It had been fourteen months since our tragic poisoning. I could see, but my eyes still didn't open and close properly. Swallowing was still difficult and my digestion has not returned to normal. I didn't have as much endurance and my muscles were not nearly as strong as before the incident. I was thankful to be able to breathe but I was always concerned about catching a cold. The only thing that was better and stronger was my love for my wife, my children, my family, my friends, my community and my life.

Bonnie's eyes still showed the effects of botulinum toxin poisoning. To me, she is still the prettiest woman on the face of this earth; however, she is still self-conscious about her appearance. She wore sunglasses during the hearing so people wouldn't stare at her.

We approached the courthouse with Rodney Bryson, Stuart Grossman's assistant. Rodney is a capable young man who has become a friend and confidant during this ordeal. The media was camped out and in scattered groups along the entry. When they saw us coming, they sprang into action. Our reply to them was simply, "No comment." Upon entering the courtroom, we walked through a metal detector. We then met with Federal Prosecutor Robin Rosenbaum. We were upset that she had plea bargained a deal with Dr. McComb in November of 2005. She explained to us that even if she tried the case and won, the sentencing guidelines would be the same; thus a trial would not produce more jail time for McComb. Sentencing guidelines are based on the monies earned, and in McComb's case, they were minimal. She assured us that he would go to jail.

The hearing began with opening arguments from Dr. McComb's attorney, Jose Herrera. He tried to make McComb out to be a victim, saying that he had no intention of hurting anyone. He injected himself with the same toxin he used on us and his girlfriend, Alma Hall. He argued that since many products used in our country are not FDA-approved, McComb's behavior was not reckless; it was an accident. "Dr. McComb did not order the toxin," Herrera said. "Dr. McComb did not mix the toxin." The judge was nodding his head in agreement. Herrera had a good point.

Because of her recurrent ear infections as result of ear surgery, Bonnie could barely hear what was being said. As the attorney rambled on, my loving wife kept leaning forward so I could fill her in. The first witness called was a woman who had been a patient of Dr. McComb. After she was sworn in, the prosecutor asked, "Did you know Dr. McComb?"

"Yes," she replied.

"Can you point him out?"

The witness pointed toward Bach McComb who actually looked to be in better health than either Bonnie or me. Alma Hall was still not well enough to make a public appearance.

"Did you have Botox injections?"

"Yes."

"How many times?"

"Two or three. I don't recall."

"Do you need to see the office records?" he asked.

"I object!" Counsel clamored, "I have had no chance to review any office records."

"Counsel?" the judge looked to the prosecutor.

"Your honor, we supplied these to Counsel," Herrera replied.

"Objection sustained. Please continue."

The witness continued with her answer, "I received them on three occasions."

The first witness was not very believable and people in the audience were smirking as McComb's attorney wore her down. "You do not know what was in the syringe, do you, ma'am?"

"No."

"So, it may have been genuine Botox?"

"Yes."

"No further questions."

Herrera called a former patient who was also a nurse. After she took the stand, he asked her about her visit to Dr. McComb's office. She replied, "The injections I received from Dr. McComb didn't work as well, so I asked for my money back," she replied.

"Did you get it?"

"Yes."

"You did not know it was not Botox you were getting?"

"It didn't feel the same."

"But you do not know what was in the syringe, correct?"

"No," she agreed.

"No further questions."

Each witness was asked the same question, "Did you know what was in the syringe?" and the answer was "no" each time. Things were not looking good and the judge was beginning to agree with McComb's counsel.

Next, Herrera called someone from List Biological to the stand. "Did Dr. McComb order this product from your company?" he asked.

"No, he did not."

"Who ordered it?"

"Tom Toia."

"How did he pay?"

"By credit card."

"Do you send botulinum to just anyone who requests it?"

"No, we only send it to businesses; never to a home address."

"So any company with a business address can order this toxin?"

"That was the case," she explained. "We changed our policy and now only research facilities can order it."

How can this be? I wondered. *Criminal Justice,* the television show, had recently aired an episode where a disgruntled employee put this toxin in the coffee pot at work and the entire office came down with botulism. What message are we sending to terrorists? Al-Qaeda could order this toxin from a US laboratory and use it to kill hundreds of thousands of Americans! Our own government arrests drug dealers on the streets, but List Biologicals, the drug manufacturer, is allowed to manufacture and distribute it. Why? Because, in my opinion, the U.S. Government is List's number one client. No wonder the government doesn't prosecute List. Any company that deals with botulinum, anthrax, or other such deadly toxins should be owned by the government and be considered part of our armed forces. These toxins cannot go unregulated. Next, a man from the New Jersey Poison Information and Education System (the Poison Control Center) was called to the stand and it was Rosenbaum's turn to begin questioning the witness. "Please state your name," Prosecutor Rosenbaum instructed.

"Dr. Marcus."

"How did you hear of this case?"

"The State of New Jersey called me when Dr. McComb and his former girlfriend, Alma Hall, were admitted to a New Jersey hospital for treatment."

"What diagnosis did you give?" she asked.

"At first, we didn't know what we were dealing with or who had been affected."

"Did you ever meet with Dr. McComb?"

"Yes, I did."

"And what happened?"

"He was ill at that point but he kept telling me the clinic diluted the toxin incorrectly." I thought the case had turned in our favor. The judge now knew that McComb was aware of what had been administered and that it was not an accident. Dr. Marcus continued, "At that point, we realized it was botulism."

"No further questions. You may cross." Ms. Rosenbaum turned and walked to her seat as Herrera came forward to question the witness. "Do you remember the exact conversation?" she asked.

"No, but it had to do with the mixing process," Dr. Marcus answered.

"Did Dr. McComb state that he mixed it?"

"I don't remember."

"Did he say whether anyone else was injected?" Herrera asked.

"I don't remember."

"You don't remember?" He acted shocked. "This was one of the largest and most widely covered media events in our country last year and you don't remember?"

We're screwed, I thought.

"Can I look at my notes?"

"Did McComb mix it?" Herrera demanded again.

"I don't know."

"Then he may not have, right?"

"He may not have."

What else could go wrong? I thought.

"Your honor," the federal counsel spoke up, "the government got its hands on the bottle of the toxin and they are testing it for fingerprints."

How can this be? I questioned to myself. *Fourteen months later and they just got their hands on it? Where has it been all this time? How could they not have this information by the court date? What a joke!*

"Your honor," Herrera stated, "they do not have the results

235

and this should not be admitted as evidence."

The judge agreed. The court was leaning in McCombs's favor. The government was blowing the case. It was up to me.

Prosecutor Rosenbaum called her next witness. "The Government would like to call Dr. Eric Kaplan to the stand."

I approached the witness stand where I was asked to raise my right hand. I did as I was instructed. "Do you swear to tell the truth and nothing but the truth, so help you God?"

"I do."

"Please take the stand and be seated."

Rosenbaum began her questioning, "Dr. Kaplan, do you know Dr. McComb?"

"Yes."

"Point him out, please."

I pointed toward the person responsible for my suffering. This was the first time I had had to look this devil in the eye. He had a smirk on his face as if to say, "I'm going to get away with this."

"Did you go to him for Botox?" she asked me.

"Yes."

"Was this your first time?"

"No."

"Was this your wife's first time?"

"No." I spoke loudly so Bonnie could hear what was being said.

"Explain."

"My wife had gone to another place before and didn't like the results because it made her eye droop. I knew Dr. Toia. He was a colleague and we felt safe going to his office for Botox."

"How long did you know him?"

"Over twenty years," I replied. "I trusted him."

"Did you know you were not getting pure Botox?" Rosenbaum continued.

"No, I did not."

"Did you ever participate in a research program?"

"No, I did not."

"Are you sure?"

"I am fifty-three years old and I have never participated in a research program."

"Tell us, Dr. Kaplan, in your own words, what happened November 23 through November 25, 2004."

I began to share an abridged version of our story as I told the court how we were injected by Dr. McComb and then began to feel ill later that day. "The doctors told us not to worry..." my voice was choked up, "they said we had the flu...eventually Bonnie and I became paralyzed. When I awoke in the hospital, I thought I was at my own funeral." The courtroom fell silent and waited for me to regain my composure.

"Is there anything else you would like to tell the court?"

I was prepared for that moment because my good friend, Richard Lubin, had called that morning to prepare me for this question. Richard is a good friend and is one of the leading criminal attorneys in the country. He was representation to the legal icon F. Lee Bailey. "Eric," he advised, "be calm and not vengeful. Let the judge see your human side. Let him know the Eric that I know. Tell him of the suffering you and your family endured. Be patient and just be yourself."

I locked eyes with the judge. "Your Honor, what happened to

us is a tragedy," I stated, "a tragedy that could have been prevented. I have heard Dr. McComb's counsel say that this was an accident, that he was not reckless, and that he is remorseful. However, I believe it was his arrogance, not his ignorance of the law or the situation, that wreaked havoc on our bodies. At first, my wife and I were 100% paralyzed. Neither of us could eat, walk, talk, swallow or breathe. I spent two months on a ventilator, my wife even longer. We literally had to re-learn how to use our bodies. It was several months before we could do anything on our own. Dr. McComb says he is remorseful. My question is, 'Why didn't he come forward early on and tell us what had happened? Why didn't he admit that he made a mistake?' There is no cure for botulism but there is an antitoxin. Had the antitoxin been administered sooner, less damage would have been done to our bodies. He met with Dr. Marcus, but even then he did not come forward and tell the truth. This is indeed reckless. He continued to practice medicine when his license was suspended for harming other people in other cases. That is arrogance. He not only practiced medicine illegally, he practiced it like Dr. Frankenstein. There was no ignorance of the law on his part. He knew what he was doing. Dr. McComb's arrogance and greed created a reckless situation." All eyes were on me as I continued, "He believes that his sentence should be reduced because he also suffered. Suppose my wife and I got into a car with Dr. McComb and he was recklessly driving the vehicle without a license. Then suppose we got into an accident, and Dr. McComb was injured right along with the other passengers. Does this excuse him from taking responsibility for his actions? Would he not be charged with a crime?" I had made a connection with the judge who was shaking his head in agreement, so I continued.

"Your Honor, I gave my watch to my son." My voice began to shake. "I told him where my will was. I said goodbye because I was dying. These two boys had to watch their parents hover at the brink of death for weeks. They have witnessed things that will haunt them for the rest of their lives. I may be alive here today but a part of me died on November 23, 2004. I am not the man I was. My wife is not the woman she was, and all because of Dr. McComb's arrogance. What happened was a tragedy that could have easily been prevented."

The courtroom fell silent. The smirk on McComb's face was gone. Herrera sat for a moment speaking with his co-counsel. After a pause, he began his cross-examination. "You were a consultant to Dr. McComb, were you not?"

"Yes, I was," I told him.

"What did you do as a consultant?"

"We reviewed billing records and office protocols. We do not render opinion on treatment."

"Did you look at McComb's files?" he asked.

"Yes."

"Were they in order?"

"Yes."

"Did you give him certain protocols?"

"Yes. But, how was I or anyone else to know whether he followed them?" I felt strength as I visualized my mother, father and uncle smiling upon me.

"No further questions."

As I walked to my seat, Bonnie smiled through her tears as I approached. My attorney, Stuart Grossman, gave me thumbs up and said, "That wasn't good; it was PERFECT!"

The court took a recess and the room was buzzing about my testimony. "You sank him," Grossman said. "He is going to jail for the entire term." Stuart went to speak with Robin Rosenbaum, then came back and told us, "Bonnie does not need to testify. You two can go home." I was relieved that Bonnie would not have to be put through the stress of giving testimony. She was emotionally drained already.

When we left the courtroom, the camera and media rushed forward, shoving microphones in our faces. "We will not make a comment to the media until the judge makes his ruling," we told them.

At approximately 7:45 that evening, after a nearly ten-hour sentencing hearing, Judge Cohn, convinced by the government's evidence and my testimony, gave McComb the maximum sentence under the plea bargain. Believing that McComb had recklessly caused harm to others, Judge Cohn sentenced McComb to serve three years in prison along with one year probation. In addition, McComb will no longer be able to practice medicine. After the sentencing, bailiffs immediately took McComb to the Miami-Dade County Detention Center where he began to serve his sentence. He will be moved to a federal prison later. I felt that justice had been served.

That night we were on every news channel and our phone rang off the hook with reporters asking for our comment. Rather than give our comment several times individually, we agreed to an interview the following day at our attorney's office.

There must have been twenty or more cameras in the room the next day when we gave our statement to ABC, CBS, NBC, CNBC, FOX, E-Channel, *Anderson Cooper 360°,* and *Inside Edition.*

"Are you happy with the outcome?" one reporter asked me.

"I am satisfied. Dr. McComb should be happy since the government reduced his possible sentence by plea bargaining a deal. He should have been tried for twenty-three counts of attempted murder. There were many others who received bogus Botox from him."

"Judge Cohn, before giving his ruling, said that in all his years on the bench he had never received so many letters of support for anyone as he did for Bach McComb. How do you feel about this?" another reporter asked.

"That shows you that Dr. McComb is not only a con man, but a good one as well."

"Do you hate Dr. McComb?"

"Look what he did to my family. Look what he put my sons through. He got what he deserved," I answered bravely. Bonnie started crying.

"Dr. Kaplan, what is next?"

"We want to eliminate this toxin and any toxin from being available to the public. It is my goal that List Biologicals will give an account for their actions and they will pay a price. As long as the government allows these and other toxins to be transported, we are all at risk. We intend to change this."

"Mrs. Kaplan, how do you feel about the outcome of the hearing?" the reporter asked Bonnie.

With tears in her eyes, she replied, "I am not happy that someone had to go to jail, but the judge was right; he had to send a message not only to Dr. McComb but to the world."

"What would you tell anyone thinking about having wrinkle reducing cosmetic injections?"

"THINK TWICE!"

The sentencing of Drs. Chad Livdahl and Zahra Karim, the owners of TRI (Toxin Research International) was the very next day. This husband and wife team had sold McComb several vials of botulinum toxin type A over the Internet. Chad Livdahl was sentenced to a term of nine years in prison, and his wife Zahra Karim was sentenced to almost six years in prison. They are also required to pay more than $345,000 restitution to the U.S. Government. Livdahl and Karim have already served a year of their sentences in pretrial detention. Karim, who is a Canadian citizen, has been permitted to serve her sentence in Canada and will be will be transferred in about nine months. Under Canadian law, she could be released to her family in less than two years.

Robert Baker, a professor for the Department of Ophthalmology and Visual Sciences at the University of Kentucky's College of Medicine, was sentenced to two years probation including 180 days of house arrest. He was found guilty of helping TRI promote the unapproved botulinum toxin by providing a testimonial letter that was used in mail brochures and Internet promotions.

The media hype and stress of the hearing was draining for Bonnie and me. I ended up with a dreaded head cold that put me to bed for days afterward. The results of the hearing gave some resolution to our case. Although our work is not over and we are still recovering, we gained enough comfort to be able to put at least part of this ordeal behind us.

In our opinion, the U.S. Government was slack and at fault in many ways. First of all, they allowed List to manufacture and distribute deadly toxins to companies like TRI who could in turn sell them to anyone with a business address. Secondly, the Government cut Dr. McComb a deal that reduced his maximum sentence if he would inform on the people he had purchased the toxin from. McComb's office had previously purchased the unapproved drug from Karim and Livdahl, the principals of TRI and had complained that it was not as effective as Botox in most patients. McComb then bought the botulism toxin directly from TRI's supplier, List Biological Laboratories. FDA investigators say that the vial from List was 20,000 times more potent than the product McComb had previously purchased from TRI. Thirdly, List laboratories, where the Botulinum Toxin Type A came from, has not been indicted. Additionally, the government never went after the Toias who ordered and cut the product even though Toia's credit card was used to make purchases of the raw botulinum toxin from TRI. He was fined $10,000 and is back in practice at another clinic in Florida. I believe he knew that Dr. McComb was mixing the toxin to create fake Botox and injecting it into people who thought they were getting genuine Botox. Otherwise, why would he have called me on the golf course to find out how I was doing after I left his office on November 23, 2004? Why else would he have come to our house to give us an IV when he knew we were manifesting symptoms? Why is the government being so inconsistent with each player in this crime sandbox?

In life you are part of the solution or part of the problem. To this day toxins like Botulinum and Anthrax can be shipped to people with no credentials. These toxins should be monitored by our government and homeland security. To acquire this or any toxin, an application and authorization should be given by our government. The utilization of Botulinum, Anthrax and other horrific toxins along with List Biologicals, the manufacturer, should be monitored. This will make the world a safer place to live.

Chapter Twenty-five

This is Why We Do It

People have asked me over and over why I had Botox injections. While I was lying in the hospital incapable of moving a single muscle, I asked myself that question many times. Why did I do it? The answer is simple: vanity. We live in a world obsessed with how we look. Our friends in Palm Beach County, Florida have had Botox injections—some at Botox parties. We had no fear of the procedure. My wife and I paid a tremendous price to look younger. We ended up looking much older. We still don't know what the long-term effects may be. My face and Bonnie's face are still partially frozen. I need glasses now and my eyes do not open and close properly. My body aches every day. Yet people are still going for shots to look younger.

My life prior to November 23 was heaven. I had the top down on my Lexus convertible and was headed to work—if you call it work. I was a retired chiropractor, acupuncturist and healthcare consultant. I was an active motivational speaker and my life consisted of teaching others the empirical formulas of success. Before that, I ran a publicly traded company on Wall Street. Bonnie and I were surrounded by wealth, opulence and perfection. We lived in a PGA national golf community in Palm Beach Gardens Florida—to me, it is paradise. The palm trees in our front yard swayed as they danced to the breeze of the Atlantic Ocean only six miles away. From the window in our family room, we could see a lake and the sixth hole of the Squire Golf Course. I even had my own putting green in my backyard. We were surrounded by beautiful real estate, nice cars, gorgeous sunsets and, of course, beautiful people. I owned two homes and had money in the bank. I had written a successful book entitled *Dr. Kaplan's Lifestyle of the Fit and Famous.* Amazon gave it great reviews and Donald Trump was on the cover calling it, "The Taj Mahal of Health Books." I was living the American dream—a blessed man married to the girl of my dreams for twenty-four years, so why would I change anything? Why would I go for wrinkle reducing cosmetic injections to remove a few wrinkles?

I was happy with my life, but like most Americans, I was never content and I always wanted more. Even with my accomplishments, I was stressed out and driven by the need to succeed. I was looking for happiness in material things and outward appearances; therefore, looking good was important to my career, self-esteem and success. As Billy Crystal said on *Saturday Night Live,* "It is better to look good than feel good." I bought into that mind-set.

When I was younger, the girls said I had a big nose. When I became a doctor, people said I was ruggedly handsome. I have been told I look like Garry Shandling. While I never considered myself a handsome man, after spending a lifetime in the sun, I was beginning to show my age. As a motivational speaker, I am a highly visible person and wanted to look my best. You might say I had the "Peter Pan" syndrome—I didn't want to grow up. I wanted to be young forever. I didn't realize that being young is a matter of mental perspective and attitude rather than the number of years a person has lived or how many wrinkles he has.

Prior to my crisis, I saw the world mostly through human filters. I perceived only through my five senses: touch, smell, sight, hearing, and taste, or by instruments that increased their range. Some people do not believe in anything beyond the scope of their senses or scientific explanation. We cannot see God, so how do we know such an entity exists? After what I have been through, I believe the spiritual world exists as surely as the physical world does. We cannot see our spirit or our soul, yet is it the essence of our very being. We cannot see love, yet we know it is real.

While I valued my family and loved my life, material objects were what gave me a great amount of pleasure before the Botox fiasco. The world continues to grow and make technological progress, and I was continuously seeking new objects in order to experience more pleasure. But they never brought me spiritual satisfaction. I never considered myself a religious man. Now I know that religion and dogma cannot compare or substitute for the bliss of knowing oneness with my Creator. By chasing material things, I never realized the true satisfaction of being in touch with my spirit. I had never given much thought to angels, but in my darkest hour, I found myself surrounded by them. No, the tragedy I faced was not a mistake. It was a valuable spiritual lesson.

Drugs are big business in America, deeply embedded in politics. Our healthcare system is corrupt and driven by money. We have more drugs and more diseases than ever before. Curing disease is not good business for doctors or pharmaceutical companies; treating illness is where money is made. We have become a drug dependent culture looking for a pill or a potion, the eternal Fountain of Youth. Drugs do not cure health problems;

they only mask the symptoms. There has not been a cure in our country for any disease since polio. We live in an overweight, overindulged world seeking something that only exists within our spirit. Television commercials are inundated with drug ads assured to ease any symptom. Everyone has headaches, sexual dysfunction, allergies, acne or acid reflux. No one can sleep, and almost everyone you know takes an antidepressant. Most people take a minimum of two drugs per day; most seniors take four to six medications per day. Adults are lazy and obese, while our children are considered hyperactive. We medicate them for Attention Deficit Disorder, then tell them to be wary of the street drug dealer on the corner. Never mind him; we know his intent! Our healthcare system is failing and in many cases doesn't care about the consumer. That is true cause for alarm.

Because of our programming, we have come to believe that there are good drugs and bad drugs. We must realize that drugs are drugs, no matter what the label says. Every drug has side effects. I never thought I was risking my life with drugs. Like every other naïve person in the world, I thought if something was approved by the FDA, or a procedure was performed in a doctor's office, or regulated and monitored by the state, it would be okay. Yet, according to a Harvard study, over 100,000 people die annually as a result of their doctor's care. According to Cyclopedic Medical Dictionary, "Iatrogenesis is any adverse or physical condition induced in a patient through the effects of treatment by a physician or surgeon." Iatrogenesis is now the fourth leading cause of death in our country behind cancer, heart disease and stroke. Taking a drug is taking a risk. If you remember or learn one thing from this book, remember that ALL DRUGS ARE DANGEROUS and

THEY ALL HAVE SIDE EFFECTS.

During my darkest hour, my son Jason reminded me that I would find a way to make good of my unfortunate situation, and I have. My goal is to save others from the harm we suffered. or at least educate people about the risk they are taking. After all, you wouldn't jump out of a plane if the pilot told you the parachute doesn't always work. Botox doesn't always work the way one might expect. In fact, many people have had unfavorable results with Botox. The problem is, if you don't like the results, you are stuck—literally—because there is no known cure or medical treatment that can undo the result. You must wait until the toxin wears off.

The real issue is not our outward appearance. The issue is our poor self-image and lack of self-esteem. Both result from an inward belief system that each of us formulates through our life experiences. When we've had negative experiences, we may believe we do not measure up to others. Therefore we judge ourselves by how we look and by other people's opinion of us. Society has set standards so high that we always feel inferior to one another. Why are we always trying to keep up with the Joneses? Because we have not learned to love, accept and appreciate who we really are. Instead, we spend our days competing with and comparing ourselves to those twenty years our junior. Think about it! A fifty-year-old man with a face-lift is still fifty years old! Changing the wrapper doesn't change the candy bar; and changing our outward appearance does not change who we are inside. We should not have to compete with thirty-year-olds to feel good about ourselves. We should be able to accept one another and ourselves, thus honoring the diverse characteristics and wisdom we each have.

Drugs are not the answer, nor is cosmetic surgery. Moses, Jesus and Gandhi never had plastic surgery! They knew their connection with God and that connection brought them the fulfillment and satisfaction they were looking for. You can fool others with your outward appearance but you know what is inside—or maybe you don't. Maybe that is the very thing people are trying to avoid: looking inside for self-worth and contentment.

How can we find peace, satisfaction, and luck? How can we attain tranquility, fulfillment, and happiness? How do we get out of the competitive rat race that compels us to look outside ourselves for approval and self-worth? It all begins with gratitude and self-awareness. Being thankful for who you are and what you have is the springboard for everything you wish to manifest. Before the poisoning, I took so much for granted—the ability to move, to walk, to talk, to breathe, to taste, to see, to smell. My experience awakened my senses. Today, I see everything as a miracle. Even the ability to shave and wash my hair is a gift. Learn from my mistake. Today, I look older as a result of trying to look younger, yet I am happier and more confident than ever. In my search for outward beauty, I found my spirit inside and awakened my soul. I encourage you to accept yourself for who you are. You can't buy youth or beauty; it must come from within. If you feel a need for a body "makeover," perhaps a mental makeover is in order. Regardless of how many cosmetic procedures you have, age will eventually catch up with you. Therefore, what is important is what *we* think of ourselves, not what others think of us. Pursuing egoism is futile. When the ego dies, the spirit is reborn.

The soul is an underestimated, under-acknowledged spiritual organ. Only those who are spiritually attuned to and familiar with their inward spiritual environment will acquire true happiness.

Sometimes we must become lost before we begin to ask for direction. It took a nasty dose of botulism for me to learn the power of my spirit and the strength of my soul. I didn't realize how far from my spiritual path I had gone until I was paralyzed and could not even look into a mirror. Then, I had to look into my heart for beauty, into my soul for strength, and into my spirit for courage. I no longer fear aging or death. Beauty, to me, rests within my soul, and the afterlife is a place for continued evolution of the soul. The power that created the body and soul also heals it. Isn't it time we cared more about the love we project than we do about our reflection in the mirror?

Since the times of Ponce De Leon, men and women have followed the eternal quest to find the fountain of youth. Aging is not fun, and it is not easy.

One recent observer asked me, "How is it that you look so good? Are you getting Botox injections again?"

"What? Are you crazy?" I responded, "Never again!"

Our journey to look younger and remove wrinkles actually made us look older with more wrinkles. I would like to say that my wife and I had been cured of our vanity, but we had not. Actually, we became even more concerned with our appearance. Once people knew our story, they would stare at us. No one wants to be the freak in the circus. My quest to look younger continues, however, no longer will I inject or recommend anyone else injecting a bio weapon and the world's most powerful toxin into their body.

On our journey we came across a product called the Athena 7 Minute Lift, by Greek Island Labs. We found a natural product that removes wrinkles and lines naturally. I wish we had known about this product sooner. It would have saved us a visit to hell and over $1 million in medical bills.

You can learn more about this product at http://www. liftingcream.com/. Imagine turning back the clock naturally without the risk of harmful injections. This technology is here today, and I am happy to share this with you. It is okay to want to look your best. Let's just do it naturally.

Everything exists and functions in accordance with strict, purposeful laws. There are laws of motion, dynamics, and rotation, the law of cause and effect and many others. There is a law in physics that states, "An object in motion will remain in motion at the same speed and same direction unless it is altered by an outside force." This event and the love of friends and family altered my direction. God wanted me to find a purpose in life. Purpose helps define who we are. Everything has a purpose. Take, for instance, the wise and logical manner in which God, or nature, created each cell of our bodies. Each cell has a precise purpose and function, but the primary question asked by the sages is, "For what purpose does all this exist?" The question remains without an answer. Or does it? Maybe we have all the answers but not the faith and the confidence to believe that we do. My lessons taught me that all the answers are inside us. There exists within each of us a power so strong it can literally lift our dying body from the shadow of death. That inner power guided Bonnie and me on this journey.

Our life is celebrated and remembered by two dates, our birth and our death. However, it is what transpires between these two dates that defines who we are. I learned to live my life as if each day was my last. Though the world has many problems, life offers boundless possibilities for true enjoyment. I encourage you to enjoy the moment, enjoy life and enjoy being a part of it all. In so doing, you'll make it that much better a place to live. This is how I now live my life. I am thankful for everything.

Chapter Twenty-six

Conclusion

At the end of life, or in life's greatest crisis, we have only three things: family, friends and our memories. These were my greatest support and I am forever grateful for the doctors, nurses, medical staff, friends and family who cared for us and believed we would recover. We will never forget you and the blessing you are to us.

Angels no longer appear to me physically, but they live in my heart and give me daily guidance. They continually remind me of the Facts of Life, the Lessons of Life and the Laws of Life. From their teachings, I drafted "Rules to Live Your Life By: Ten Golden Nuggets to Daily Empowerment." These mantras have become my way of life and I am happy to share them with you:

1. **Let Go of the Past.** Before any of us can create a better future, we must let go of the pains in our past. Failing once does not mean we will fail forever. Even if we fall flat on our face, we are still moving forward. We need to get up and brush ourselves off. Learn from the past, but don't hold on to it or let it stand as an obstacle between you and your future. I had to let go of my past or I would have remain diseased. I am no longer mad at myself for what happened. I learned from my mistake and have come to cherish my life.

2. **Success Stays Forever.** Just as important as learning from and overcoming past failure is recalling past success. Hold on to everything good in your life. Memories are magic, memories create miracles. No matter who you are, you have succeeded at something in your past. Don't forget those moments. You have earned those memories. They are your right of passage. Use them. Replay them to remind you that you can achieve your goals. Bonnie and I successfully beat botulism by holding on to all that was good in our lives, and by remembering the good things about our past. It was my past memories and past victories that gave me my greatest success.

3. **Visualizing is Realizing.** Fairy tales can come true, and they can happen to you. Whatever you visualize, you have the power to realize. Close your eyes and see yourself as who and where you want to be. You can create a better life. Look to your inner eye to see and create the future of your dreams. I never saw myself in a wheelchair. I never saw myself as the world saw me until *Primetime Live*. Even then, I saw myself in the future as a healthy person. Yes, you can realize what you visualize. I am living proof.

4. **Be a Dreamer.** We need dreams and desires to inspire us to take action and gain achievement. Dreams are powerful affirmations. Let them guide your physical body and remind you that your goals are within your reach. If you don't get excited about what you have planned for the future, you will never find the inspiration or the power you need to change your life. I dreamed every day of getting better. It was my imagination that helped guide me to a new reality. Dreams are real. They are superconscious powers from other states of reality. Harness your dreams and you

will harness a super power that rests within your soul. While I was paralyzed, it was my dreams that gave me life, restored my hope.

5. **Work to Change.** No matter how badly you want something to happen, change will never result from thinking alone—you must take action. Work is a four-letter word, but so is love and so is hope. Hope, work and love will help you change. The world is swimming in dreamers, but only those who act on their desires, and only those who are willing to change, can achieve truly remarkable results. As Winston Churchill once said, "Never give up." Work is a way of life. My wife and I worked hard to regain our ability to walk, talk, eat, and breathe, and it was worth the price.

6. **Maintain Healthy Habits.** There are good habits and bad habits. Know the difference. The best way to break a bad habit is to drop it. Healthy habits will help you realize your goals and dreams. Remember there is no right way to do the wrong thing. Being healthy in mind and body is a full-time job. You must eat healthfully and exercise. Eating, exercising and breathing are gifts of life. Develop habits that can save your life, enhance your life. These habits may one day save your life. The fact that Bonnie and I exercised regularly and didn't smoke cigarettes probably saved our life. Instead of a coffee break, take a family break, and call and give thanks to your family.

7. **Life is A Team Sport.** Achieving a goal or dream requires a team effort. One of the surest ways to overcome setbacks in life is to have the support and guidance of a partner. Share your dreams and goals with your family, friends and community. There will be times when you feel like giving up or when you feel like things are too much to handle. Remember you are not alone in this universe. Ask for help! I was never alone in my journey to health. I

was guided by angels from life and the afterlife. The universe works in harmony. Each person is like a cell. We are all interconnected in the cosmos.

8. **Get Excited About Your Future Today.** You are on your way to getting everything you have ever wanted! Now is the time to get excited and inspired about what your future holds. Imagine living your ideal life, then make it happen. Enjoy the moment as if this day would be your last. In my case, one day I was healthy and the next, without warning, I was totally paralyzed. Such is life. Don't regret what you can't do or what you should have done. Enjoy your future as if it were here today.

9. **Plan Your Life and Live Your Plan.** Goal-setting is important. You must focus on your tomorrow by planning today. Set aside at least ten minutes each night to review your day and plan for the next one. Utilize this time to set goals, affirm what is good in your life, to visualize your future as you want it to be. You can see the future today. A goal without a plan is nothing more than a wish. I first visualized this book while I was in the throes of recovery. I set a goal and then made a plan. Plan your life, work your plan. Don't wish for a result; work for it, plan for it.

10. **Be the Best You Can Be.** At the end of each day, look in the mirror and ask yourself, "Was I the best me I could be today?" The mirror never lies. Each day we must work, plan, visualize, dream, appreciate, exercise, eat responsibly, give thanks, give love, and give hope. What we think about comes about. We must cherish the past and anticipate the future. Our lives are merely a reflection in the mirror. We must carry this reflection with us every day. I am now a better person. I am a more patient, more loving person. I may not be Super-Eric or a superhero, but I know I am the best

"me" I can possibly be.

There is a story of a man who went to Heaven and said to God, "I know I was not the man that Abraham was, but I did not have his strength or his tools." God responded, "All I wanted was for you to be the best you could be and meet your potential." Have you met your potential? Make every day a better day. Be able to look yourself and the mirror at the end of the day and ask yourself if you were the best you could be today. Raise your standards. Expect more out of yourself than anyone else. Accept nothing less than your absolute best in all that you do and you'll have no problem creating your ideal life. Before any positive changes can take place, you must take responsibility for your position in life. You are in control of your future and you are the only one who can guarantee a better life. If you play the role of a victim, giving up control and ownership of your life, you will never enjoy the amazing opportunities that life offers. I live my days by these codes and I know they will work for you.

Our experience was a fairy tale. All fairy tales offer adventure and outlaws. Hansel and Gretel defied the wicked witch and her house made of cookies and candies. We defied botulism. Fairy tales always have a superhero with the ability to conquer evil. I now know that everyone on this planet is a hero. We are powerful spirit beings living in a suit of flesh, ready to learn our lessons and evolve.

What would you do if you were in a situation where you had lost control of all your physical abilities? Would you have faith in your body to heal itself? You are connected with a power stronger than yourself. Would you have faith in that power in your time of need? If you believe in the order of the universe, or if you believe in God, you are on the path of healing regardless of your religion. And for the atheists who may read this book, trust me, in your hour of need you will pray for someone, anyone to assist you. You may call it Mother Nature, Higher Self, Buddha, Jesus, Allah, Creator, Source, Angels, Spirit or any other name you choose, but I assure you there are powers that watch over us and help us—regardless of whether we can see or feel them. We cannot see electricity but we use it in our homes. We cannot see the wind, but we can feel it and see its effects. We have all encountered this Universal Intelligence or God because God is love. If you can feel love, then you have encountered the strongest power in the universe. My gift to you is to remind you that you are not alone in your struggles. There are powers in the universe available to you. Just look inside.

Recovery

It's amazing and fun when the right person just seems to *show up* in your life right when you need them. While playing golf, I met this interesting, passionate woman who helped me understand how important feeding your brain is for any illness and especially for my recovery.

Chris Carley, one of Herbalife's top producers and now one of my golf buddies, reminded me what I had known and taught for years: our brain is the control tower for our entire bodies, including our emotions, personalities and well-being. If we do not feed this wonderful power organ the right nutrients (gasoline) our bodies cannot respond at a top level.

Chris drives an Aston Martin and she said, "Would you put

sugar water in your Ferrari or my car? No. Absolutely not. It would destroy the entire system. The car would be sluggish if it even worked at all. Well, why would you even think of putting it into yourself?"

She pointed out that the bodies of most Americans are breaking down because of what they are putting into them: sugar, processed foods, alcohol and add to these the reality that our soils are depleted of most of the nutrients we need, and include the pollution in the air we breathe. Cancer, diabetes, heart problems, just about any disease can be linked back to what we feed ourselves.

"It is sad that we will treat our cars better than our children and ourselves," she told me. She went on to explain and give me products that really changed my recovery and my life.

Flavonoids (vegetables and fruits) Anthocyanins, (antioxidant pigments) and her favorite: Omega 3's help us, as the saying goes, to live to fight another day. We need these daily to counteract autoimmune conditions, cancers, fatigue, and to help us prevent heart disease, depression and in my case, recovery. She reminded me that it was hard to get antioxidants and vitamins from our foods nowadays. Tons of fruit and vegetables come onto our country with **no nutritional value left!** They are sprayed with pesticides, dipped in wax, shot up with hormones and steroids.

It was fun watching her talk. The more she said the faster her hands waved and the more emotion she exhibited. I discovered that Chris had literally helped hundreds of thousands of people get better. I was shocked when she mentioned she had also helped hundreds make more money, even to become millionaires!

There is no cure for botulism. I had to rely on my body and

products from Mother Nature to heal both Bonnie and me. I went back to my roots as a doctor and considered the phrase, *physician heal thyself.* I needed to do everything and anything to make my body stronger to get my life back. The more I studied the more I learned.

Imagine, the nutrients found in Omega Three antioxidants, known as probiotics, have been shown to **reduce** premature brain aging and enhance memory. "When you understand this and you help others to understand it as well, helping them change their lives forever, you have the best job in the world, not to mention an incredible lifestyle change for yourself," Chris said. Now that is anti-aging naturally: from the inside out, not from the outside in, which is how I got into this mess.

During recovery, it is amazing the people you meet and the stories you hear. Chris's story is one such amazing story. Upon further questioning, I found that she had been a Boeing factory clerk working the midnight to 7 am shift. Her pay was about ten dollars an hour. She had become very sick, depressed and could hardly get out of bed. She had also gained about fifty pounds. She stumbled across a product from Herbalife that changed her life. Signing up just so she could get the products for wholesale (and losing fifty-four pounds in nine weeks!), she accidentally earned two hundred dollars in five days. Everyone asked her what she was on! Chris had no background in sales and no money to advertise but realized she was a walking advertisement. She started with hand-written flyers and leaving cards with anyone that wanted to lose five pounds (everyone). By her ninth month she was earning close to eight thousand dollars a month and became a millionaire after her first year. By studying another sales person, she developed a training system that anyone in sales could use to double their own business. She went on to break many company records, and in just three years she was earning seven figures each year! These are ordinary people doing extraordinary things.

Chris went on to explain that it wasn't just about getting lucky. The company is amazing. Right now the President and a former CEO at Disney, Michael Johnson, has brought the earnings to the three billion dollar mark in sales per year.

"Michael is this gorgeous, fun man who not only runs marathons and is a good family man, he devours the products. I don't know about any other company's president, but Michael treats us like movie stars," she explained.

Chris went on to tell me about one of their top people, Susan Peterson, who does business in almost fifty countries. She and her then husband, John, really turned their lives around from once financially broke, home decorators with twins. They helped open Mexico and now Mexico is one of the strongest countries Herbalife has.

"Can you imagine," she said, "they showed how the products had literally saved Susan's life, and now thousands of people in Mexico have had their entire lives changed!"

That day, golfing was pleasurable, but Chris's energy was amazing. It was good to be alive and listen to a person who was so enthusiastic about her life and about her health. Chris was a ball of energy, while my great friend Bill Meyer and I enjoyed listening to her recount her success and talk about the people who had helped her.

Chris talked about Doran Andry as a unique, top sales

example and a person who has become a wonderful friend to her. "Without knowing a word of Japanese, Doran became one of the biggest and most influential people in Herbalife. Along with Susan, and with help from Bob Anderson and Paul Michaels, we have worked together to developed a system to help train people all over the world," Chris said.

When I got home, I got on the Internet and looked into the business side of Herbalife. Now, being one of the world's most persistent skeptics, I wanted to do my homework to verify what Chris had been saying. I discovered that Chris's friend, Susan, had been the top earner for the last five years. The company is traded on the NASDQ and the stock is consistently strong. On the Heralife website there is story after story of people, young and old, coming from nothing and making good incomes, even great incomes.

I next met Chris for lunch to learn more about her company, her success, and her healing. Chris really honed in on the fact that not everyone automatically makes it. She talked about how important it is to work smart. She pointed out that there are thousands of people who think sales is easy and that all anyone has to do is place an ad.

"Each person is responsible for his own success. I see people every day fail in business because they just didn't try to understand the basics. They blame it on others, even the company, when no one has guaranteed their success—ever," she explained. "You've got to understand that not only did Herbalife save me physically, it gave me a world that I had always dreamed about. I have been a member of Donald Trump's Mar-a-largo and his famous Trump International Golf for six years now. I was the youngest single female to ever join both. Donald has introduced me to President

Clinton, Barbara Walters, Katie Couric and many more—me, a ten dollar an hour factory clerk. This is all because of Herbalife. I have traveled the world in private jets, helicopters, yachts, attended parties in Monte Carlo, Hotel du Cup, and done so many things, all because I helped people feel better."

By the time Chris was done telling me about her products, I knew that *I wanted whatever she was taking.* I wanted to feel as strong and as vibrant as Chris. She was right. The products changed my life, NATURALLY.

This story, like my story, reflects these truths:

- No matter what your state of health, you can always get healthier.
- No matter what your state of wealth, you can always get wealthier.
- What you think about can actually come about.
- We live in a world abundant with resources. There is nothing in life that is not possible.
- The sky is not the limit; it is only as far as you can see.
- The universe, like each of our physical and economic potentials, is infinite.
- If you can see the invisible, you can do the impossible.

My encounters throughout my journey with people like Peter Brock, Bill Meyer, Chris Carley, Chris Cuomo, Donald Trump, Mark Victor Hansen, Marla Maples—where do I end?—and my visits to places like Big Canoe, Shepherd Center, and chance encounters which ultimately led me to my favorite publisher, Valerie Connelly and Nightengale Press, reaffirm all I have learned.

There are no mistakes in the universe, only lessons. In those lessons, there are ups and downs. You cannot have darkness without light. You can not have right without wrong, male without female, joy without sorrow, winter without summer, hot without cold, day without night, health without disease. As surely as spring follows winter and day follows night, you can believe that health will follow disease and happiness will follow sorrow. If you learn anything in a situation, it renders the situation a vital learning experience no matter how bad or unfair it may have seemed. People have asked me over and over what I have learned from all I have been through. My answer is short and sweet: GOD IS REAL.

The past is history. The future is a mystery. This moment of life is the gift. That is why we call it the present. Take your present, unwrap the gift of life and remember: Life is for living, loving, laughing and learning. Not just whining, worrying and working.

Prior to having wrinkle reducing cosmetic injections, I was dying to be young. After almost killing myself in my pursuit of youth, I have been reborn. The old adages, "Youth is wasted on the young," and "Life is too short," are absolutely true and have more meaning to me now than ever. I am no longer dying to be young; I am living to be old with my wife and ...my wrinkles.

Epilogue

Facts About Botulism and Botox

History of Botulism

At one time, food poisoning from botulism was considered a dinner table threat in most American households. Since the toxin is rendered inactive when heated at boiling temperature for ten minutes, the only way a human may contract the bacteria through food is when contaminated sources are not properly heated before consumption. This used to be the case with improper home-canning processes that were common before so much of our food came packed full of preservatives.

Botulism-causing *Clostridium botulinum* bacteria and their spores are found in fruits, vegetables and seafood worldwide. The bacteria and spores themselves are harmless, but as the bacteria grows, it produces a dangerous substance called botulinum toxin that may enter the human body through contaminated food or exposure in an open wound. Once the toxin is in the body, it irreversibly binds to nerve endings where the muscles and the nerves join. The toxin blocks the release of acetylcholine thereby rendering the nerves unable to send signals to the muscles to contract. Weakness and paralysis starts in the head and moves downward through the body, affecting the person's ability to breathe. About eight percent of those who contract botulism will die. For those who survive, recovery may take years. What makes our case unique is that we were directly injected with the raw toxin. Recent reports have revealed that we received 2,800 times the amount of the clinical dosage contained in cosmetic Botox. This made us candidates for death as well as the record books. What happened to us has never happened to anyone before. Our goal is for this to never happen to anyone again.

Botulinum toxin is the most poisonous substance known to man. Because of its extreme potency and lethality, the ease of production, transport, and misuse, botulinum toxin is considered a bioweapon. A single gram of crystalline toxin, evenly dispersed as an aerosol and inhaled, would kill more than one million people. Since aerosol dispersement is difficult, terrorists might instead use botulinum toxin to deliberately contaminate food sources. Development and use of botulinum toxin as a biological weapon began during World War II. Terrorists attempted to use botulinum toxin as a bioweapon in Japan in the 1990s but these attacks failed, either due to faulty microbiological technique, deficient aerosol equipment, or internal sabotage. After the Persian Gulf War, Iraq admitted to having produced and loaded into bombs and military weapons enough concentrated botulinum toxin to kill the entire current human population by inhalation. You may not sleep as well tonight after you know that the whereabouts of those toxic weapons is still unknown.

In a protein-purified form, botulinum toxin is licensed for medical treatment of muscle spasms in the neck and eyes, cross-eyed vision, involuntary muscle contractions, migraine headaches, chronic low-back pain, stroke, traumatic brain injury, cerebral palsy, clenching of the jaw muscles, urinary bladder muscle relaxation, the management of tics, writers' and musicians' cramps, and difficulty swallowing due to failure of the esophageal muscle. A purified and greatly diluted version of the botulism toxin is manufactured and distributed by Allergan and marketed under the trade name Botox. It is used to minimize facial lines and wrinkles by paralyzing the muscle and causing it to relax. Botox is an FDA-approved and licensed Botulinum Toxin Type A derived from the waste of the bacterium *Clostridium Botulinum*—the same toxic byproduct that causes botulism food poisoning.

Botulinum Toxin Today

Millions of people have been injected with Botox but most do not realize that the serum is a weaker version of botulism bacteria. The media, pharmaceutical companies, and doctors have made it seem so safe that many people receive this plastic surgery procedure at a social event known as a Botox party. This social gathering is thought to be more economical and help reduce the anxiety associated with getting an injection. Imagine going to a party, drinking a glass of wine and enjoying hors d'oeuvres with your friends while waiting your turn to receive plastic surgery or a medical treatment. Then you return to your peers in the waiting room for their approval. They may even tell you how much better you look after being injected with the toxin.

In a country concerned about homeland security, the raw botulism toxin (intended only for animal research) given to us could ironically be purchased over the Internet. That means anyone could use it as a bioweapon. What about the antitoxin's availability? Government regulation for the antitoxin to treat an overdose mandates that a police escort deliver it to a hospital where it will be administered by a doctor from the Centers for Disease

Control from Atlanta, Georgia. Nerve damage in our bodies increased by the minute while we waited hours for the antitoxin to arrive. Even after receiving the antitoxin, we remained completely paralyzed and unable to breathe or function without life support. We struggled for our lives in Palm Beach Gardens Medical Center for nearly six weeks before being moved to a rehabilitation center in Georgia where we were weaned off life support. We continue to recover almost two years later, not knowing how much of the neurological damage is permanent or what side effects may occur later. Wouldn't we all be much safer if the toxin were as hard to get as the antitoxin and vice versa?

Appendix A

Mother's Facts of Life

- Life is for living, loving, laughing and learning.
- Life begins with love.
- Love is life, and God is love. Wherever there is love or life, there is God.
- God has granted every soul the power of choice, but choice should be governed by wisdom.
- Nothing is ever gained or lost in the universe—only transformed.
- The more good you do, the stronger your spirit and soul become.
- People must evolve by using their free will to make choices that lead to peace.
- Whether we choose to do good or bad, we will all eventually reach the same destiny—awareness of our oneness with God.
- Accept the idea that we are love, and as such, we are one with God.
- THERE IS NO DEATH! There is only life and afterlife.

Uncle Herb's Lessons of Life

1. You will receive a body. You may love it or hate it, but it will be yours for the entire period of your life. It is the vessel which contains your spirit. If you are good to it, it will be good to you.

2. Your life is a series of lessons. You are enrolled in a full-time informal school called Life. Each day in this school you will have the opportunity to learn lessons. You may like the lessons or think them irrelevant and stupid; however, all days, all encounters, good or bad will contain a lesson.

3. There are no mistakes in Life; only lessons. Growth is a process of trial and error through experimentation. The "failed" experiments are as much a part of the process as the experiment that ultimately works.

4. A lesson in Life is repeated until learned. A lesson will be presented to you in various shapes and forms until you have learned it. Only when you have learned it can you then go on to the next lesson.

5. Life's lessons never end. There is no part of your day or your life that does not contain lessons. If you are alive, there are lessons to be learned. The wise person learns from his/her lessons.

6. Being "there" is no better than being "here." When "there" has become "here," you will simply obtain another "there" that will look better than "here." The grass is not greener elsewhere, so learn to live in the moment.

7. Others are merely mirrors of you. You cannot love or hate something about another person unless it reflects something you love or hate about yourself.

8. What you make of your life is up to you. You have all the tools and resources you need. What you do with them is up to you. The choice is yours.

9. All of Life's questions and answers are inside you. All you need to do is look, listen and trust. You must have faith in your body, your mind, your soul and your spirit. Your inner voice and your innate intelligence will provide you with answers to all questions.

10. The secret of life is "I am." You harbor the strength and power of the universe. When you accept responsibility for your life and your actions, you will learn to harness the power of the universe. You must take responsibility for your life.

Father's Laws of Life

- Life is about choices; choose wisely.
- We are put on earth to grow, to evolve.
- Only humans have free will. Will to be free.
- You must know the difference between right and wrong.
- Follow the path of your heart and you've made the right decision.
- There is no right way to do the wrong thing.
- Manifest your life as you choose and the universe will assist you.
- Death is simply a passing from one dimension of life to another.
- Those who seek truth are seeking to be one with God. God is truth.
- The future of your life is in your vision today; see clearly.

Thoughts for Success

- You can never change your outer world without first changing your inner thoughts.

- Don't just wish for things to get better in your life, but actively work to make things better in your life.

- Be solution conscious. Focus 10% on the problem and 90% on the solution.

- The future is your tree; plant it today. The choices you make today will shape your tomorrow.

- Build a reputation on delivering more than you promised. It comes back to you like a tidal wave.

- No one can stop you from reaching your goals unless you give them permission to do so.

Bibliography

Goldrick, Barbara A. PhD, MPH, RN, CIC. "Emerging Infections: Botox Goes Black Market: New dangers arise for those wanting to look young." *American Journal of Nursing.* March 2005, Vol. 105 Number 3. Pages 30-31. <http://www.nursingcenter.com/library/JournalArticle.asp?Article_ID=573349>.

Perry, Gordon Randall. Registered Respiratory Therapist, Certified Pulmonary Function Technologist at Vanderbilt University Medical Center in Nashville, Tennessee. Personal interviews October–December 2005.

"Tracheostomy & Ventilator Swallowing and Speaking Valves." Passy-Muir Glossary of Respiratory Care Terms. 1 December 2005. <http://www.passy-muir.com/education/glossary.aspx>.

About the Author

As a businessman, Dr. Eric Scott Kaplan has turned companies with million-dollar-a-month losses into profitable entities with his style of practice management. From 1978 to 1993, Dr. Kaplan founded and owned six integrated clinics with annual revenues in excess of $2.5 million. Dr. Kaplan is the past President and COO of Complete Wellness Centers, a publicly traded company. A retired chiropractor and acupuncturist, Dr. Kaplan is currently on the editorial advisory board of *The American Chiropractor* magazine.

Dr. Kaplan is a renowned motivational speaker and healthcare consultant. Audiences flock to hear his profound and practical advice for achieving and maintaining maximum health and wellness. He remains a nationally sought-after personality whose credits include appearances on ABC, CBS, NBC and Fox networks. *Primetime Live* aired an interview with the Kaplans' in February 2005 during their recovery from botulism.

Dr. Kaplan is the best-selling author of *Dr. Kaplan's Lifestyles of the Fit and Famous,* which has sold over 50,000 copies since it was published by Starburst in 1995. His book was endorsed by the likes of Donald Trump, Norman Vincent Peale, Mark Victor Hansen, and Earl Mindell—to name a few. Dr. Kaplan plans to release two more books within the next two years including a series of health books geared toward children. Go to www.dyingtobeyoung.net for more about Dr. Kaplan.

A Note from the Author

Living to Be Young

There are days that I wake up thinking the past three years have been just a dream but then reality sets in. My wife and I literally almost died trying to be young. But they say what does not kill you makes you stronger. No one should experience the cosmetic nightmare we did. It was through this process we experienced the love of family, friends and faith in God that created my spiritual awakening. Now instead of chasing vanity and Dying to Be Young, my wife and I are actually Living to be Young. There is no magic pill or potion that will restore youth and keep you young. What I learned is that a youthful spirit and appearance, like most good things in life require commitment, hard work and a positive outlook. The *secret* is doing it NATURALLY.

The principles of books like the *Secret*, are based on the concept that a person's thoughts (conscious and subconscious), emotions, beliefs, and actions attract corresponding positive or negative experiences. I believe this is true to a fault. Nothing we did or thought attracted this catastrophe upon us. To insinuate it in any way would be purely perverse. However most books or philosophies have limits, have weaknesses. The true *secret* is staying positive in the moment of adversity. We only wanted beauty, to look younger; never could an outcome like ours be imagined, consciously or subconsciously. Our thoughts do carry actions, which correspond to outcomes. Our *secret* was we never would accept a life of disability, we willed to live free. Free of disability, free to love again, to be happy again, to look good again.

Each and every day Bonnie and I only look to attract what is good what is natural in the universe. We recognize our health has been compromised, but our spiritual awakening also has us give thanks to life each and every day.

This book was only the beginning of our healing process. We did not write this book to make money, we wrote this book to make a difference. This book is our way of saying thank you to our friends and all of the people who prayed for us. We are grateful for all the good reviews on our book and we even reached #1 for a short time on one of Amazon's bestseller lists. Imagine #1 in the WORLD. Our book is proof that sometimes good comes from evil and that nice guys, gals, don't always finish last.

Three years ago we were literally Dying to Be Young, now our journey has changed course where now we are Living to Be Young. As our wrinkles reappeared our health returned. Imagine rooting for wrinkles. Each wrinkle represented that the botulinum toxin damage was giving way to new cell growth and activity. We wanted this toxin out of our system. Our barometer was wrinkles. However we reached another dilemma. Although we wanted to feel good, as our health returned so did our vanity.

What a conundrum, wrinkles were desired, yet we also wanted to look good. Is there such a thing as good wrinkles? Our faces now looked weathered, people stared. We did not want to be remembered in the tabloids as the Bogus Botulinum couple. Where do we turn, yet where do millions of American turn? We need a new health paradigm, a new solution to youth, so like any pioneer, my quest began in earnest. Like Ponce de León, I began my own search for my fountain of youth. I wanted a natural solution to the anti-aging epidemic that is sweeping the country, the world.

Instead of just trying to look young, my mantra, my life's quest, became Living to Be Young, naturally. To find natural solutions, natural alternatives, and to bring these alternatives to the masses. I started my journey with friends, with peers, and on the internet.

A World at War

As my quest began I learned that we are a world involved in a significant war. A war so far reaching, that the casualties will exceed any war know in history. A war so bold, so disastrous, that not one of the presidential candidates dare to discuss it. This war is the "Health care War" sweeping America. Just consider these facts:

• Health care spending in our country exceeds 1.8 trillion dollars, which is four times the amount spent on national defense and forty times the amount spent on homeland security.

• According to a recent Harvard study, 50% of all bankruptcies in our country are the direct result of excessive medical spending. This is compounded by Warren Sick's, article in the *Washington Post*, where he reported, every thirty seconds someone files for bankruptcy due to serious medical problems.

• Some experts believe that a retiring couple will need between $200,000 and $300,000 just to pay for the most basic medical coverage.

If this is not enough to make you sick, in a recent article published in the *Journal of the American Medical Association (JAMA)*, Dr. Barbara Starfield of Johns Hopkins School of Hygiene and Public Health listed the negative health effects in the U.S. system itself, including:

- 7,000 deaths per year from medication errors in hospitals
- 12,000 deaths per year from unnecessary surgery
- 8 million unnecessary hospitalizations
- 3 million unnecessary long-term hospital admissions
- 199,000 unnecessary deaths per year
- 20,000 deaths per year from other errors in hospitals
- 77 million unnecessary prescriptions
- 77 billion in unnecessary costs

Imagine: AIDS takes less the 20,000 lives per year and the publicity is enormous, yet 199,000 unnecessary medical care deaths every year and this statistic, this epidemic, seems to be ignored. According to Dr. David Himmelstein, associate professor at Harvard Medical School, states we are all one serious illness away from bankruptcy. Another Harvard professor, Dr. Steffie Woolander said in an interview, "Even the best policies in this country have so many loopholes, it's easy to build up thousands of dollars in expenses."

In our case we had insurance, which we believe was wrongly denied, and after paying for health insurance our entire lives we were left with over $1 million in medical bills. It appeared the system wanted to silence us, have us just become another statistic. But if botulism poisoning, being paralyzed 100%, taught me anything, it taught me to fight. So I made a commitment, not only to get myself well, but to talk and write about what politicians dare not, or refuse to talk or write about. My objective in life became making a difference in the "Health care Crisis." The adulation of drugs and surgery that dominates our countries consciousness needs to be changed. We need to stop treating the symptoms; we need to treat, remove, the cause. Now I must do more than LIVE TO BE YOUNG, I must now get myself healthy, healthy enough to lead by example, strong enough to tell my message.

Over the past year I knew I was making progress through exercise, diet, vitamins, as well as massage, chiropractic, Lipomassage through Endermologie, accupucture. We were looking better and our journey led us to Athena Greek Island and their wrinkle removal formula. Imagine companies whose business and success are based on keeping people looking young naturally. We felt better about ourselves and like any athlete we started training for the big day, that day was *Good Morning America.*

What show is bigger than *Good Morning America*? How would the world perceive us? Bonnie stayed out of the public eye; she was still not happy with her appearance. In my eyes she was her old beautiful self again. Yes, Bonnie was back. Nobody wants to be stared at for the wrong reasons; this was our chance, our *Rocky* moment. Our moment to show the world we not only survived, but we won the battle and would continue to fight the anti-aging wars. You must understand people stared at us for so long we didn't know how we really looked. Heck, anything was better then how we were. (Go to dyingtobeyoung.net to see pictures.)

The day came for *Good Morning America*. Being a public speaker, I was not nervous about the appearance on national television. I was more worried to see Chris Cuomo again. Chris Cuomo did the segment on us two years prior for *Prime Time Live*. At that time, Bonnie was still not able to talk, I was still on a ventilator. Rarely in one's life do you meet a person that makes you want to be your best, that motivate you to take yourself to another level. Chris did that for us, in his caring, in his eyes, and in the feature ABC did on us. It was honest, it was pure.

Now two-plus years later, here we were again. Then it happened, he looked at us, did a double take and smiled. "You look great," he echoed. "I can't believe my own eyes." Victory at last, I was now being looked at as a person again, not a victim. I never wanted sympathy. I knew what it was like to be the freak in the circus. Everyone wanted to see us, how we looked, what had happened, many for curiosity, others just for love. Mr. Cuomo cared, plain and simple; his smile electrified my wife and me. It was a warm and fuzzy moment, one we will always cherish. It was our best day.

"I am so proud of you, you guys are amazing. How do you look so good?" A speaker loves a question. Now the floor was mine and I went on to tell my story of my quest for the fountain of youth. "Chris," I went on to elaborate, "an amazing thing about healing, once we started to get well, our vanity returned almost as strong as ever. What were we to do with our wrinkles now? Injections or fillers were no longer an option. We decided, if it wasn't natural, it wasn't for us." I went on to tell him of a product that we found that literally changed our lives— ATHENA 7 MINUTE LIFT. It isn't, it is my testimonial that natural products do work and make a difference and you do not have to inject yourself with a toxin to look younger and remove wrinkles. If only we would have known this sooner. Lifting cream worked, no injections, no fillers, just products from God's earth" (Go to www.liftingcream.com.)

It was great to look normal again. It was great to be treated like an equal again and not a freak. I felt it was my role in life, my purpose, to educate the masses in natural ways to look and feel younger. Why else would God have put me through such an ordeal? There had to be a reason, a purpose.

We went on to do the show and it was great and well received. At the end of our segment he brought out two boxes of Ray's Pizza. This brought a tear to Bonnie's eye. When we were at the Shepherd Center, not able to eat, to drink, to breathe on our own, we missed the little things that life has to offer. It was during our first meeting he asked what I missed the most. I told him pizza, Ray's Pizza. Ray's Pizza is one of the top pizza franchises in all of New York City. The beauty of Mr. Cuomo was that he remembered. Approximately two-plus years later, he remembered a promise he made to a broken, beaten, and weathered man. I made a promise to him, to myself, to come back whole, to be the old Dr. Eric again. On this day we both kept our word.

Chris Cuomo is a bright man, a loving man, educated as an attorney. It was great to see him again, to see happiness in his eyes versus the fear and pity we saw in the past. He meant so much to us, to our recovery, this was a great day. We talked candidly, like two old friends reunited after years of being apart. He soon asked what I was doing now? I told him my next book, like this chapter, would be entitled LIVING TO BE YOUNG. This book would be about anti-aging naturally. My hours of healing and recovery were spent doing research, researching historical beauty secrets. Cosmetic injections, Restyline injections, as well as many wrinkle fillers and remedies only became FDA approved this century, what did people do 100 years ago? One thousand years ago?

The Greeks were renowned for their beauty secrets, way before chemical peels, injections or any form of plastic surgery. They relied on natural remedies products that were readily and naturally available. The Greeks utilized many ingredients like Lavender oil. The more I read, the more I researched the more it became apparent. We have become the "Chemical Generation," looking for drugs or potions to look good, feel good, or for basic virility. Something had to change; someone had to change this paradigm.

I went back to the basics. I met with my good friend Thierry Phillipe, I spoke with him about my quest. Mr. Philippe is the President of LPG World. They are the founders of Endermologie. I explained to him how we used his Well Box on our muscles, a form of Endermotherapy. We were taking responsibility to look good naturally. He agreed and told me he also was taking an interest in responsible beauty, that he was touched by my book and by our dilemma. He agreed something had to be done and we agreed to do it. To alert the world that there are risks associated with any procedure and that there are natural alternatives that often work as well, if not better. It is time for the consumer to take responsibility of their life, their looks. Now is the time for RESPONSIBLE BEAUTY

There is nothing wrong with wanting to look your best, to be your best. In a recent article by Meredith Bryan in *Marie Claire*, she wrote, "How Much is Too Much?" Her article hit home. She went on to report her views on cosmetic surgery. In her article she stated that the American Society For Aesthetic Plastic Surgery revealed that 63% of women in the country approve of it, though just 34% would consider it for themselves. Were we making a difference? Did our poisoning wake up the world? If so, if we saved other families from our tragedy, then and only then was it worth it. Our goal was to make a difference.

The world was now awakened to cosmetic risks, Meredith Bryan's article helped to confirm it. She went on to report that many doctors persuade their patients against constant procedures. One doctor, a facial plastic surgeon from Chicago, stated he dissuaded 40–50% of his patients from procedures due to risk. If only someone would have dissuaded us. "Responsible Beauty" as Mr. Phillipe explains is a proactive, natural approach to anti-aging. He goes on to state how France and other parts of Europe look to natural means to look good. Yes, it is ok to be vain, but be responsible. Any cosmetic procedure has risk. Why not limit that risk?

Many actors and entertainers have had so many procedures they just don't look good anymore. Mickey Rourke, Burt Reynolds, and Melanie Griffith just don't look the same. Brittany Spears now wants to drink and eat junk food, believing she can continually go for liposuction. Could all this surgery, all this anesthesia, have altered her mental state? Then there is Michael Jackson, enough said. "Responsible Beauty" is taking responsibility for looking good and not looking for ongoing surgical intervention. "Responsible Beauty" should be the new paradigm. The French, the Greeks, worlds leaders in the beauty field, have know this for years. Let me share some of their secrets.

Lavender oil is one of the most widely used essential oils and is native to the Mediterranean region. It was used to heal wounds in ancient Greece and Rome and still is today. In addition to its calming, relaxing fragrance, the lavender flower has natural antiseptic and astringent properties when applied to the skin that were recognized centuries ago. (In fact Greek and Roman soldiers often carried lavender oil in medical kits.) Because it is high in esters, lavender oil can help sooth irritated skin and protect it from further damage.

Now combine this with jasmine oil which is known for its antiinflammatory properties, its deep rich scent, and its ability to help calm and restore the skin. It is often called the "king of essential oils" and has been trusted for centuries for its soothing effect on skin irritations, along with its ability to help calm and restore the skin.

The more I researched the Europeans, the history of beauty, the more I learned. The past would become a part of my future. Why would we throw away thousands of years of success? Imagine a simple thing like a lemon peel. Introduced to Europe by the returning Crusaders in the Middle Ages, lemon peel oil helps bring balance to the fluids in the cells of the skin. It helps stabilize the pH of the skin by counteracting the acidity on its surface. Lemon oil also helps calm redness and irritation and freshen dull, dry skin. Dry skin is not healthy skin.

So what do you do for dry skin naturally? Orange peel oil helps sooth, soften and clarify the skin. It helps protect the skin against free radical damage because, just like lemon peel oil, it is a concentrated form of vitamin C, a powerful antioxidant. It adds an enchanting, floral note and was used in ancient Greece and Rome.

My wife had her glow back, she looked like her old self again, and she had her pride back. Imagine something as simple as vitamin C, can change your appearance. High in vitamin C, grapefruit helps protect against free radical damage and has a cleansing effect on the skin. It is also used in anti-cellulite treatments and in massage oils. As with all citrus oils, grapefruit peel oil helps to brighten dull, tired skin.

Combine this with rose petals and almond oil. Edgar Casey, one of the fathers of naturopathy, called almonds the KING OF NUTS. Almond trees are believed to have originated in the Mediterranean area around Greece. Sweet almond oil is obtained from dried kernels of the almond tree. This oil is an excellent emollient and helps the skin to balance its loss and absorption of moisture. It is a light, non-greasy, penetrating oil, rich in essential fatty acids and vitamins A, B1, B2, B6 and E.

Now combine the almond oil with sesame oil, why? The use of the healthful properties of sesame seed oil can be traced back almost 5,000 years. It is a natural skin moisturizer and antioxidant, rich in lecithin, Vitamin B complex and Vitamin E, and is easily absorbed into the skin. Are you starting to get the picture? You can look young naturally and you can start your future today.

My wife and I went to the past to find the secret to our future. We learned from the Greeks. Imagine if we knew this prior to our injections. I was now convinced. I found a formula to change the way we looked we were thrilled. We found a formula to take away our wrinkles using products of nature. For more information go to www.liftingcream.com.

We didn't stop there, we learned the secrets of the ages and we want to share them with you.

Anti-aging starts with attitude and nutrition. Not with drugs or potions. Great nutrition is essential to aging gracefully. To age well you need to eat well. Eating the right kind of food will have an immediate impact on the way you look—and on the way you feel.

Energy, vitality and zest for life come from within—from a body and brain supplied with the essential nutrients needed for optimum performance.

Good nutrition is also vital for skin tone and muscle tone—every cell in your body needs essential nutrients to regenerate and repair. Eating the right things has a huge impact on the way your skin looks and how well it copes with the passing of time.

This part of the site is all about anti aging nutrition with the focus on good food eaten with enjoyment. Enjoying what you eat is such an important part of eating healthily.

You won't find recommendations that you eat something just because it's the latest anti aging wonder food.

So start now—put the best food choices up there on your weekly shopping list—very soon you'll find you enjoy what you eat, feel fantastic and look years younger!

Kaplan's Anti Aging Tips — Top Ten

Anti aging doesn't have to mean turning to cosmetic surgery or chemicals.

If you really want to look younger and stay healthy, here are my top ten anti aging tips:

1. Quit Smoking

One of the most important anti aging tips of all. If I could do it you can. If I was a smoker at the time of our injections, I would be dead. I have come to learn your lungs are everything and as important to your heart. Once we got off the ventilator and were able to breathe on our own our strength returned.

If you smoke, STOP NOW. It's as simple as that. Over time You may able to completely reverse the damage smoking has done to your skin but you will stop the damage getting worse. With the right anti aging skin care, proper nutrition and a good multi vitamin skin supplement—you should begin to look younger and healthier than you have for years, if we could do it so could you..

Smokers do not usually have healthy skin. So, do your face, your body, your lungs a favor and quit smoking now. Kick start your cessation program with acupuncture or laser therapy - you're more like to succeed with help than cold turkey.

If you do choose to continue smoking be prepared for the consequences. Smoking accelerates skin aging by encouraging the destruction of collagen. Reduced levels of collagen are one of the primary reasons your skin ages so a smoker's skin ages much faster. The tell-tale signs are dull, grayish, dry skin, increased wrinkling around the eyes and the puckering wrinkles from drawing on cigarettes—"smoker's face."

Is it really what you want for your skin?

2. Protect Your Skin From The Sun

Sun damage is the number one enemy of younger looking skin. My friend Dr. Zwecker still yells at me on the golf course, "Wear a hat, utilize sun screen." Where did my wrinkles come from? How did I get into this mess? The sun, naturally. I as a youth overdid it on my days at the Belmar, New Jersey beach.

Getting a sun tan leads to photo-aging, a process that produces deep wrinkles in leathery textured skin and will cause premature age spots.

Use a moisturizer combined with a broad spectrum sunscreen. Have sunscreen always with you in so you never get caught out—great to slip in your purse or golf bag. And—if you want a tan—fake it. Most of Hollywood does anyway.

3. Eat a natural and high antioxidant rich diet

Antioxidants are a group of vitamins, minerals and carotenoids that work against the damage caused by free radicals that weaken the skin's structure. For maximum anti aging protection eat fresh fruit, vegetables, fruit and whole grains. For younger looking skin make sure you get plenty of vitamins A,C,E and Selenium (ACES). These vitamins work together to restore collagen in your skin. You also need plenty of Omega 3 essential fatty acids—which will aid in a healthy heart. Omega 3s maintain the structure and fluidity of cells and help moisturize the skin from within—an essential part of your anti aging diet.

4. Take a vitamin supplement for younger looking skin

Boost your antioxidant intake with a daily supplement. Go for one with the highest levels of the key vitamins and minerals for younger looking skin and all round health.

5. Add green tea to your day

Drinking green tea is an anti-aging tip you may not have considered. Green tea is an amazing anti-aging powerhouse—recent research findings show that taking sufficient green tea during the day can protect you from all forms of cancer, build your resistance to heart disease and dementia and contribute to your body's ability to burn fat—especially abdominal fat—resulting in possible weight loss and increased energy, even where there is no change in your daily diet. To get the wonderful anti-aging effects of green tea in concentrated form take a high strength green tea powder.

6. Moisturize and exfoliate

A great anti-aging moisturizer, when applied properly, will provide continuous hydration—essential for mature skin—and protection from further free radical damage. Choose the best moisturizer you can afford. Make sure it has high levels of proven effective ingredients like peptides that work to reverse the aging process and reduce wrinkles.

You have to exfoliate for younger looking skin. Without exfoliation, anti-aging skin creams can't work their magic on the skin. Follow a disciplined and consistent skin routine and exfoliate twice a week to ensure that fresh, live skin is soaking up moisture. Bonnie is great at this and I am so proud of her.

7. Exercise more

I had to learn to walk again, utilize every muscle again. To maintain my lungs and health, exercise is part of my life. I don't love doing it, I love the way I feel after. Exercise is my KEY anti-aging tip—exercise will give your more energy, build muscle mass, increase blood flow to your skin, help prevent high blood pressure, reduce anxiety, strengthen bones and raise your metabolic rate so you lose more weight more quickly.

With all these anti aging benefits—exercise doesn't have to be a chore. Go for exercise that gives you a cardio workout as well as developing core strength and fighting abdominal, buttock and thigh fat. So if you haven't already—put exercise at the heart of your anti-aging routine.

8. Moderate your alcohol intake

My wife and I still enjoy a glass of wine. Wine is loaded with phenolic compounds and flavonoids, with high anti-oxidant value. The key is doing it in moderation. We all know that drinking too much can lead to serious health problems. What is less talked about is the aging effect of alcohol on the skin. Alcohol is bad for your skin as it is has an inflammatory and dehydrating action which accelerates the aging process. Excess alcohol blocks the absorption of key nutrients you need for antioxidant protection. The key is to drink eight ounces of water for every four ounces of wine and two ounces of liquor.

9. Stress less

We are all under pressure in life. Pressure to perform, to be the best dad, best mom, and best employee. We all feel the pressure to succeed. Athletes feel pressure to win. Pressure is part of life, just accept it and don't let it in to your consciousness. Once you do, once you obsess over pressure, then pressure becomes stress. When you're under stress your body releases stress hormones which—over a period of time—suppress the immune system and accelerate the aging process. As a result of prolonged stress, the cells in your body—including your skin cells—are unable to regenerate properly and become more susceptible to the aging process. The result is premature lines and wrinkles. Stress really does get etched on your face.

So anti-aging tip number nine is to learn to recognize that pressure is ok but stress is not, so manage it effectively.

10. Drink more water

Nothing on this planet would survive without water. Not cola, water. You need to hydrate your body, your skin, from within. Skin cells need water just like every part of your body including your brain. Without sufficient water your skin will dehydrate and essential anti-aging nutrients cannot be delivered to your system. You should aim to drink around eight eight-ounce glasses every day just to replace the water you lose through sweating and urination. If you want to look good longer you need to make sure water is an essential part of your anti-aging routine.

Just about every dermatologist out there tells us we should drink water for skin health and to hydrate the skin. I did a quick review and found that respected dermatologists like Daniel Maes (Head of Research for Estee Lauder), Nicholas Perricone, Dr. Murad and countless others all say drinking water is required to keep skin hydrated. And hydrated skin is younger looking skin, as we all know.

Loss of hydration in the skin shows in all sorts of ways—dryness, tightness, flakiness. Dry skin has less resilience and is more prone to wrinkling. Water is essential to maintain skin moisture and is the vehicle for delivering essential nutrients to the skin cells. As water is lost in large quantities every day, it stands to reason you have to replace it somehow.

Taking water into the body by drinking during the day is important, but most dermatologists will tell you that to maintain the skin's moisture levels you need to keep it there too. The key is to drink water throughout the day at regular intervals; this makes it easy and fun.

So—that's it—ten great anti-aging tips to help you look younger and feel great—all you need to do is follow them!

Anti-aging skin care is not for the faint-hearted.

There are literally thousands of anti-aging creams to choose from, with new must-have magic ingredients appearing weekly in the beauty press. Anti-aging is big business and millions of dollars are spent every year on the search for the ultimate anti-aging cream. Wrinkles is a billion dollar industry.

That's it—retraining your body and face can go a long way to preventing wrinkles and giving you younger looking skin and a healthy body.

You might be clear about the benefits but have you really taken the time to consider the risks? Start here with ten things you need to know about cosmetic procedures or any form of plastic surgery BEFORE your book your appointment or have any treatment.

1. Results are not guaranteed. Everyone is unique and your physical make up and genetics will determine the outcome as well as the skill and performance on the day of the physician you choose. Just because someone you know has had a great result does not mean the outcome for you will be the same.

2. It will cost you—a full face lift may cost anything from $6,000 to $15,000 in the U.S. Lower level procedures—half face lifts, brow, or eyelifts are less but you're still talking a lot of dollars.

Never cut costs in your choice of surgeon or clinic—you could endanger your health and your looks.

3. Any invasive procedure or surgery is a risk—plastic surgery included. With the best medical facilities and a top-class surgeon, complications are rare but they do happen. Some health conditions —for instance diabetes—place you at much greater risk from plastic surgery. An invasive procedure such as a facelift will involve a general anesthetic and this is not something to undertake lightly.

4. Recovery is slow and often involves pain and discomfort. TV makeover programs frequently gloss over the slow and painful part. You could be in a condition to scare the dog for several weeks afterwards and it will take many weeks after that—possibly even months—for your face or body to fully recover.

5. During recovery you will probably need time off work and help with basic needs like shopping, errands, housework. You'll also need to buy products to help you heal more quickly—dressings, creams, lotions, pills and supplements. All this needs planning —not least from a financial point of view.

6. Any procedure, injection, or plastic surgery can have a bad effect on the physiology of your skin and underlying tissues and can actually speed up the aging process. Remember you look great.

7. Stretched skin will sag again over time. More plastic surgery may not be the way to go if you want to avoid a distorted, unnatural look. So you may end up with just a temporary reprieve or—with frequent facelifts—a slightly scary result.

8. If you're squeamish—forget it. You won't even be able to cope with the pre-surgery discussions.

9. You still need to spend money on anti-aging skin care. Even plastic surgeons now acknowledge that you need more than plastic surgery for younger looking skin: www.liftingcream.com is a great alternative. In fact, after any cosmetic procedure you need to be even more careful to follow a regular anti-aging skin care regimen with the best products you can find.

10. Topical anti-aging treatments should always be the first step. If you've neglected your skin in the past try out some anti-aging creams and lotions first. You may be very surprised by the results you can achieve over three months of careful use.

So—take your time. Find a board certified surgeon with a lot of experience in the type of cosmetic procedure you are seeking. Spend a long time on the research. Get names of previous patients and talk to them about the doctor, their experience and the process.

But there's one piece of advice you should listen to if you're considering any cosmetic procedure. Ask yourself who are you doing this for? Who are you trying to impress? Remember, a sixty year old man or woman with a face lift is still sixty years old. You can lie to your friends, even the mirror, but you can't lie to your heart, your lungs, your liver, your spleen or gallbladder.

Remember that true, pure anti-aging is an inside job. The key to RESPONSIBLE BEAUTY is to take responsibility for not only how you look but what you do, or put into your body. There are many natural products and natural alternatives to Liposuction, facelifts, fillers, and injections. Don't risk DYING TO BE YOUNG, but rather, LIVE TO BE YOUNG, naturally.

Let's go back to the basics, let's start liking ourselves for who we are, not what society wants us be. My final advice, thinking about any cosmetic procedure, or surgery, THINK TWICE. We wish we did.